"I absolutely love this book. Couldn't put it down once I started reading. It is entertaining, interesting, and factual, with some humour thrown in. A wonderful mix of people, their interactions with their neighbours, and the indigenous population around them within the time frame in which they lived. Neill McKee has created a wonderful history of the growth of the US and Canada. The way he included stories of people living at the time and places our ancestors lived made history come alive. Great job!"

—*Gwenda McCurdy,* Avid Reader, Brampton, Ontario

"Neill McKee has personalized the history of North America since the arrival of his ancestors on the *Mayflower* like no author I have ever read before. While the story follows the McKee and Neill/Haskins family experiences, it also speaks to the broader settler-indigenous relations, conflicts, and struggles still unfolding in the 21st century. Drawing on family stories and his interactions with concerned people on both sides of the Canadian-USA border, McKee describes cultural distinctions that significantly inform contrasting assumptions about governance and the Rule of Law, including gun culture and socio-religious underpinnings. All of this is done through vivid descriptions, dialogue, poetic prose, poetry, analytical opinion, and loads of images—a most enjoyable and informative read."

—*Ken Frey Ed.D.,* Management Consultant, Milton, Ontario

"After reading *Guns and Gods in my Genes,* as a Canadian, I was overwhelmed at the thought that my North American family history stretches so far back in time and is such a significant part of United States history. I was thrilled to learn about the remarkable men and women who lived through all the wars, endured religious strife, and carried on with family farming. I loved the stories of the life and times of my paternal grandfather, a Methodist minister, who ventured into the American West as far as Newcastle, Wyoming, a place with a two-story brothel and a sheriff who carried a gun with 20 notches on its handle. A wonderful historical memoir which, I believe, has universal appeal."

—*Catharine Neill,* Richmond, British Columbia

"A truly masterful work compiled and written by Neill McKee, detailing the history of our mutual McKee ancestors before and after their arrival in Canada, and his Neill/Haskins ancestors in Canada and the United States. This has been skillfully interwoven with detailed accounts about national history in both countries. McKee possesses a great talent for describing the past in a way that brings it into present-day issues, particularly with regards to guns and law and order. I was very surprised to learn about his mother's side which connects him to all those wars in American history, and the coming of the English Pilgrims on the *Mayflower* in 1620. This book is definitely a must read for anyone who is interested in family history and genealogy. My thanks to Neill McKee for a job well done!"

—*Kenneth McKee,* Listowel, Ontario

# GUNS
## *and* GODS
### *in* MY
## GENES

# GUNS
## *and* GODS
## *in* MY
## GENES

A 15,000-mile
North American
Search Through
Four Centuries of
History, to the
Mayflower

# NEILL MCKEE

NBFS CREATIONS, LLC
*Albuquerque, New Mexico, USA*

NBFS Creations LLC
Albuquerque, New Mexico, USA
neillmckeeauthor.com
© 2020 Neill McKee

Note: This book is a work of creative nonfiction reflecting several years of genealogical research undertaken or commissioned by the author. The historical accounts and family stories contained herein are based on the readings, investigations, and experiences the author encountered while traveling to collect material for this book. The dialogs contained herein have been recreated to the best of his memory and are not intended to represent word-for-word transcripts of the many conversations that took place during the author's journeys. Some names and identifying details have been changed out of respect for the privacy of the people involved.

Literary editor: Pamela Yenser, NM Book Editors, LLC
Book and cover designer: The Book Designers, bookdesigners.com
Final copy editor and proofreader: Barbara L. Daniels
Maps: Doug Nelson, DCNmaps

Photographs are by the author or from family sources, unless credited otherwise. Photographs by the author of the Plimoth Plantation, pp. 245-46, 251, 253-54, 256-57 are published with the permission of the Plimoth Plantation (plimoth.org).

Publisher's Cataloging-in-Publication Data

Names: McKee, Neill, author.
Title: Guns and gods in my genes / Neill McKee.
Description: Albuquerque, NM: NBFS Creations LLC, 2020.
Identifiers: ISBN 9781732945739 (pbk.), ISBN: 9781732945746 (ebook) |
Library of Congress Control Number: 2020918847
Subjects: LCSH McKee, Neill—Family. | McKee, Neill—Travel. | United States—
Description and travel. | Canada—Description and travel. | United States—History.
United States—Social life and customs. | Canada—Social life and customs. |
Firearms—Social aspects—United States. | Firearms—Social aspects— Canada. |
United States—Church history. | BISAC BIOGRAPHY & AUTOBIOGRAPHY /
Personal Memoirs | BIOGRAPHY & AUTOBIOGRAPHY / Historical | HISTORY
/ United States / General | TRAVEL / Special Interest / Family | TRAVEL / Essays &
Travelogues Classification: LCC E185.97 .M575 2020| DDC 917.303/092—dc23

*To the memory of my cousin,
the late Linda (Smith) Driedger,
who started me on this journey*

# Contents

# Acknowledgments

My sincere thanks go to the following people and organizations for their help in my research on parts of this book:

- Timothy May, Verifying Genealogist, General Society of Mayflower Descendants, Plymouth, MA

- Sarah Dery, Researcher Services Manager and Researchers of American Ancestors & New England Historical Genealogical Society (NEHGS), Boston, MA

- Ancestry.com, Fold3.com, Findagrave.com

- Plimoth Plantation, Plymouth, MA

- Ronald G. Taylor, President & Museum Director, Allegany County Historical Society, Andover, NY

- Michael J. F. Sheehan, Senior Historian, Stony Point Battlefield, NY

- Eric Schnitzer, Park Ranger and Military Historian, Saratoga National Historical Park, NY

- Paul R. Ackerman, Museum Specialist/Conservator, West Point Museum, United States Military Academy, NY

- Staff of the Windsor Historical Society, Windsor, CT

- Stephen Williams, President of the Pawlet Historical Society, Pawlet, VT

- Jerry Wellnetz, Curator, Sheridan County Historical Society, Rushville, NE

- Larry Miller, Pastor, Extension Community Chapel, White Clay, NE

- Leonard Cash, local historian, and staff of the Anna Miller Museum, Newcastle, WY

- Lynn Lubkeman, Wisconsin Methodist Conference Archives, Sun Prairie, WI

- Esther Wonderlich, Iowa Methodist Conference Archives, Mt. Pleasant, IA

- Tamara Jorstad, Haskins family researcher, Sunrise Beach, MO

- Library and Registrar staff, Garrett-Evangelical Theological Seminar, Evanston, IL

- Ralph V. Stevens, family historian, Campbell, NY

- Edith and Dan McCaw, local historians, Coe Hill, ON

- Archivists, Wellington County Museum, Fergus, ON

I would like to express my deep appreciation in memory of the late Linda (Smith) Driedger for her extensive preliminary research on the Neill and Haskins families, and to Gwenda McCurdy for the Neill/Haskins family insights, memories, photos, and the stories she shared. Likewise, I would like to thank Catharine Neill, for her stories on our Neill/Haskins ancestry, and the war story of her father. I very much appreciate the work of Kenneth McKee, who, with help from his brother, Randy, captured many McKee family stories and reflections from his late father, John F. McKee, before his death.

My sincere gratitude also goes to Gayle Lauradunn, Poet and Author, Albuquerque, NM, for offering a very helpful critique of each chapter of the manuscript as it developed and for her pre-publication review. I'd also like to thank the following people for their suggestions and corrections on all or parts of the manuscript and/or reviews before publication: Ken Frey, ON; Gwenda McCurdy, ON; Catharine Neill, BC; Kenneth McKee, ON; Christopher Smart, ON; Charles M. Rolison, NM; Leonard Cash, WY; Rev. Brenda Torrie, WY.

*The past is never dead. It's not even past.*

—WILLIAM FAULKNER

*Long before you knew what death was you were wishing it on someone else. When you were two years old you were shooting people with toy guns.*

—RAY BRADBURY, *The Veldt*

*Puritanism, the haunting fear that someone, somewhere, may be happy.*

—H. L. MENCKEN

*The truth is the great Gods of this world are God-belly, God-wealth, God-honour, God-pleasure, etc.*

—REVEREND ROGER WILLIAMS,
Founder of Rhode Island and Providence Plantations

# The Author's Genealogical Map

Principal North American Ancestors in the Chronology of this Book

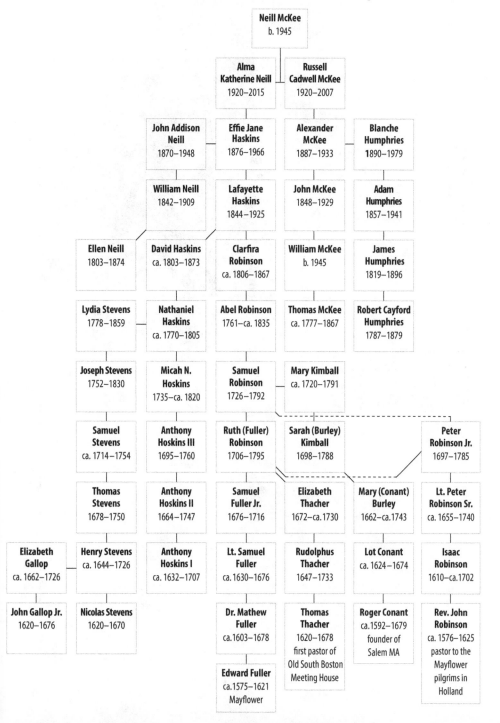

# Sites Visited in the Eastern United States and Canada

MAINE

QUEBEC

Montréal

VERMONT

NEW HAMPSHIRE

Ticonderoga

Pawlet

Salem

Boston

Plymouth

Crown Point

MASSACHUSETTS

Springfield

RHODE ISLAND

Old Scotland Cemetery

Fort William Henry

Fort Edward

Saratoga Battlefield

Stockbridge

Windsor

CONNECTICUT

ONTARIO

Montréal

Rose Island

Coe Hill

Belleville

Asphodel

Niagara Falls

Bath

Campbell

West Point

Tappan

New York

NEW YORK

NEW JERSEY

DELAWARE

Cape Croker

Colpoy's Bay

Clifford

Glen Allan

Elmira

Toronto

Ohsweken

Alfred

Andover

PENNSYLVANIA

Valley Forge

MARYLAND

Washington D.C.

Wilderness Battlefield

OHIO

Bull Run Battlefield

VIRGINIA

WEST VIRGINIA

*DCN Maps*

# Sites Visited in the Midwest and Western United States

# 1

# THE CEREMONY
## *and the* MASSACRE

Annual McKee deer hunt, 1990s

*The Deer Hunt, November 1961:* For my first deer hunt, a boy not quite 16, my father loaned me his old Lee-Enfield .303 rifle. Stationed on a rock in the middle of a field—so quiet, just a sprinkling of snow on the ground—baying hounds awoke me from a daydream. I surveyed the far hillside, saw a deer, aimed, and squeezed the trigger. The animal flinched and then took off. I thought I had missed, but joining Uncle

Gerald and the hounds, we followed a dark red trail—so easy to find the doe. Celebrations followed at lunchtime for that first kill of the season: a toast with sweet red wine, laughter, slaps on my back, my father so proud of me. But all seemed much too easy, with four more days to go.

In the afternoon we resumed the hunt. A cold wind had blown in from the north. I sat on a small hill crowned by rock. Again, hounds broke the silence, bushes rustled, hoofs pounded, a startled young buck darted from the woods, leaping up the slope. I fired as he sprung over me, but I missed and cocked the gun. The bullet jammed, then slid in, I swung and pulled the trigger again. The deer dropped close to me—blood gushing from its throat, sputtering, gurgling. Uncle Archie emerged from the woods to shake my hand; his words muffled by those sounds. My stomach churned and I vomited on the ground while Archie shot it in the head. The woods fell silent as we dragged the carcass out.

For me that evening, another toast, more pats on the back. I went out with the gang for the rest of the hunt, but never killed another deer and never fired a gun again.

I grew up with a fascination for guns as a child in the small town of Elmira, Ontario, Canada. My father and most of his brothers loved blood sports, and so I was educated in how to hunt. But killing that second deer close up, in November 1961, helped change the course of my life. I never became an anti-gun activist or a pacifist, but I tried to stay clear of firearms wherever I went on my life's journey—and I went pretty far.

After university, I volunteered as a secondary school teacher in Sabah, Malaysia (North Borneo) during 1968-70, where I also became a documentary filmmaker. I lived in some far-flung places—Asia, Africa, and Russia—for 18 years, and I traveled on assignments to more than 80 countries. In 1970, while in Tokyo, I met an American woman, Elizabeth, and we were married when I was on a filming trip in Zambia in 1972. At the end of 2012, I retired from a fulfilling career in international film and multimedia production. In 2015, we decided to settle in Albuquerque, the largest city in New Mexico, USA, known for its sense of community, sunshine, and mountains—a high desert country. I loved our new home and had been thinking about becoming an American citizen, but hadn't yet decided whether to go through with the application because I'd always thought of myself as a Canadian. Besides, I never liked America's freewheeling love of guns.

On June 11, 2016, I found myself in a gathering of 140 of my mainly Canadian relatives at Union Cemetery in Glen Allan, Ontario. I felt much at home for my parents met in the church in this village in the mid-1930s, when my mother's father was the minister. The sun broke through early morning clouds, revealing a colorful late spring day in the Conestoga River Valley, much like I remembered from my childhood. The occasion was the dedication of a newly renovated tombstone for our paternal great-great grandparents (2nd great-grandparents in "genealogical speak"). By sending emails about the project from my new home in Albuquerque, I had raised most of the balance of funds needed from cousins for the refurbishing. I billed the event as a family reunion. In addition to the Ontario crowd, family members arrived from places as far away as Santa Ana, California; Vancouver Island in British Columbia; and Calgary, Alberta.

I had started researching my ancestral roots in 2013, looking backwards to reflect on my family's foundations, wanting to discover factors that had propelled me to do what I had done with my life. As part of my discovery process, I joined *Ancestry. com*, spat into a tube, and mailed it off, hoping to find DNA links with previously unknown cousins—parts of my large family lost in the fog of time. The ceremony in the cemetery and the party that followed were the finale of three years of research, writing, preparation, and organization.

As it evolved, my interests eventually led me to focus on the religious inclinations and the attitudes towards guns of my Canadian and American ancestors in North America, rather than to undertake a full effort at tracing their European origins. Little did I know when I started my journey that it would take me back through 400 years of North American history, while traveling over 15,000 miles (over 24,000 km) through Ontario and 22 US states. I would unearth plenty of surprising discoveries, gather both humorous and tragic stories, meet distant relatives and interesting characters, collaborate with devoted historians and genealogists, confirm many facts, discount a few false claims, and come to some dead ends, leaving some stories never to be known, at least by me.

My 2nd great-grandparents, William and Margaret (Fleming) McKee, settled on the land that became our pioneer family farm around 1850. Wind and rain had corroded their old tombstone, first put in place in 1882 after William died. The roots of a lilac bush had pushed it at an angle. It looked like it could topple any day. The original tombstone was an impressive affair—seven feet tall. I asked the folks at the monument company to match its dimensions and color, using new gray granite, but to retain the original phallic spire. I had them place William's name on the west-facing surface, and Margaret's on the southern side. By my instruction, they also inscribed the original Christian verse below William's name and dates:

> Sweet is the sleep Our Father takes.
> Till in Christ Jesus he awakes.
> Then will his happy soul rejoice.
> To hear his Blessed Saviour's Voice.

There was room on the sides for the names of five of their children: two bachelor sons, as well as a son and two daughters who had died of various illnesses in their early adult years. The younger ones had been buried beside the larger memorial but their small

William and Margaret (Fleming) McKee's old and new tombstones

markers had so corroded that, for the correct names and dates, I had to depend on a cemetery inventory taken in 1996.[1]

During my childhood, my father, Russell Cadwell McKee, made sure my siblings and I knew this cemetery well, trying to instill in us an appreciation for our heritage. He frequently brought us to this sacred place. Dad's greatest challenge involved trying to find the burial place of Thomas McKee, his 2nd great-grandfather, and my 3rd, the first to come from Scotland. Before Dad passed away in 2007, for many years he had searched graveyards in the area, never finding a trace. I followed him in this endeavor by examining all the Methodist and Presbyterian church burial records available, including those in church archives in Toronto. I came no closer to discovery, but learned the pleasure of this kind of hunt.

Dad's brother, John Fleming McKee, once told me, "You know, there's a story that old Thomas could have been buried behind the farmhouse. He died during the winter when the cemetery would've been closed. Come spring, the family probably decided not to disturb him. Sometime in the mid-1930s, a sinkhole opened up in the garden behind the house. Brother Jim did a little diggin' but found nothin', and we didn't investigate further. The land settled again. Maybe that's where he was meant to rest."

The original tombstone had one free side on which I asked the memorial company to inscribe: "In Memory of Thomas McKee, born ca. 1777, died 1867, Father of William McKee. He came to Canada from Scotland in 1843." At least he'd be remembered.

In spite of this rather grand memorial, by all accounts my ancestors had been unassuming lowland Scots. I didn't understand why the family had decided on such a final statement for William—and that spire—it was like an exclamation mark pointing to heaven. Was it reverence for him or mere peer pressure to match similar gravestones in the cemetery? Or, perhaps they had simply succumbed to the sales pitch of a persuasive memorial salesman.

Part of their story had been published years ago in a Maryborough Township history.[2] Thomas McKee and his son, William, had been handloom weavers in Bridgeton, Lanarkshire, a village that is now part of Glasgow, Scotland, the place of William's birth according to his death certificate. They wove in linen and wool and probably belonged to a craft guild.

Dad always said that Thomas McKee came with two families by the names of MacKay and Cadwell (sometimes spelled "Caldwell"), who had sailed at the same time. I had found some evidence that they landed on June 16, 1843, at Quebec City, Lower Canada, on a ship named "Jane Duffus."[3] On this sailing ship's passenger list, the names of two of the Cadwell boys, John and Joseph, are entered. They match the names and ages of those who settled in the same area as the McKees. At the time, captains tried to hide the number of adults on their ships to avoid fines for overloading. But there was a total of 251 souls aboard the Jane Duffus, probably including my 3rd great-grandfather, Thomas McKee.

When he sailed, Thomas was a widower of about 66 years of age, so these younger Cadwell and McKay families probably took care of him while his son William remained in Scotland to make enough money for his own passage. I imagined Thomas, an old man for that era, riding the storms of the North Atlantic on his journey to a better life. What forces had driven him to leave the only home he'd ever known and embark on this perilous 3,000-mile (4,828 km) journey, never to see Scotland again?

My father also told us the McKees originally came from Ayrshire, a county in southwest Scotland. I searched many genealogical records but found no trace of them there. However, in the most southwest corner of Scotland lies the Region of Galloway, where a strong branch of the McKees, first spelled MacAodha or MacEth, and then MacKie or MacKay—as well as other variations—had been recorded from the 10th century.[4]

If my McKee ancestors originally came from Ayrshire or Galloway, they may have arrived in Bridgeton after losing their land, or the land on which they had been tenant farmers, during the evictions of the 1700s. Most people who know a little history have heard of Scotland's highland clearances, but the same took place in lowlands such as Ayrshire and Galloway. Popular opinion holds that the English were responsible for these evictions, but I learned they had been largely the doing of land-owning Scots. The clearances happened gradually in the lowlands, beginning in the first half of the 1700s. Landlords turned hilly lands into sheep farms and devoted lower flatlands to cattle raising and production of cash crops. By the 1820s, the lowlands had attracted international attention for innovations in agronomy—the first successful threshing mill, the improved light plough, Aberdeen-Angus cattle, and Clydesdale draught horses.[5]

My ancestors were not really part of the "Scottish Enlightenment" of the 1700s and early 1800s, when universities in Edinburgh and Glasgow threw off the stranglehold of John Knox's dogmatic Presbyterian Church. These institutions fostered new channels of human thought in religion, philosophy, law, politics, science, and technology. While my ancestors tilled the land or wove, their educated countrymen invented the modern world—the steam engine, coal-gas lighting, new canal designs, iron-hulled ships, the threshing machine, printing technologies, the first *Encyclopedia Britannica*, as well as new university disciplines such as economics and sociology.[6]

There is little distance by sea between Northern Ireland and southwestern Scotland—only 12 miles (19 km) at the closest point—and for centuries there had been considerable interchange of people and culture between the two lands. In fact, the "Scoti" or Scots, a warlike tribe from Northern Ireland, invaded western Scotland, beginning in the 4th century, joined with the

Picts to defeat the Romans, and eventually blended with them and others through Christianity.[7]

Close ties remained throughout the following centuries between Northern Ireland and Scotland in kinship, marriage, and migration for work. Starting in the mid-1770s, the Glasgow area attracted Protestant Irish weavers, who joined Protestant Scots, and places like Bridgeton became centers for the trade. By 1830, Glasgow had emerged as an industrial powerhouse of the British economy. The steam engine, power loom, and "spinning jenny" upended my ancestors' means of livelihood—handloom weaving. Large steam-driven mills dominated the industry, fed by an abundant and cheap supply of "slave cotton" from America's southern states. Unskilled Irish Catholics flooded in, searching for factory jobs. Glasgow grew from a city of around 30,000 people in 1750, to 77,000 in 1801, and 275,000 by 1841. Political and labor unrest grew, then conflict flared between Protestants and Catholics. Slums expanded in the city's smog-laden air. Polluted water sources brought cholera, typhus, and typhoid. A period of rapid economic growth in the early 1830s turned into a great depression later in the decade. Handloom weavers like Thomas and William could make only a few shillings a week.[8,9] Like many economic migrants at the time, they searched for a way to escape conditions of life in and around Glasgow.

After landing at Quebec City, Thomas McKee and his friends probably traveled up the St. Lawrence River by *bateaux* and overland on horse-drawn carts to reach the port of Kingston, then the Capital of Canada. From there, they likely sailed west by steamboat over Lake Ontario to Hamilton, where they hired carts once more to take them to Wellesley Township in Waterloo County, Upper Canada (the original name for Ontario).

In 1844, William, then 28, also crossed the ocean to join his father. The McKees helped the Cadwell and McKay families settle on their land and likely did some weaving to earn cash for purchasing their own farm. In Wellesley, William met and married Margaret Fleming, then age 16, who had also recently arrived with her family from Scotland. Accompanied by Thomas, they settled in Maryborough Township, Wellington County, about 15 miles away from her family's farm.

It is a true testament to William and Margaret's fertility and economic success in Canada that, in addition to the five children inscribed on the new tombstone, they managed to raise six other offspring who lived full lives and married, producing many descendants, some of whom flocked to Glen Allan that June day—a true gathering of the clan. The bagpipe music suggested by my brother Philip, provided some dramatic flair. I agreed to hire a professional piper, dressed in a kilt, because this music has become a Scottish Canadian tradition. I had to admit that it added an extra element of emotion to the prayers, hymns, and short sermon in the service conducted by my cousin, Reverend Keith McKee, a Presbyterian minister. Tears came to my eyes when the piper played the *Skye Boat Song* in the middle of the proceedings. But I doubt that my McKee ancestors would have had such an emotional reaction to the sound of bagpipes. Most likely, they seldom heard this whining cacophony in Scotland, and I doubt that they ever wore kilts.

The original long version of the kilt was banned in the Dress Act of 1746, after the bloody Battle of Culloden, when the highlanders were finally defeated by the English. The British implemented this ban as a measure of control over the clans. However, as the Scots gradually assimilated into British culture and the military, a modern version of the Celtic bagpipe and a shortened kilt were created. Many tartans and family crests were artificially associated with Scottish surnames—Victorian inventions, some created for the visit of King George IV to Scotland in 1822.[10, 11] The kilts and tartans subsequently became a big business, especially in North America, where Scottish ancestry identification caught on as a craze, partly driven by a lucrative commercial use for new chemical dyes. By 2018 in the US alone, there were 160 clan societies, nearly 2,000 pipe bands, over 150 highland-dancing schools, and 70 annual highland games.[12]

My ancestors may have been a part of the Protestant revival of the 1830s and 1840s, which spread through parts of Europe and North America. They could read because near-universal public education was another Scottish innovation.[13] They most likely read the Bible a lot. They first attended a nearby Presbyterian Church and moved to a Wesleyan Methodist congregation in Glen Allan, once it formed, avoiding a fundamentalist "Primitive Methodist" church, which favored American-style camp meetings with all-day prayers, songs, and preaching events. Other settlers, mainly Scottish, Irish, and Germans, surrounded their farm in Maryborough Township, on land that had been opened for settlement in the 1840s.

The ethnic mix of settlers in English-speaking Canada was much like parts of the northern United States, and gradually the two countries grew close in popular culture. But a stark difference emerged in the way the two societies evolved regarding the regulation of firearms. Canadians passed increasingly tighter rules on the ownership and use of guns. As early as 1892, the Canadian Criminal Code required a permit for a handgun, unless the owner had cause to fear assault or injury, and it was an offence to sell a handgun to anyone under 16 years of age. By 1913, carrying a handgun outside one's home without a permit could land a person in jail for up to three months.

In Canada, the regulations for handguns grew more stringent, including registration with local police in the 1930s, and a central registration system for handguns and automatic weapons by 1951. Beginning in 1995, rules strengthened into new legislation that required permits for all firearms by the end of the decade. Purchasers faced strict background checks, waiting periods, and police-supervised safety courses, along with stronger penalties in the criminal code for unlawful possession and use. A strict three-tiered classification system was implemented: prohibited, restricted, and non-restricted firearms. A person wishing to acquire a restricted firearm had to obtain a registration certificate from the Royal Canadian Mounted Police (RCMP).[14] In 2012, under a Conservative Party Government, many of the requirements to register restricted and non-restricted firearms were dropped in every province and territory except Quebec. But more recent legislation by the Liberal Party Government has reversed many of the former government's moves and added new controls.

As the dedication ceremony ended and we headed for a party in a nearby community hall, I looked at the aging faces of my Canadian brothers, sisters, nephews, nieces, cousins, in-laws, one of three remaining aunts, and my only surviving McKee uncle, John. The first five generations in Canada had left a real legacy (Table 1). I felt uplifted by the sight of many McKee children running around. I thought about what had compelled me to do all this family research, organize the tombstone renovation, and lead this commemoration. Suddenly, I had a nostalgic feeling that, after all my worldwide travels, I had come home to where I belonged.

That same day—though unknown to me at the time— 1,300 miles (2,092 km) to the south in Orlando, Florida, an

American-born Muslim, Omar Mateen, son of Afghan-born parents, prepared his *SIG Sauer MCX* semi-automatic rifle and *Glock 17- 9mm* pistol for an assault on a gay nightclub, where he would kill 49 people and injure 53 more, before dying in a shootout with police. A security guard with a gun license, Mateen had easily and legally purchased his weapons at a gun shop a few days before, despite the fact he'd been questioned by the FBI three times for possible but unproven terrorist links. What drove him to this act? Were these interrogations triggers? Was he a closeted gay, as some have suggested, or just an angry and frustrated young man born in a gun-loving society, where many people consider his religion and heritage to be alien, even un-American?

The next morning when I learned of the late-night Orlando massacre, I was truly shaken. Some of my cousins questioned my sanity for living in the US with all its gun violence. Had Elizabeth and I made the right decision to settle in Albuquerque, where the sound of gunshots sometimes ring out at night?

# 2

## RETURN *to the* McKEE FAMILY FARM

Aerial view of the McKee pioneer family farm

A COUPLE OF DAYS AFTER THE CEMETERY CEREMONY, I returned to the McKee pioneer farm where my father was born. During the past three years, I had made many visits to this place. It's located near Glen Allan, about 20 miles (32 km) northwest of my hometown of Elmira, on Concession Road 3. The farm consists of a rectangular 100-acre (40.5 hectares) lot, with a long straight lane running halfway into the property. On a sunny day in June of 2014, Richard Carothers—a friend from my filming days in Africa—flew me over the area in his 1972 Piper Cherokee

140, so I could take photos. Our view included a branch of Lake Conestoga, an artificial body of water created by damming the Conestoga River and its tributaries in 1958. From the air, the land itself looked so tame and flat, except near the original entrance road along the valley, where trees now hide a community of summer cottages. When my ancestors settled here around 1850, they found the land covered with forest and the soil full of rocks.

One of our family's stories, which my father often repeated, came back to me as I surveyed the property from the air: "The McKees didn't like the soil in Waterloo County, where the Mennonites had settled after moving from Pennsylvania in the early 1800s. Instead of looking for walnut trees, a sign of dark loam fertile soil, our ancestors searched for clay soil with plenty of thistles and rocks, just like in Scotland." But I could see no remnants of Scottish-looking rock walls. Besides, the census records and old maps I studied revealed that, by the time the McKees arrived, they probably had little choice because most lots in Waterloo County had already been granted to others. So, they took the best land available to them that was not too far away from Margaret's parents and siblings, as well as their friends, the Cadwells and McKays.

I visited the farm to gather family stories from Uncle John Fleming McKee. He had taken over the property in the 1940s—the only one of nine children, including seven boys, who wanted to farm for a living. I drove up the long lane toward the striking red barn. As I came closer, the fine details of the farmhouse became clear as well.

In the 1990s, my cousins had stripped away layers of old shingles, wooden boards, and tar paper from the outside walls—five layers, marking the five generations before them. They revealed the great logs our 2nd great-grandfather William had put in place 160 years ago. He and his aging father Thomas, and his son John, who was born in Canada in 1848, felled the surrounding trees—elm,

McKee pioneer farmhouse, completed ca.1860

oak, maple, and white ash—with axes and saws. Employing horses, they dragged the best logs to the site of their new house, where they swung their adzes day after day to square them.

During their renovation, my cousins came upon old family letters in beautiful longhand hidden in the walls, waiting to be discovered. I read one dated August 15, 1867, to William from a childhood friend, John Erskine, in New York. It was written on the occasion of the death of William's father, Thomas. It contained passages reminding William of how the two young men had lived in Scotland:

> I have been thinking of the old shop you worked in, the kind of webs we wove, the patterns they were, what thy looms looked like. The flowers in your window that you used to take so much delight in nursing and trimming and fixing up, and watching their growth.

My cousins also had removed some boards in the upstairs ceiling to uncover a skylight above the room where William had kept an old-time loom and spinning wheel. He worked there every winter until his death, leaving an unfinished woolen blanket in place. He died at age 66, "Cause of death: Inflammation," as noted on his death certificate. Considering his previous less physically demanding occupation in Scotland, it's possible he suffered from severe rheumatism brought on by over 30 years of hard labor—clearing trees, plowing, sowing, weeding, reaping, and harvesting. How his life had changed from his youthful days in the old country.

Uncle John's beautiful wife, Ruth, had died of cancer in 1963 at the age of 39, and he never remarried. His only daughter, Judy, had also died of cancer in 2008 and his oldest son, Ross, had passed away in 2015, after a nearly lifelong battle with rheumatoid arthritis. Uncle John and his two bachelor sons, Kenneth and Randy, now in their 60s, were the three remaining McKee occupants and possibly the end of our line on the farm, unless a family member buys the place from them or from their estate. In Canada, it is unusual for a farm property to be occupied by one family for 170 years through six generations—their names, birth and death years now held firmly in my brain:

1.  Thomas McKee (ca. 1777-1867)

2.  William McKee (1815-82) and his spouse, Margaret (Fleming) McKee (1829-1903)

3.  James McKee (1854-1918) and Archibald McKee (1860-1911), followed by their older brother John McKee (1848-1929) and his spouse, Mary Jane (Doren) McKee (1854-1932)

4.  Alexander McKee (1887-1933) and his spouse, Blanche (Humphries) McKee (1890-1979)

5.  Uncle John Fleming McKee (1921—still living at the time of my visit) and his spouse, Ruth (Lavery) McKee (1923-63)

6.  Uncle John's remaining sons, Randy and Kenneth McKee

This record of tenure represents a pretty straight line of succession, except for James and Archibald—two bachelor brothers who squabbled and split the ownership of the land down the middle, each taking 50 acres (20.25 hectares). In 1910, they finally sold out to their older brother, John, my great-grandfather.

As I reached the house, Uncle John emerged from the tractor shed with my cousin Kenneth. Uncle John, age 95 at the time of this visit, didn't have an ounce of fat left on his bones. He once stood about five feet six inches, but had shrunken and probably weighed less than 90 pounds. He was wearing overalls splattered with dirt and manure, the mark of his trade. He had mustered enough strength to make it to the tombstone dedication and had even risen to his feet at the dinner party to give a short speech, thanking me for organizing the event. He referred to the fact that he would soon be buried in the same cemetery with his wife, two eldest children, and our ancestors.

Cousin Randy had gone out on an errand, but Uncle John, cousin Kenneth, and I went into the house to talk. The inside looked plain, rugged, and dusty—obviously lacking a woman's touch for many years. I apologized for not making an appointment, but they didn't seem to mind. We started with their health. Uncle John told me he had terrible pains in his feet, but that didn't stop him from driving the tractor, although no longer every day.

I had collected many stories from him on previous visits, so I soon got down to my main line of enquiry, "Uncle John, do you have any guns on the farm?"

He looked a little perplexed and Kenneth answered, "We've got three guns, a shotgun and two .22 rifles. They're under Randy's name. He has his license but doesn't much hunt now. We use them to kill groundhogs or sometimes when we have to put an animal down. I've never hunted. Dad, when he was young, liked to hunt just like your father and our uncles."

Kenneth had learned every one of Uncle John's stories by heart, and when you listened to him, he sounded like a recording of John in his younger years. He also wrote well, passing on many of his father's tales to me by email.

Uncle John added, "The hunting never came from the McKee side. That was the Humphries, my mother's side. Her father, Grandpa Adam Humphries, had a big farm down near Peterborough. He hunted almost until the day he died—an expert at shooting deer and foxes. When we were kids, we used to take the train down there and hunt with him in the fall and winter."

Uncle John's statement made sense to me. My thoughts drifted momentarily to my findings on the Humphries family in eastern Ontario. I had visited their former land, with its stately gabled farmhouse in the rolling countryside of Peterborough County. Great-grandfather Adam Humphries (1857-1941) descended from Robert Cayford Humphries, born in England in 1787 of Welsh-Norman descent. He and his younger brother Job, left England as young men in their 20s with the intention of going to the West Indies. Their ship was on the way to Boston when it had to put into Halifax for repairs. The two young men liked the place and decided to stay. Robert particularly liked the look of Catherine McGuire, a young lady he met in Halifax, and he courted and married her. The brothers decided to continue on with Catherine to Pennsylvania, where their mother's brother had settled, but for some reason they didn't stay there.[1]

The War of 1812 had ended in 1815, at which point the Americans had to face the fact that they were not going to take over all of British North America. I speculate that the Humphries, who had grown up under the Crown, decided to throw in their lot with the stability it represented, so they headed north—late United Empire Loyalists.

In 1821, Robert and Catherine, with their two small children and brother Job, made their way in a light wagon pulled by one horse through Pennsylvania and New York, probably crossing into Upper Canada by ferry at the eastern end of Lake Ontario. When they reached Asphodel Township, Peterborough County, they decided that this land suited them just fine.[2] They gazed upon forests full of deer, bears, wolves, rabbits, and foxes—rolling and fertile land for farming, once cleared. I believe that they

**STILL HUNTS REYNARD**

Adam Humphries hunting

must have brought their long-barreled, Pennsylvania-Kentucky rifles, used in the US for both hunting and warfare. Their design included spiral grooves in the barrel called rifling, which made the bullet spin and increased its accuracy, even up to 200 yards (183 meters).[3] I could imagine my ancestors easily shooting deer—even moose—and bringing home good supplies of meat. A cousin sent me an old newspaper clipping with a photo of Adam Humphries still hunting foxes and trapping muskrats at the age of 82.

The influence of my paternal grandmother's side on my father and his brothers must have been considerable in their formative years. A perfectly preserved photo of my Humphries great-grandparents and their many children demonstrates prosperity and education beyond the level achieved by the McKees.

Adam and Mary Ellen Humphries & family ca. 1918—Mary Blanche at top row, farthest right

Refocusing on the McKee family, I listened to Uncle John continue. But I had to pay careful attention since his jaw had shrunk considerably and his false teeth flopped around in his mouth when he tried to speak. To remedy this, he held them out beside his face. I found myself looking at his waving dentures instead of his eyes as he said, "Anyways, for a long time on this farm, the McKees never had much use for guns."

"But Uncle John, what about the powder horn that cousin Bill has?"

A few months earlier, when gathering photos from cousins for our family history, I had received an email with an image of a powder horn attached. My cousin, Bill McKee, wrote that he had the real article. His dad, Uncle Bud, had given it to him before he died. It was inscribed with the name "Ross William McKee." (William never used his first name "Ross," for some unknown reason.) Bill mentioned that he didn't have the guns that had been charged with powder from this horn and didn't know what had happened to them.

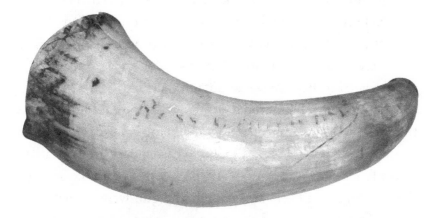

Powder horn of Ross William McKee. *Photo by Bill McKee*

Uncle John scratched his whiskers, "Ya, there were a couple of muzzle loaders around here when I was growing up. They were really old and in pretty bad condition."

I pulled out a copy of William McKee's will, dated April 16, 1883, and offered it to Uncle John, "I want to give you this. I found it in Wellington County Museum."

The inventory included in the will listed everything William had left to his wife, Margaret: every animal and farm implement, six tons of hay, and bushels of grains and peas. According to the list, their household furnishings were only worth $20.00 Canadian. The inventory's total value amounted to almost $6,000, but most of that was for the land and buildings (Table 2). (To arrive at the farm's current Canadian dollar value, one would have to multiply by at least 400. The value per acre has risen exponentially since my ancestors' time.) They had risen out of abject poverty to a relatively wealthy situation through years of back-breaking work. How had they managed in this land and climate, so very alien to them?

As I looked around the dusty room at the well-worn furniture, I had to remind myself that my uncle and cousins were far from poor. I knew the old guy to be a penny pincher.

I pointed to the will, "Look, no muskets in the inventory."

Uncle John squinted at the list, "That's quite a find. There's a lot of detail here. Don't know why the guns aren't listed. They were here when I was a kid in the 20s." He started to chuckle, "I recall when brother Jim was about ten years old, he decided to try out one of them. He poured in gun powder and wadding, primed the barrel with the ramrod, and popped in a musket ball. He was afraid to actually hold and shoot it in case it backfired, so he tied it to a fence post with a rope. Then he fastened a long string to the trigger, stood back, and pulled. The gun went off with such a bang that Father heard the noise and came running out of the barn. He was really angry and gave Jim a good swat—could have killed himself or one of us. After that, Dad decided to get rid of the guns. He wrote to Charlie Gunter in Saskatchewan, his sister Margaret's husband, and asked him if he would take them. Charlie agreed, so Dad shipped them out West."

I dug a little deeper concerning his father, my grandfather Alexander, a name which was usually written in the short form "Alex" but pronounced "Alec." I asked, "So, Grandpa Alex and our ancestors didn't seem to have much use for guns? Do you think they were pacifists?"

"Don't know about our ancestors, but I don't think my father was ever a pacifist. Maybe there'd been too much killing. The First World War had just ended."

"It's strange that the family didn't list them in William's will. Do you think they just didn't want guns mentioned there? They were pretty religious."

My grandparents, Alex and Blanche, on their wedding day

"Could be," Uncle John said.

I remembered the old family story that William did some lay preaching in his Methodist Church, and also was a social reformer. He and his son, John, helped build the log schoolhouse on Concession Road 3 at the edge of the McKee property. That's where my dad and his siblings attended school. My grandmother had once taught there as well.

Thinking of my first childhood association with guns—playing cowboys and Indians with our cap pistols and homemade bows and arrows—I asked, "When Thomas and William first settled here, do you think they met any Indigenous People in this area?"

Uncle John asked, "You mean Indians?"

"Yes," I nodded, but smiled a little about the term he used. "Indians" is now recognized as a symbol, or symptom, of structural racism in Canada. Even "native people," and "first nations" are also disappearing from use in favor of "Indigenous People." Compare this to New Mexico, where I have met Native Americans who proudly continue to refer to themselves as "Indians."

Kenneth jumped in, "There used to be a Wyandot reserve over on Concession Road 5, across the creek. There was a butter and cheese factory there, and after it was abandoned the township bought the property. When I went to school there in the 60s, both the factory and the school still had the name 'Wyandot.'"

"Do you think the reservation was there when our ancestors settled here?" I asked.

"I wouldn't be surprised," Uncle John offered.

The Wyandot, or Huron Nation, a northern Iroquoian-speaking people, had settled on the north shore of Lake Ontario and migrated toward Georgian Bay on Lake Huron. Once a nation of at least 20,000, they had been reduced to 600 or 700 people by the time my ancestors arrived in Canada. Diseases brought by early explorers and settlers, and their involvement in inter-tribal wars, had decimated the Wyandot in Upper Canada.[4]

I changed the subject, thinking of the huge surge in gun sales to conservative whites after President Obama had been elected in the US, "When I was a kid, I remember Dad saying something about a black family around here. He showed us some small houses on Concession 3."

Uncle John replied, "Yes, a couple of African families lived down at the crossroads of Concession 3 and Dorking Road. There's an old African cemetery someplace over there. My dad used to employ a black man by the name of Bill Alestock. He worked as a hired hand for different farmers around here. I heard he descended from former slaves who came from the US by the underground railway. The white people usually got along with them in this area, but I recollect that some of the children in our school were a bit bigoted; probably learned it from their parents. When Bill drove past the school on his bicycle one day, some of the boys called out a racist rhyme. We McKee boys weren't involved.

"Bill got so angry that he stormed into the schoolyard and gave the children the talking to they deserved. Then he turned and started to walk into the schoolhouse. A few of the boys had rushed in ahead of him to warn our teacher that Bill was coming. She replied, 'We don't want any niggers here.' Bill overheard this as he entered and he stepped in front of her and shouted, 'You should have your ears boxed!' Bill Alestock made his point that day and for good reason."

I found it interesting that even in the 1920s, Bill knew how to stand up for himself. Things had been pretty peaceful in this place between whites and the few blacks who remained here. But my deeper research into the history of the area revealed a more complicated account.

The McKee farm had been carved out of an area once called, "The Queen's Bush." Around 1,500 escaped slaves from the US settled on it in the 1820s and 1830s. The Government of Upper

Canada allowed them to squat on the land, some of which had originally been reserved for the Anglican Church. They established settlement centers in Glen Allan and the nearby villages of Hawkesville and Wallenstein. They had the reputation of being a hardworking and self-reliant people who built schools and churches. However, in 1848, the Canada Company, based in Guelph, was granted a license to survey and sell the Queen's Bush on behalf of the Crown. Because most of the black squatters could not afford to pay for the land they occupied, the Company pressured them to leave, sometimes by nefarious means. They moved farther north and west in Upper Canada.[5] Many returned to the US to fight for the Union side in the Civil War. Some decided to remain there after the Union Army's victory, and they brought their families with them.[6]

My 2nd great-grandfather, William McKee, was one of those settlers who petitioned for his 100 acres from the Crown. As far as I could determine, he had not chased off any black families from his parcel. It took William until April 21, 1875 to receive his papers on the Crown Deed, according to the archival records in Wellington County Museum. It appears from the long period he took to complete his payments that it was far from a free grant.

Uncle John grimaced due to the pain in his feet. I suggested, "Maybe you need to take a nap while Kenneth shows me around the farm." John's eyes closed as we quietly exited.

Kenneth and I walked outside toward the barn. On the left, I saw a small herd of goats enclosed by a wire fence. "So, which of you bachelor brothers keeps the goats and who keeps the cattle?" I was making a reference to our great-grand uncles, Archibald and James, who had divided the farm in half after taking over from their father, William. One preferred to raise sheep and goats and the other cattle. They lived together in the farmhouse, but didn't see eye to eye on many things.

Kenneth laughed, "We don't have a division of ownership or labor for animals. We all like goat's milk and we make our own goat's milk cheese. It's healthier because it's designed to grow a much smaller animal, closer in size to humans."

I asked, "Is there anything left of the wall that divided the farm between cattle versus sheep and goats? My dad told me there was a wall running right through the whole farm."

"Maybe they ran a cedar fence through the fields but not a stone wall. Let me show you something." We went through the barnyard as Kenneth continued, "See those stones? That's all there is left of the wall in the barn built by James and Archibald. It used to run through the whole barn and you couldn't get from one side to the other without going outside until Great-Grandfather John constructed a doorway. In the 1930s, Grandpa Alex and Uncle Jim broke down most of the remaining wall. We tore the last part out in 1983."

McKee barn and goats

Kenneth's eyes sparkled as he told me this. It became clear to me that he thrived on such stories—inseparable from his life, like the air he breathed.

We walked to the back fields where cattle grazed: purebred French Limousins, which were most certainly the center of their farm operation. Kenneth watched cattle prices on the Internet and also played the stock market a little. We reached a place near the edge of the property where the land began to slope downwards into the valley that now formed Lake Conestoga. Like my father and his siblings, and McKee children before them, I had played in this valley and fished in its creek when I was a kid. I remember standing in the same place before. My father had brought me and my brother Glen here to show us where the original McKee cabin had been built in the late 1840s. Dad had found some old ceramic shards in this place, which seemed sacred to him.

I had located their records on *Ancestry.com* for the 1851 and 1861 censuses of Upper Canada. My excitement in finding them probably matched my father's when he found those shards. There, on the 1851 census, I saw a family from Scotland living in a log shanty: Thomas McKee, a widower (with an inaccurate estimated age of 80, when he was probably about 74 at the time), William McKee, age 34, and his wife Margaret, 20. Also listed in that census were their first four children, including my great-grandfather John, then age three. At the time, they registered ages "at next birthday," a strange thing to do, I thought, when survival year-to-year was precarious.

There's an old family story about our ancestors' encounter with a bear. I asked Kenneth, "Do you think they had those old muskets for protection from bears?"

"If they had guns, they weren't so keen on using them. The story I heard was that when the McKee family went to town to shop one day, a black bear broke into their cabin. They returned home to find the bear still inside, making a real mess. William climbed up on the roof, carrying a hammer. He tapped loudly on the chimney. That scared the bear and it ran away."

"Maybe they left their guns inside the cabin. Would they have taken one on their outing?"

"It was pretty wild here, but I doubt that they would have taken a gun to town."

I imagined the area at the time—dense mixed forests with thick underbrush and plenty of bears and wolves. When the McKees started to clear their land, only about 600 people lived in the whole of Maryborough Township, according to the 1851 census. They entered their lot on a road running along the valley. William and John helped to build it, laying logs across some parts prone to flooding, a so-called "corduroy road."

I asked Kenneth, "Why do you think Great-grandfather John left the farm to go to Hastings County in eastern Ontario? It doesn't make sense to me that the first-born son would give up his natural title. They were doing relatively well."

"Hard to tell. Maybe he just wanted adventure and decided to leave it to his younger brothers, like your dad did."

I'd seen references in the old letters found in the walls indicating that Great-grandfather John had done some carpentry or building work in Galt, a town about 40 miles to the south. Then he married Mary Jane Doren, a Cadwell granddaughter, and settled in Hastings County in eastern Ontario. I had traveled to Hastings in June 2014, but couldn't locate the former McKee homestead there.

I asked, "Do you think that he took those old muskets to Hastings County? Compared to here, it must have been an even wilder country."

Kenneth nodded, "Now, you may have a good theory there."

Great-grandfather John was definitely a character I wanted to learn more about. I remembered some family stories of him in his dotage. He and Mary Jane had eight children in Hastings before they moved back to take over the farm from his squabbling bachelor brothers. He had become the only hope for McKee family continuity on the property because one brother, Thomas, born in 1851, already had his own farm; Alexander, born in 1862, moved to Vancouver Island to become a missionary-cum-trader; and David, born in 1865, became an accountant and chose to go to India to work at a mission church and school.

McKee children never roamed or worked the fields again until 1920, when my grandparents, Alex and Blanche, took over the farm to relieve his aging parents. They brought two children with them and seven more were born here, including my father, Russell Cadwell, and his identical twin brother Gerald Humphries. By 1929, four adults, including the two grandparents, and nine children, ages one to fifteen, lived in the tiny farmhouse.

I remembered a story from my father. Great-grandfather John lived to a good old age, lending a hand on the farm as best he could, while Mary Jane helped raise the brood. Then, on Thanksgiving Day 1929, in his 82nd year, John worked all morning clearing brush and sat down to a feast at noon. He felt some indigestion so he went outside for air, returned to get some water from the cupboard, then suddenly crashed to the floor. They carried him to the sofa where he expired within minutes. Mary Jane lived for about three more years but passed on peacefully, leaving more room for the growing children.

My thoughts drifted to all the McKees who had lived and died on this land. Kenneth brought me back to the present when he stopped and said, "Here's the spot where our grandpa Alex had the accident."

I had heard the story from my father many times but Dad never told us that it happened in almost the same place where the first McKee cabin had been built. It occurred in July 1933, one day before Grandpa Alex's 46th birthday. I had found Grandpa's death certificate online: "Kitchener-Waterloo Hospital, July 7, 1933, fracture of 4, 5, and 6 cervical vertebrae, fell from a load of hay."

I said, "I think the accident was part of the reason why my dad and Uncle Gerald wanted to leave the farm as soon as younger brothers could take over. As you know, their company, McKee Brothers, made hay harvesters, which didn't require standing on moving wagons, spreading hay around. Their inventions could be safely run by one man on a tractor."

Kenneth said, "You're probably right, there."

As we walked back to the house, my thoughts returned to the landscape—it was like a book full of stories, some of them so tragic, including the premature death of my grandfather. Dad told us he had been driving the wagon that day, and I wondered if that made him become such a slow and cautious driver.

We entered the house again, finding Uncle John awake and somewhat refreshed after his nap. The pain in his feet had temporarily subsided. I wanted to get his perspective on what had happened that day. But I wasn't prepared for the implications.

*The Hay Wagon, 1933:* As a boy, I knew my father to be a cautious driver—gas pedal, brake, gas pedal, brake, rocking, watching, weaving, avoiding bumps, potholes, and cursing "knuckleheads" on the road. As we lunged along, he'd sing a popular song to sooth his nerves: "Irene goodnight, Irene goodnight, goodnight Irene, goodnight Irene, I'll see you in my dreams." The whole family would join in the chorus: "Sometimes I live in the country. Sometimes I live in the town. Sometimes I take a great notion, to jump in the river and drown."

Even with Dad's erratic driving, he lived to a good old age. Just before he died, he repeated the story of his own father's death: "On July 4th, 1933, when I was just 13 years old, I drove our team of Clydesdales, while my father forked hay on the wagon behind. I heard a gunshot in the nearby woods, the horses bolted, he lost his balance and fell to the ground. We carried him to the farmhouse and called the doctor, but his neck was broken and he passed away."

When I asked Uncle John to tell me his memory of that fateful day, he told a different story, "I was 12 that year and my job was to follow behind, gather up scattered hay, and shout when things went wrong. As your father turned the horses, the back wheel hit a rock. The wagon lurched upwards, then came banging down. Dad lost his balance, pitchfork shot into the air. Falling backwards, his head hit a rock on the ground. All was still for a moment, then I heard him moan, 'Oh my Lord, what a stupid thing to do.' We carried him to the house, called the ambulance, but he died three days later. His coffin sat right there by the window and we all sang 'There is a land that is fairer than day.'"

"But tell me about the gunshot!" I demanded, like a lawyer in court.

"There was no gunshot. The wheel just hit a rock."

As I left the farm, driving down the lane, I checked my rear-view mirror for that hay wagon piled high with guilt; my father with the Clydesdales, him holding those reins so tight. And as I drove, I sang to him "Irene goodnight."

# 3

# REVISITING
## *the* WILD COUNTRY

The Irish Brothers, Rose Island, Ontario, 1960. *Painting by Frances (McKee) Gregory, from a photo by Gerald McKee*

I FOUND THE PAINTING IN A COUSIN'S BASEMENT IN Elmira—two old geezers with guns. The taller one had obviously tied his pants up with a cord. Their place looked more like a shack than a proper home. Had they just come back from hunting or were they hillbillies keeping intruders away?

After doing some traveling in the US, I returned to Ontario in July 2016, to investigate the early life and times of my paternal great-grandparents, John and Mary Jane McKee. He had left the family farm, married, and settled in Hastings County—wilder country to the east. My primary question remained: Did he take those old muskets with him as protection from hillbillies or only for hunting game? Searching for details of the lives of our ancestors involves real detective work. Most databases can only give you names, dates, and places—no real stories. On my visit to Hastings County two years before with my brother Glen, a local historian in Coe Hill, Edith McCaw, gave me the names and telephone number of a couple of elderly "Irish brothers." She told me they just might know the whereabouts of the former McKee place. I mentioned the Irish brothers to cousin Kenneth on the McKee farm, and he remembered a painting that used to hang in our Uncle Gerald's house in Elmira. My sister, Frances, had painted it from a photograph Gerald had taken on a hunting trip in the early 1960s—a 25th wedding anniversary present from the family.

My great-parents didn't leave a tidy trail to follow. During the earlier trip, my brother and I had turned up a few clues, but when we stopped to take photos or knock on doors for information, swarms of mosquitoes attacked us. This second visit by myself in late July, I accurately calculated, would be less tortuous, for mosquito populations usually decrease by then.

According to family stories, John and Mary Jane McKee settled in a place called "Rose Island." On the earlier visit, I had found a short history of the place titled *The Loon Calls*. It stated that Mary Jane had named the settlement,[1] but I couldn't find any islands or lakes on maps of the area, and if wild roses once grew in this wilderness, they were no longer evident. I couldn't help but think that Mary Jane had named the village "tongue in cheek." To me it didn't seem rosy at all.

John and Mary Jane were latecomers to the settlement process in Hastings County. The region consisted of bushland with a thin

Great-grandparents, John and Mary Jane McKee, ca. 1920

layer of soil covering the Canadian Shield, a layer of rock that had been scraped clean by glaciers during the last Ice Age. In the late 1800s, free grants of 100 acres were offered to anyone willing to build a house of at least 20 by 20 feet (about 6 by 6 meters) and to keep a minimum of 12 acres (5 hectares) under cultivation for five years. But I knew from my previous visit that no lots were marked, so their former property would be hard to find.

Before this second visit, I had also completed more research on *Ancestry.com* and other sources, and made more contacts. I found John, Mary Jane and their growing family in the censuses of 1891, 1901, and Mary Jane and three of their children in 1911. (By then, John had returned to the family Farm in Wellington County to prepare for the move.) But I couldn't find an exact record of their property. This time, after only an hour on the microfiche reader in Hastings County Archives at Belleville, Ontario, I discovered they had acquired Lots 30, 31, and 32 (each 100 acres) on Concession Road 12 (Rose Island Road), Wollaston Township, Hastings County.

With photos of my sister's painting in hand, I drove to Madoc,

Ontario, to meet Delbert Irish, age 89, a well-known local whittler, and his elder brother Leslie. I had called them to make an appointment and to be sure I'd be welcomed. When I arrived, Delbert was whittling one of his pieces for sale, but he put down his tools and his brother joined us. I showed them the photo and asked, "Do you know these guys?"

Delbert replied, "Why that's Uncle Raymond and Uncle George. Where'd you find this?"

I explained the origin of the painting and asked, "Is this at Rose Island?"

"Sure is," Lesley said. "That's at the old Irish property."

"They both have shotguns, looks like. Did they keep those for safety in that wilderness?" I asked.

"Those are rifles, not shotguns. Our uncles loved to hunt deer and so did we. There's a lot of deer in that area, still today."

The photo set off a long discussion about Rose Island, during

Delbert and Leslie Irish holding a photo of the painting of their uncles

which I discovered that Delbert and Leslie, with their parents, had lived during the 1930s on the former McKee property after my ancestors had sold out and left. They told me they still called it the "McKee place" at the time, 20 years after the McKees departed. The Irish brothers were most helpful in describing what to look for along Rose Island Road in order to locate the place.

From Madoc I drove to Coe Hill, where my ancestors had shopped for provisions and caught the train. I stopped for lunch and bought a T-shirt and baseball cap printed with the words "Coe Hill Billy," then I headed west on Rose Island Road, a narrow track through the bush.

The author of *The Loon Calls* mentions that the Rose Island post office opened in 1887, and John McKee served as postmaster for over 25 years.[2] In an earlier discussion with Uncle John, he told me that his grandpa John operated a sawmill and was said to have made and sold cedar shingles for roofs and siding. He grew and milled grain for his family and also ground grain commercially for the community. Uncle John said, "The local farmers would load their wagons with grain and haul it to Grandpa's gristmill. Everyone knew him as a kind-hearted and generous man. He used to feed hay to the farmers' horses while they waited. If it happened to be at meal time, he would often invite them in. Not sure what all that socializing cost him, but he was sure liked by his neighbors. Probably, he got extra business that way."

As I drove westward down the gravel road toward Rose Island, I felt totally alone. I could see no sign of people—no ongoing farming or other economic activities. In places, I saw the remnants of old cedar fences, but no farm animals to enclose. I drove past a deserted-looking house on the north side of the road

Remains of agricultural activity at Rose Island

and a broken-down barn with a few old sheds on the south side. The buildings looked like the McKee place the Irish brothers had described, but I wasn't sure so I drove on.

A letter from Mary Jane to her in-laws, written in 1876, and another from John in 1877, had been found by my cousins within the walls of the McKee farmhouse in Wellington County. The address on the letters indicated that my great-grandparents first lived across the line in Chandos Township, Peterborough County, also part of Rose Island settlement. I reasoned they had followed her uncle Thomas Cadwell to this place. He was part of the Cadwell family who had brought old Thomas McKee to Canada in 1843 (Chapter 1). Thomas was a brother of Mary Jane's mother, Elizabeth, who died when Mary Jane was young. After Elizabeth's death, her husband, John Dorrien (a maiden name that Mary Jane simplified to "Doren"), departed with all of Mary Jane's siblings for Cleveland, Ohio, leaving her with her grandmother, Isabella Cadwell.

*The Loon Calls* also contains a mention that John and Mary Jane had given away some of their land on the Peterborough side of the county line for a church and a cemetery.[3] My brother and I had seen a cemetery on our earlier visit and I wanted to talk to someone about it. I saw a car approaching and stopped to wave it down. I had no problem bringing the driver to a halt.

"Sorry to bother you, but I was here a couple of years ago and I saw a cemetery and old church on this road. Do you know anything about them?"

"Sure do. My people are buried there. Down the road on your left side."

"So, your family's been here a long time? Would you happen to know if any Cadwells live around here?"

She laughed, "I'm a Cadwell. It's my maiden name. You'll find many of us in that cemetery."

"Do you know of Thomas Cadwell, the first to settle here in the late 1800s?"

The former Presbyterian Church on Rose Island Road

She chuckled some more, "That's so long ago. I'm no historian. Best check the cemetery yourself, or maybe the one at Coe Hill."

After driving a short distance, I located the cemetery but not the church. Then I recalled it was farther down the road. It was easy to find again. Probably, it had been moved and converted into a summer residence some years ago. I knocked on the door. No one answered.

I drove back to the cemetery, which appeared to be well-kept. No swarms of mosquitoes attacked me this time as I got out of the car, but when I walked through the grounds, deer flies dove at me like spitfires, biting my face and neck—the major pest of mid-summer in the Ontario bushland. I quickly located the tombstone of Albert Cadwell, a son of Thomas. I couldn't find Thomas' grave, but I saw a whole row of Cadwells, some recently buried.

I headed back on the road towards the county line where I happened to see an old man with a long white beard repairing a hay mower—the first person I had seen on any property. When I drove up the lane, I could see that his face looked younger than I had anticipated. As it turned out, he was Jim Eadie, a farmer who had recently retired from a career as a forensic expert with the Ontario Provincial Police. We engaged in a good conversation on living in the US versus Canada. He told me that one time he was loaned to the Los Angeles Police Department to help solve the O. J. Simpson murder case. But now, incongruently, he raises sheep. He also is a ham radio enthusiast, connecting to the world from his isolated location.

I asked him, "Did you ever hear of the name McKee around here? They used to have a farm and ran the post office."

"Can't say that I've ever heard that name. But you might ask Merle Post in the second house to the left, after you cross the county line."

He told me he had done a little investigating around the abandoned buildings I had seen on my way in. We discussed the possibility that a sawmill and gristmill had once been there because the place had a water source. He also mentioned he had seen ruins of an old schoolhouse up on a small hill at the county line. This was promising since I knew Grandma Blanche (Humphries) McKee had taught school in the area—the reason she had come to Rose Island in the first place. But my priority was first to find the former McKee place.

I thanked my new forensic expert cum sheep farmer acquaintance and drove to Merle Post's place. The name "Post" rang a bell. I had read in *The Loon Calls* that a John Post had been the second person to take over the Post Office—a vocation well suited to his surname—after the McKees left Rose Island.[4] As it turned out, Merle Post knew nothing about a McKee family, but she gave me the number of Mac Wilson in Coe Hill, who had once owned the abandoned farm I'd seen. I was getting a little "warmer" in this search.

I returned to the broken-down buildings to investigate. I knocked on the door of the small house on the north side, probably built in the 1940s or 1950s, but no one answered. I walked around the back and saw something strange—the remains of an old log foundation. I recalled what Delbert Irish told me, "the McKee place was a big two-story, frame house—kind of T-shaped. But it burned down some years ago." I could see that the logs had been partially charred. I'd found what I was looking for.

Straight back from the house I spotted a small lake—more like a swamp full of old stumps attracting mid-summer frogs and insects. The creek ran from the swamp, down alongside the house, and under a bridge to the other side of the road—a perfect location for water-powered mills.

I investigated the creek. It reminded me of my childhood

occupation of fishing in such places. It looked pure and inviting, and I wondered if it contained trout. The old barn beside it had a stone foundation much like that on the McKee home farm. It was built quite high, obviously good protection against spring floods. The barn appeared to have been built or rebuilt in the mid-1900s.

I walked back to the house and used my cell phone to dial the number given to me by Merle Post. Mrs. Wilson answered and passed the phone to her husband, Mac. I told him about my mission and where I was standing.

Mac spoke in an enthusiastic and helpful way. "Yes," he told me, "I owned Lot 30, Concession Road 12 from 1956 to 1972 where the McKee place was. I also owned Lots 31 and 32. The large house had burned down by then. I purchased the lots from Jerome Campbell, who built the smaller house sometime in the early 50s. I worked the farm there until I retired. Had to close down due to loses."

"What kind of loses?" I asked.

"Cattle rustlers, actually."

"In Ontario?"

"Yep. You could find thieves anywhere those days."

"Did you have to guard your place with guns?" I asked.

Mac laughed, "Nope. We had guns for hunting but let the police deal with thieves."

"Were there any police stationed in Rose Island when my great-grandparents lived here?"

Mac paused and then replied, "I doubt it. But it must have been a pretty wild place, even wilder than when we lived there. There's no real record."

Then I asked, "What about the creek? Did you see any traces of an old mill there?"

What he told me was music to my ears. "Yes, I recall some

The remaining original log foundation of the McKee property

Abandoned barn rebuilt in the 1950s by Mac Wilson

stories that the McKees ran their mills with a big waterwheel. They had a gristmill and a sawmill."

"Did you see any sign of a mill powered by a steam engine? The water from the creek wouldn't power a mill year-round."

"Can't say I saw anything like that," Mac said.

I was testing a theory. The husband of the helpful local historian in Coe Hill had suggested this possibility on my earlier visit, and it made sense to me because Grandfather Alex and his older brother, Harvey, had both become steam locomotive engineers after they left this place. How else could they have learned how to run such technology out here in the wilderness?

After we'd ended our conversation, I stood there staring at the old foundation. During the years they had lived here, my great-grandparents carried on the farm family tradition of populating the land, bringing eight children into the world—four girls and four boys, including my grandfather, Alexander, born in 1887 (Table 1).

Along with operating Rose Island Post Office, John and Mary Jane McKee also earned an income from selling groceries, hardware, and fuel. Most likely, Mary Jane and their older daughters did the cooking and looked after both the store and post office, while the sons helped their father with running the sawmill and gristmill, clearing and ploughing the land, as well as raising hay and grain crops for their animals.

As it turned out, the land on which my great-grandparents had settled did not match their marital fecundity. The thin soil required years of lying fallow between crops in order to be productive. In addition, the Coe Hill area did not remain prosperous. An iron mine near town closed in 1885 because the ore contained too much sulphur. John and Mary Jane's children had no interest in carrying on in this desolate place, and they left Hastings County—except for one daughter who married a farmer in the next township. By 1910, John and Mary Jane had decided to sell their land and move back to the McKee family farm in Wellington County. Eventually, many of the other families who settled along Rose Island Road sold out and left. Over time, the forest advanced and erased most signs of those better times.

I could imagine John and Mary Jane packing their belongings, including those old muskets that went missing from William McKee's will, and putting them on the train. The powder horn used to charge those firearms had William's name etched on it. William probably thought his son John could make more use of the old guns in this wilder country. Or had there been a disagreement about the need for guns at all? This was pure speculation on my part, as I searched for reasons why John had given up his chance to take over the McKee family farm as a young man, being the first-born son.

While preparing to leave Rose Island, I remembered the forensic expert cum sheep farmer's talk of the remains of a school. John McKee had been a school board trustee who helped to build a one-room schoolhouse designated S. S. No. 3.[5] For many years, his family had boarded the teacher. With all this history in mind, I drove back to the county line, hiked up a steep bank, and walked into the woods. There I saw it, just where he told me it would be—the remnants of the school where Grandma Blanche once taught—now only a few layers of rotting logs above the ground.

Listening carefully amid the rustle of wind in branches and bird songs, I imagined I could hear the rhythms of Grandma's voice as she recited a poem to her students over 100 years ago. The oft-repeated family story of her arrival at Coe Hill train station came to mind. She was only 16 years old, the new elementary

Remains of "The Red Schoolhouse," Rose Island

school teacher, fresh out of high school—very smart and ready to go to work. She met my grandfather at the station—the beginning of a union that led to my dad's birth, my own, my son and daughter's after that, as well as throngs of aunts, uncles, and cousins. I could visualize their first encounter as a love story.

*Meeting the train, 1906:* It was a winter's day and Alex McKee, then only 18, had been assigned by his father to meet Mary Blanche Humphries with a horse-drawn sleigh. I suppose the train was late and they only had moonlight to guide them along Rose Island Road. A cold night with light snow falling. Had I been sitting behind them, I might have seen her thin coat, requiring them to share a woolen blanket, to move a little closer together than was proper at the time. I would have caught a whiff of that light perfume she applied to her neck just before the train arrived. As I imagined their conversation, I could sense Alex's pulse increasing and the moisture on his palms within thick mittens. I could see their eyes meeting ever so fleetingly. She asked many questions and he knew the country well. But from behind, I could have only read their body language, heard her laugh, and noted his shy reactions. Would I have noticed his mind wandering, losing focus on steering the sleigh through the shadowy woods? How fortunate for me and my family that horses are wise animals who can compensate for human emotions and frailties, finding their way home by themselves, remembering the oats and warm hay awaiting them in the stable.

I left the ruins of the schoolhouse and drove eastward away from Rose Island. After I passed the old McKee place, I entered a more forested area. In places, the woods almost enveloped the road. Suddenly, a deer rushed out of the trees on one side and dashed into the undergrowth on the other. In that instant, I remembered what my father had told me on my one and only deer hunt when I was almost 16: "Down this road is the place where your great-grandfather John had a store and post office."

I don't think Dad actually showed me the buildings, but just like the deer that had leapt from the bush, his words darted out of the deep recesses of my memory. I'd been here many years before when I shot those two deer with Dad's old Lee-Enfield rifle—the day I gave up on guns for good.

I concluded that, in spite of Great-grandpa John's love for those old muskets, the McKees belonged to a certain breed of lowland Scots-Irish weavers and farmers. They had little interest in the fighting spirit exhibited by their highland Scottish compatriots, who had battled the English. With their spare time and spare cash, they socialized—without alcohol—and joined community efforts to build churches and schools. But during his sojourn at Rose Island, John kept his guns ready for action against all wild things, real or imagined.

When I reached Coe Hill, I woke from my reverie and began to ponder my mother's side of the family, the Neills. I knew they were more religious than the McKees, or I had always assumed so. Would I find them to be just a peaceful lot with few interesting stories of guns and wars to write about? I have to say, I was surprised by what I discovered.

# 4

## THE NEILL FAMILY *and* MY CONNECTION *to the* USA

Aerial view of Neill farms (lower left, far side of road), near Clifford, Ontario (upper right)

THE DAY I FLEW OVER THE MCKEE FAMILY FARM WITH my pilot friend from my Africa filming days, we also inspected the property on which the Neill family settled in the 1860s. It's located about 25 miles to the northwest in Howick Township, Huron County, Ontario. In the summer, this land is reminiscent of the gently rolling green hills of County Armagh, the place they had left behind in Ulster (Northern Ireland).

My mother was christened Alma Katherine Neill. For some reason, my parents gave me her maiden name as my first name. Whatever their intention in doing so, it resulted in a lifelong struggle for me, with the misspelling of my first name by every official or new acquaintance who wants to correct it by dropping an "l" or inserting "ea" in place of "ei." Some British and Irish people I meet even revert to the old spelling "Niall," the legendary 5th century Irish noble who kissed an ugly witch in a forest, turning her into the most beautiful woman on earth. She, in turn, granted him the kingship of all of Ireland.[1]

The surname O'Neill is actually an Anglicization of the original Irish *Ui Néill*, (*Ui* which became "O'" means "grandson" or "descendant"). There are different unrelated interpretations of the meaning of *Néill*, such as "cloud," "passionate," or "champion."[2] I like the latter because, taken together with my surname, McKee (originally *Mac Aodha* meaning "son of *Aodha*," a Gaelic word which translates to "fire"), I am able to tell people that my name means "Champion of Men, Son of Fire." So, who can argue with me?

The O'Neills were once chieftains and landowners in Ireland. Due to English invasions and domination, and to Irish uprisings against this, many of the O'Neills lost their lands. Most of those who converted to Protestantism dropped the O' from their name. In the face of growing prejudice against Catholics, dropping the prefix made it easier for Protestants to find work.

I had visited Howick Township in 2013, taking along my brother Glen and my mother. I had photographed the crumbling foundation of an old barn that probably once belonged to William Neill, my great-grandfather, or his brother James. But no one was home at the farm and I had no proof that I had the right place. We had also visited the public cemetery in the nearby town of Clifford and easily located William's tombstone.

A few days after the McKee tombstone dedication in 2016, I returned to Howick Township with two of my Neill cousins and my youngest brother, John. On this second visit, I had more luck. The farmer and his wife were home, and they invited us in for

Remains of William Neill's barn, Howick Township near Clifford, Ontario

Tombstone of William Neill and his wives     William Neill ca. 1880s

tea and cookies. The lady of the house pulled out a large green book, *The Lines of Howick*, a history of the township. It only took her a minute to verify that their farm had once been in the hands of William Neill. Starting in 1872, he held 50 acres of land on Concession Road 15, Lot 32, and lived in a house (no longer standing) with his brother James, who owned the adjacent 50 acres to the west. William took over his brother's property in 1885 and sold both lots in 1910.[3]

William Neill had come to Canada in 1860 as a teenager with four of his siblings and his mother, Ellen Neill née Stott, after her husband, John Neill, died. He had been a handloom weaver, like my McKee ancestors in the Glasgow area of Scotland. There's a family story that indicates he had learned his trade while working in Scotland, then left to establish a weaving business in Ulster, specializing in Paisley shawls, the pattern of which he brought from Scotland. This teardrop design originated in Persia and reached Scotland on textiles from British India.[4]

Around 1832, John Neill married Ellen Stott, who was born in Ulster in 1803. They moved to Tandragee, a small town in Ballymore Parish, County Armagh. But John had chosen a problematic vocation. Like my McKee ancestors, he fell on hard times, due to competition from steam-powered mechanized weaving. Then, the potato blight hit, and their main source of food disappeared. Meanwhile, the ruling English continued to export tons of wheat and other grains from Ireland, while many Irish starved. By the late 1850s, Tandragee had become an impoverished town, like many parts of Ireland. When the domestic linen industry and trade declined sharply, many weavers and their families grew vulnerable to hunger and disease.[5]

The eldest son of John and Ellen, Jeremiah, died in Ulster in 1855 at the age of 14. John may also have died around the same time. To date, no records have been found. I can envision John returning to Ireland with such high hopes and then seeing those dreams dashed by forces far beyond his control.

Ellen Neill somehow had the foresight, connections, and good luck to get out of Ireland with her five remaining children: Elizabeth, James, William, Jacob, and Joseph. They immigrated to Upper Canada and settled in Huron County where, according to one unverified family story, Ellen's brother had already established a homestead. William and his brother James, plus another brother, Joseph, set down roots in Howick Township. William married Eleanor Bruce and had two children: a girl named Mary Eleanor and my grandfather, John Addison Neill. (See Table 3.)

The records of the Neills in rural Ontario paint a picture of quiet family life with nothing more than reunions to write about—no wars and no guns. As a child, I could usually tell if visitors to our home were Neills because all of my mother's brothers stood at least six feet tall and acted in a more refined manner than my McKee uncles. The rules allowed only polite, controlled laughter. They said long prayers and sang hymns at our family picnics. I associated this serenity with the fact that my late Neill grandfather had been "a man of the cloth," and his sons grew up to be peaceful souls: a tailor, two store managers, a tobacco salesman, a radio operator, a construction worker, and a horticulture professor. I initially doubted that I could discover any interesting war stories from the Neill clan.

Then I learned from my cousins that one of the general store managers, Uncle Leigh, had been wounded in the arm in April 1917 during World War I in northern France, at the Battle of Vimy Ridge, in which four divisions of the Canadian Corps fought. A total of 3,598 Canadians died and 7,004 were wounded before they finally took control of the ridge from the Germans on April 12, 2017.[6]

Also, during World War I, my oldest Neill uncle, Millard, learned to become a "gas instructor" in the UK and was given the rank of sergeant. The Canadian Army sent him to France to teach soldiers how to cope with deadly mustard gas used by the Germans. According to his own notes and clippings from newspaper interviews, Millard taught soldiers in the trenches to roll up blankets and soak them with Lysol, protecting themselves against gas attacks at night. He took part in major actions such as the Battle of Arras, the Battle of Passchendaele, and the Battle of Amiens, which began on August 8, 1918, in the opening phase of the "Hundred Days Offensive." It ultimately led to the end of World War I.[7] Millard survived all of this action and returned home to marry and raise a family in London, Ontario, where he became a tailor, made children's toys, and did fine weaving.

My cousin, Catharine Neill, sent me a copy of the World War II story of her father, John Wesley Neill,[8] a quiet horticulture professor. He had written and published the short book himself, but never distributed it very widely. Uncle John had commanded a tank troop during the war. In August of 1944, he was posted to the 27th Armored Regiment known as the "Sherbrooke Fusiliers," a unit of the 2nd Canadian Armored Brigade. They blasted their way through France, Belgium, and into southern Holland. He was responsible for the opening move of an important battle in the drive to cross the Rhine River. With one of his tanks bogged down in mud, he led the other two, including "The Bomb," in which he rode, to take out the so-called "Pimple," a high point of land held by the German Army on the Siegfried Line, near Calcar. The Germans had used it to guard the entrance to the Hochwald Forest in Germany. In 1945, the Canadian Army awarded my uncle the Military Cross for his gallantry.

Neill McKee with "The Bomb," once commanded by J.W. Neill

One time during a visit with our son, then living in Sherbrooke, Quebec, I mentioned this story. He opened the curtains of his kitchen window and pointed, saying, "That might be it." Sure enough, on closer inspection I found it to be Uncle John's tank.

Although they all volunteered to fight, Uncle John Neill and his older brothers, like many former soldiers, seldom talked about their war experiences. Upon further investigation, I found that these uncles had joined the two world wars against their parents' wishes. In the Neill family, boasting too much about one's achievements or prowess was taboo, and doubly so if it involved talk about wars, violence, or guns. I wondered about the contradiction between my uncles' voluntary enlistments and their peaceful lives once they reached home. Unlike my dad and his brothers, they did not keep guns at home and never went hunting. I felt a connection with these tall uncles, and found myself wanting to dig more deeply into the roots of the Neill family.

My maternal grandfather, John Addison Neill, was born in 1870 and grew up on the family farm in Howick Township, as mentioned above. He attended primary and secondary school. His mother, Eleanor Neill née Bruce, died from tuberculosis in 1885 when she was only 52. According to a family story, John Addison didn't want to farm like his father, William; he hoped to become a pharmacist. His mother's brother, James Bruce, had left Canada to become a storekeeper, pharmacist, land owner, state legislator, and the mayor in Rolfe, Iowa. But John Addison promised his mother on her deathbed that he would fulfill her wish and become a Methodist minister instead.

When William Neill remarried, young John Addison didn't get along with his stepmother. He dreamed about getting off the farm and possibly joining his relatives in America—the land of opportunity. About 850,000 people migrated from Canada to the US during the 1870s and 1880s.[9] This included his aunt Elizabeth, who had married a Methodist minister by the name of Robert Smith, and left with him for Tennessee and then Wisconsin.

Ellen Neill, John Addison's grandmother, had also moved to Wisconsin to be with her daughter. In addition, he probably heard stories of his uncle, Jacob Neill, who had moved to Indiana around 1869. After Jacob's wife died in childbirth, he gave his child to her parents in Buffalo, New York. They blamed him for taking their daughter into what they thought of as "the wilderness of Canada" to perish. Then Jacob left Ontario and wandered through Indiana, Kentucky, and Tennessee for a few years as a Methodist "Circuit Rider"—lay-preachers who traveled about, often on horseback, to proselytize to people in remote places. Around 1873, he finally settled in Reno County, Kansas, where he farmed, married, and had a family, while also serving as postmaster.

These stories must have occupied John Addison's mind, for in 1899 at the age of 19, he enrolled in Garrett Biblical Institute in Evanston, Illinois, the first Methodist seminary in the American Midwest. He had already gained his full height of 6 feet 3 inches (190.5 cm), not someone you could miss in a crowd. On arrival, he slept outside or wherever he could find shelter, so the family story goes. He had to wash dishes and wait on tables to pay his way through college.

In the 1890s, Evanston was a town of about 9,000 people. It is located 14 miles (24 km) north of Chicago, which had become a haven for criminals by the late 1800s. John Addison had left the comparatively peaceful world of rural Ontario to live near one of the growing hot-spots of crime in America. Guns were readily available and loosely controlled; for instance, the "Chicago Palm Pistol" was popular—a small revolver with a barrel that protruded between fingers, firing seven .32 caliber cartridges before reloading.

Men didn't need much education to join the Chicago police force, and they received little training. Corrupt politicians or criminal gangs easily influenced them. Gun control laws were minimal. I can imagine Grandpa reading the Chicago papers in the college library, perhaps becoming increasingly concerned about the choice he had made to attend college in the US.

On May 23, 2017, I drove through Chicago to Evanston during what I call my "Epic Journey of 2017." I wanted to track down the places where Grandfather Neill lived, worked, preached, married, and had children. While sipping a cappuccino at a

Starbucks in Evanston, after many tries I finally got through to a real human being at the reception desk at the Garrett Evangelical Theological Seminary, now part of the campus of Northwestern University.

When I reached Garrett, the receptionist directed me to the library, where I met a librarian who appeared to be overwhelmed with work because her colleagues were on leave. I asked her how I could confirm whether my grandfather had studied at Garrett. She led me to shelves full of the minutes of Methodist annual conferences in different midwestern states. Delving into these books, I soon realized I was looking for a needle in a haystack. I returned to the librarian and asked if she had any record of graduates of the Seminary during the 1888-94 period. She said she would try, but this would take a while.

So, I took a walk around the campus. For a half-hour, I sat alongside the brown and churning waters of Lake Michigan. A cool spring wind blew off the lake, but direct sunlight warmed me, along with a few students studying on the rocky shoreline. I imagined my grandfather sitting in this same place over 125 years ago.

Next, I found a cafeteria to have lunch and kill time, hoping the hassled librarian would have some luck with my request. She could have been officious and asked me to make an appointment for another day. But she was a very accommodating person.

When I returned to the library, she showed me an old book and said, "I found a record of all the graduates of the Seminary from the time it opened until 1900, and I am sorry to say, your grandfather isn't here."

A dark question came to mind. Had my grandfather been a fake? When I attended Grandma Neill's funeral and burial in 1966, I saw his tombstone for the first time, or at least the first time I can remember. It read "John Addison Neill, Ph.D." I asked Uncle Millard, "In what subject did he, a rural minister, have a Ph.D.?"

Millard replied, "Oh, he studied different things all the time. I think it was in economics."

"Wow, how could he do that while being a full-time minister?"

Uncle Millard replied, "A correspondence course, I believe; or maybe it was just an honorary degree."

This seemed a bit far-fetched to me. Did he get the degree from one of those US universities where you can practically buy a certificate? Did he not even earn a first degree or diploma in theology?

Tombstone of John and Effie Neill, with daughter, Eleanor, Hillside Cemetery, Ridgeville, Pelham Township, Welland County, Ontario

I asked to inspect the book myself, just to be sure, and the librarian offered it to me in exchange for my driver's license. On my returning it in disappointment, she suggested I check with the Registrar's Office upstairs. This involved another wait because the office had closed for lunch. Finally, when it opened, I told a friendly African American lady my quandary. She immediately started to rummage through old files until a colleague entered and offered another source, saying, "Let's try the President's vault. He's away but I have the keys. He has some old records there."

The lady left and returned in about ten minutes with a tattered ledger in hand, saying, "I found him, I think. But the name and dates are a bit confusing: "Neill Jno. Addison Clifford, 1889-90, 1890-1."

I pointed out "Jno." was short for "John" and "Clifford" was in the column for place of birth. I'd found my grandfather, but I realized immediately the lack of diploma in the last column. The lady confirmed that it would have taken three years of attendance and passing exams to receive a diploma. She said, "Many people preached without diplomas in those days."

"Well, at least I found his record of attendance. Maybe he just couldn't afford the fees for a third year," I offered in my grandfather's defense. I thanked her and her colleague and left—mission accomplished.

Part of a page of the old registry, Garrett Biblical Institute

From Evanston, I headed northwest on Illinois tollways and into southern Wisconsin, checking into a hotel near Madison. In the morning, I set my GPS to "Indian Creek Cemetery, Muscoda, Wisconsin" and glided through sunlit hilly countryside on narrow highways, passing multi-green colored woods and small dairy farms dotted with Holstein cattle grazing after morning milking. My GPS led me onto Highway 60 in Richland County, a route which parallels the Wisconsin River, at that time overflowing due to heavy spring rains.

After about 90 minutes, I reached the cemetery, situated right beside the road. I walked through the gate and looked to the left. There I saw it, the shape I'd seen on the Internet. I had downloaded a photo of Ellen Neill's tombstone from *Findagrave.com*, but didn't expect that it would be so easy to locate it here, under a great elm tree.

As noted above, Ellen, my oldest ancestor on the Neill side in Canada, had moved to the US from Ontario, following her daughter Elizabeth and husband, the Reverend Robert Smith. Little is known about Ellen's life. She passed away in 1874 at the age of 71. Through consultation with the Wisconsin Methodist archives, I later found that Elizabeth and Robert were living, at the time of Ellen's death, in the town of Orion, less than a mile from the cemetery. But soon after the burial, they moved on to other Methodist postings in Wisconsin, leaving Ellen behind, surrounded by strangers.

I knelt down by Ellen Neill's tombstone, thinking about her journey from Ireland to Ontario in 1860, a widow with five children, including her precious daughter Elizabeth, who probably loved her mother for her sacrifices and bravery. Amazingly, I

could read Rev. Smith's dedication on the 135-year-old memorial—still visible in fine script.

Above the tombstone inscription, I could see a hand with a
raised index finger. At first, I was reminded of the mythological
severed red hand of Ulster. In some versions of the legend, it is
the hand of the chief of the *Uí Néill* clan, or Niall of the Nine
Hostages himself who, in a very close contest to reach the shore
of Ireland first, and thereby become the king, cut off his hand and
threw the bloody thing onto the shore in one grand gesture.[10] On
further study, I learned that as the Irish became Christians, they
used the pointing hand symbol to represent souls aspiring to an
afterlife in heaven. How our tribe had been tamed!

I lay down beside Ellen's tombstone to think about what
really brought my ancestors to Wisconsin, a state that's posi-
tioned at about the same latitude as our part of Ontario, where
she had first settled. Unlike southern Ontario, Wisconsin is not
surrounded by the modifying influence of three Great Lakes.
It's open to westerly winds from the prairies, so the winters are
colder and longer. In addition, the Rule of Law at the time could
be described as rudimentary, at best. Wisconsin, like most midwestern states, had recently emerged from more than a century
of violent conflict with Native Americans. In addition, many
men had returned a few years ago from killing and wounding
their southern brothers in the Civil War. Most of Ellen's new
neighbors were Germans or Scandinavians who could not speak
English well. Her closest neighbor in the cemetery was a Chinese
immigrant. His tombstone, chiseled with Chinese characters,
had toppled and been propped up against the elm tree. Compared
to her previous predominantly Scots-Irish settlement of Howick
Township in Ontario, Ellen had come to a land of strangers. As
I rested beside her tombstone, I thought about her life and her
burial place, so far from home.

Ellen Neill's tombstone

Inscription: "Erected by Rev. Robert Smith in memory of his mother-in-law"

*Meditation by the Wisconsin River:* Born in Northern Ireland in 1803, I don't pity this poor immigrant who found the strength and means to escape famine, chaos, death, and bring her children to a new beginning in a land of promise. But why did her daughter leave her here with strangers, by a river she hardly knew? I spoke to her, "Am I the only descendant son in the last 100 years who has visited your courage in this lonely place, this alien land?" But the only answer that came was the distant sound of rushing water.

As I lay there at the grave of my ancestor from Ireland, I felt the urge to explore Wisconsin further—to find more details that might point to why my grandfather Neill had also chosen to come to this land.

# 5

## MY NEILL GRANDPARENTS
### *in the* MIDWEST

United Methodist Church, Cadott, Wisconsin

ON SUNDAY MAY 28, 2017, I DROVE UP TO THE METHODIST
Church in Cadott, Wisconsin. The building looked much like the
old photo I found on the Internet, but with a more recent extension to the left. A parishioner entering the side door saw me park-
ing my car with its New Mexico license plate. He asked, "Are you
going to join our service?"

"If I can," I said. "My grandparents were married in this church in 1895."

"Wow," he said. "Come in and meet our pastor and some folks. We always start our Sunday meetings with coffee before the service."

I joined them and met the pastor. I briefly told him and a group of parishioners the family story, "My grandfather was a visiting preacher here, sometime in the mid-1890s. In the middle of the Sunday service, he looked at the organist and lost his train of thought—apparently rare for him—and decided that he wanted to marry her."

Pastor Patton and his friends laughed but then carried on with the banter that had begun before I arrived. Their conversation didn't exactly connect with my feelings about the building I had just entered. A few minutes later, as I entered the vestibule leading to the new worship hall, the man I walked with told me that the church only had about 40 members. He mentioned that they had tried to unite with another Methodist congregation, but it had been too liberal. With my goatee, the guy may have assessed that I leaned on the liberal side. Had he given me a "heads up" about what to expect in the service? I thought to myself, *Oh boy, what have I got myself into?!*

The service started off tame enough, with a participatory preacher who encouraged the congregation to speak out. But as I looked at the order of service, I could see the slant. It happened to be Memorial Day weekend, when Americans honor the military personnel who died while serving in the United States Armed Forces. The hymns were all of that ilk: "America the Beautiful," "There's a Star-Spangled Banner Waving Somewhere," "The Battle Hymn of the Republic." Where were all the sentimental hymns of my Canadian Methodist childhood?

In my small notebook held on my lap, I recorded that the

preacher read from the Old Testament, Isaiah 5:20-24, and I became fixated on these verses:

> Woe to men mighty at drinking wine,
> Woe to men valiant for mixing intoxicating drink,
> Who justify the wicked for a bribe,
> And take away justice from the righteous man!
>
> Therefore, as the fire devours the stubble,
> And the flame consumes the chaff,
> So their root will be as rottenness,
> And their blossom will ascend like dust....

This scripture harkens back to the fire and damnation of the old Methodists. Had it only been this reading and the chosen hymns, I might have become less alarmed. But when Pastor Patton got to his sermon, simply titled "Liberty," flames issued from his mouth. He ranted and railed against the Quran being allowed in American schools but not the Bible, the pro-choice murder of the unborn, euthanasia, and other devilish attempts to social engineer our lives, the "deep state" administration in Washington, and alternative lifestyles that are protected by law, whereas the traditional family is not. He didn't say anything about guns but I calculated by all the other militancy expressed in his sermon that he backed the National Rifle Association (NRA) and the Second Amendment on the right to bear arms.

What would my grandfather have thought of all this? I knew this preacher probably wasn't representative of more modern thinkers in the United Methodist Church of today. Could he be a throwback to my grandfather's days in America? If so, I wondered how he had dealt with such theology.

As I sat there, for relief from his diatribe, I diverted my

thoughts, trying to recreate the scene of my grandfather looking
at the organist and losing his place:

> ***My grandparents' meeting:*** Did he look down at her from the
> pulpit when she closed the last hymn with an organ flour-
> ish? He stumbled a little, whereas he usually spoke with elo-
> quence. I could see her being watched by him, the flicker
> of their eyes meeting and then turning away, maintaining
> a proper posture but feeling something more—an increase
> in heart beats? Perhaps a slight rise in temperature and mild
> lightheadedness? I could imagine him regaining his place,
> fingers catching the right line, a slight clearing of the throat
> before he began to speak again. Did the congregation notice
> any of this at all?

When the service ended that day, my grandfather asked for
the name of the organist and they were introduced. Her family
invited him to lunch at their place, and so the "dance" began. They
married in this church on March 6, 1895. He towered at least 14
inches over her. Although in the late 1800s, it was not obligatory for the man to stay seated for a formal portrait, I expect the
photographer decided on that arrangement so my grandmother
wouldn't appear to be so short.

No organ remained in the church, only an electronic key-
board, and the woman who took my grandmother's place annoy-
ingly chewed gum through the whole service. I tried not to look
at her. Then, near the end of the proceedings, the New Testament
reading of Galatians 2:4-5 caught me by surprise:

> Yet because of false brethren secretly brought in—who
> slipped in to spy out our freedom that we have in Christ

John Addison Neill and Effie Jane Haskins, 1895

Jesus, so that they might bring us into slavery—to them we did not yield in submission even for a moment, so that the truth of the gospel might be preserved for you.

Wait a minute… "false brethren"…was he talking about me? How had he predicted my coming and chosen this reading?

To Pastor Patton's credit, during the service he asked me if I would like to tell the story of my grandparents' love affair, beginning in their church. I elaborated a bit, mentioning that my grandmother, Effie Jane Haskins, was born in their town in 1876. She became a school teacher in Cadott, in addition to serving as church organist. Her parents were Lafayette and Sarah Alma Catherine Haskins. He fought in the 7th Wisconsin Regiment during the Civil War. (*A great idea to mention this on Memorial Day weekend day,* I thought.)

I went on to describe a little of my grandparents' lives, having children and ministering to Methodist congregations across Wisconsin and farther west, and then going back East to Ontario, where he came from. The congregation seemed to be entertained by my story and some people surrounded me afterwards, making sure I stayed for their monthly potluck luncheon. I sat and chatted with a couple, ate, and then said "so long," feeling a little like an intruder, being a non-believer myself—"false brethren secretly brought in"—despite the contribution of the entertaining story about my grandparents' meeting.

To learn more details about my grandparents' lives, I called the Wisconsin United Methodist Church and left a message with the archivist. I wanted to understand how my grandfather had become a preacher in Wisconsin without a diploma from Garrett Biblical Institute. It took me a few weeks to learn the full story. In the meantime, I traveled to where he preached, according to the places written in their family Bible, where they had also recorded all of their children's births.

Following his two years at Garret, Grandpa Neill had undergone a rigorous apprenticeship from 1891 to 1895. The Methodist archivist explained in her message how, during the old days, prospective preachers were assigned readings and then had to pass written and oral examinations, while working with senior ministers. He completed his formal studies, then was "elected" and ordained. In 1891, he was "Admitted on Trial" and appointed to Woodville and Potterville in Eau Claire District. (I was relieved to hear that my grandfather had not faked his credentials.) During this period, he acted as a kind of circuit preacher, a job which had led to his meeting Effie Jane Haskins in Cadott.

After my grandparents married, they moved to Ironton, La Crosse District, an iron ore mining and railway town where my uncles Millard and Leigh were born—the boys who later fought in World War I (Chapter 4). Millard had a twin who died at birth, posthumously named "Willard." His parents were devastated but carried on with procreation. When not giving birth or caring for children, Effie Jane actively participated in women's groups and often played the organ or piano in church services. She also led the choir—the ideal pastor's wife.

The Methodist archivist reported that Rev. Robert Smith, the man who had buried my 2nd great-grandmother, Ellen Neill, preceded my grandfather in West Wisconsin Conference, first in Eau Claire District and then in La Crosse District, even being appointed to the same charge back-to-back with him in the town of Ironton. This made perfect sense. I also learned that, despite his good works, a tornado took Rev. Smith's life near Oakdale, Wisconsin on July 3rd, 1907. What a way to be raised to heaven!

I drove to Ironton, only to find the Methodist church building vacant and for sale. A man next door told me that the original building, in which my grandfather had preached, burned down years ago. More recently, the congregation became too small for the replacement building and was amalgamated with one in an adjacent town—sign of a by-gone era, I thought.

My grandparents "grew no moss" on their soles—or their souls. In 1898, the church appointed Grandpa Neill as pastor in Tunnel City and La Grange, La Crosse District, where he stayed for only a year. By 1900, they had moved on to Soldiers Grove, an old sawmill town on the Kickapoo River. That's where their first daughter, Eleanor, was born in January of 1902. Later that year, the church moved Grandpa to South Wayne, Platteville District, and then in 1903 to Maiden Rock, Eau Claire District—too many moves for me to investigate during one trip.

I did, however, visit their former church in Maiden Rock. The town is located beside a wide stretch of the Mississippi River, called Lake Pepin. The small Methodist Church he preached in is still standing there, perched precariously on a steep road. I speculated that a run-down house sitting beside the church may have been the parsonage at one time. Earlier, in a phone call to the preacher who serviced this church, I had learned that it had only nine remaining members.

In contrast to the beauty of the setting, that Sunday the town had been invaded by at least 100 members of a motorcycle gang who were boozing it up a few blocks from the church—a

Lake Pepin on the Mississippi River

Memorial Day celebration. They hung out around a tavern beside the railway tracks, which ran along the shoreline—a different kind of congregation, I thought. The reading from Isaiah still rang in my head: "Woe to men mighty at drinking wine, Woe to men valiant for mixing intoxicating drink." How disgusted my grandfather, a teetotaler, would have been had he observed such an invading host.

Grandpa Neill could not have started his new career in America at a more difficult time. The whole country had plunged into a depression. The Panic of 1893 had been set off by the failure of two of the country's largest employers, the Philadelphia & Reading Railroad and the National Cordage Company. The stock market collapsed. Banks, railroads, steel mills, and many other businesses went bankrupt—15,000 in all. Unemployment rates soared. People became homeless when they couldn't pay their rent or mortgages.[1] It must have felt like the American Stock Market crash of 1929 and the subsequent Great Depression, or the recession of 2007-08.

The effects of the Crash of 1893 continued for a decade or more, badly affecting farm prices and the finances of families in their congregations. My maternal grandparents lived on a meager salary. This was evident from my memory of an old family story:

*The Lean Christmas, ca. 1903:* Grandma Neill remembered it as the hardest Christmas ever, for she didn't even have any scraps of cloth to make the kids some toys, nor wool to knit socks or mittens. On Christmas Eve, they didn't have enough money to buy the children oranges or nuts. After the kids had gone to bed so excited about Christmas, Grandma sat down and cried. Grandpa came in and saw her tears. He knew why she was crying and suggested that they kneel down and talk to

God about it. While they were praying, they heard a knock on the door. Grandpa went to answer while Grandma wiped her tears. Some friends entered whom Grandma knew from her childhood. They had brought presents for each of the children.

Our family also preserved a less endearing story. True to form at the time, men kept women in their place. One day, Grandma washed clothes in the basement of one of their parsonages, while he read poetry to her from the top of the stairs. From that image, I began to think of him as a romantic wanderer, trying to adapt to domestication.

Their daughter Eleanor developed chronic asthma and they decided to move farther west, hoping to find a better climate for her. In 1904, Grandpa Neill was transferred to Northwest Iowa Conference "on account of the health of his family," so the Methodist archive read. My intention had been to follow their trail west to Nebraska and Wyoming, where they went after leaving Iowa, but my long journey had already taken its toll. (My travels did not match the chronology of this book. Starting on April 15, 2017, I had already driven from New Mexico to Ontario, New York, Virginia, and many of the northeastern states, then to Illinois and Wisconsin.) Exhausted, I decided I'd had enough traveling for the year. On May 29th, I drove to Minneapolis to meet a distant cousin. From there, my new plan was to head south through Iowa toward New Mexico.

Fostoria, in northwestern Iowa, struck me as a depressing little place on one of the flattest and most barren plains on earth. In late spring, I saw no sign of crops, just dry brown fields. My grandparents only stayed in this place for a few months, probably the hottest ones of 1904. The area was then, and still is, tornado-prone.

I found it easy to locate the United Methodist Church, but the building in which my grandfather preached had been replaced by a cement-block affair, erected in 1965. I investigated an old church bell in front of the new building—the only remnant of their time in Fostoria—raised up on an ugly platform and out of reach. I wanted to ring it, as he may have done, but couldn't reach the lever.

I stopped at the US Post Office to ask directions to a local museum, but I didn't bother to go there. I was just as anxious to escape the area as I suppose my grandparents might have been, judging from their short stay. They must have missed the rolling hills, green woods, and rushing rivers of Wisconsin.

The old bell of the former Methodist Church, Fostoria, Iowa

I drove south to stay overnight at Council Bluffs, Iowa. The next day, June 2nd, I traveled southwest through Nebraska and into Kansas. Looking at my map of the Midwest, I realized Dodge

City was on the route home—one of the main places of my boyhood gun-slinging fantasies—and I decided I had to stop there. When I reached the small city, I checked into Wyatt Earp Inn, a cheap hotel run by immigrants from India. Then, I drove out to a site overlooking the Arkansas River Valley and one of the largest cattle lots I had ever seen. The wind blew from the southeast, bringing with it the odors of cattle manure—a vile and pungent smell so intolerable that my eyes stung. I could only look for about a minute before diving back into my car. As I drove off, I thought of all those cattle being fattened and awaiting slaughter for the meat markets in Chicago and farther east—the original reason for Dodge City's creation.

Next, I headed down Wyatt Earp Boulevard, an ugly strip lined with commercial properties along the railway line, just south of the main residential area. There, I located Dodge City Museum, a replica of Old Dodge next to Boot Hill, where many gunslingers and innocent victims of gun violence had been buried. It wasn't at the actual location of the original cemetery and it lacked tombstones. As I inspected some cheap-looking signs

Memorial signs of men killed in gunfights

plunked into the soil, the images I'd seen in old Western Movies as a kid came back to me.

After a quick look at the museum, which focused a lot on popular Hollywood images of Dodge City, I walked down the town's boardwalk. I couldn't see the wide and dusty street where Wyatt Earp won gunfights against ruthless outlaws in films and television shows. But I did witness a mock gunfight between lawmen and a gang of outlaws. They played it as a farce with most of the outlaw actors dying in a spectacular blast of six-guns at the end.

I came to understand that this drama characterized America's showdown over the Second Amendment of the Constitution—the right to bear arms versus gun control. The actor playing Wyatt Earp, like the fictional character Matt Dillon from the television series *Gunsmoke*, demanded that everyone follow the rule the town council had passed—no guns allowed in town north of the railway line, except those worn by lawmen.[2] This was historically accurate.

Likewise, on October 26, 1881, in Tombstone, Arizona Territory, when Wyatt Earp and his brother Vigil, along with Doc Holiday, gunned down a group of rowdy outlaws in the gunfight

Fake gunfight in Dodge City, Kansas

popularly known as the "O.K. Corral," the outlaws had invited their own demise by breaking a similar town ordinance—no guns allowed in town.[3]

I realized that this theme—attempts at controlling armed men by regulations—ran through most of Wild West history. Without such local laws, America would have been robbed of a lot of stories and drama—a mythological tradition as the gunfighter nation and Hollywood might never have become so successful.

As I read a little more about the history of Dodge City in a book[4] I bought at the museum's gift store, I had my suspicions confirmed: Wyatt Earp had been a real person, but stories about him were wildly exaggerated. He came to Dodge City in 1876 and left in 1879—a restless man who kept moving, like my grandfather Neill. But unlike my grandfather, Wyatt Earp entertained himself through a whole variety of occupations throughout his life—bison hunter, saloon keeper, miner, boxing referee, gambler, brothel keeper, and lawman.

The next morning, I got out of Dodge, taking two-lane highways that cut southwest across the heart of Kansas into Oklahoma, shooting as straight as an arrow toward my home state, New Mexico. I sped through dry plains, only slowing down for small towns, all uniformly built south of grain silos and the railway line. No traffic, no police, and perfect sunny weather for thinking about my grandparents and all their moves. I regretted not having the energy to explore their time in Nebraska and Wyoming. That would have to wait until the following year.

# 6

# REVEREND NEILL
## *in the* AFTERMATH *of*
## WOUNDED KNEE

Rolling plains and bluffs of northwest Nebraska

IN SEPTEMBER 2018, I DROVE NORTH FROM ALBUQUERQUE
into northwest Nebraska. I'd much writing, research, and reading to do, and didn't get back on the trail until then. On a Sunday
afternoon, with a final thrust up the less frequently traveled State
Highway 71, I arrived at the famous Fort Robinson. From 1876
to 1890, it had been the main center for the American Army's war
against the Native American population of this region, especially
the Lakota Sioux.

Before Columbus arrived in the hemisphere in 1492, millions of Indigenous Peoples lived throughout the North American continent. Estimates vary widely—from as low as 2.1 million[1] to as high as 18 million.[2] In the 1700s and early 1800s, as Europeans advanced westward, they thought they had come to a nearly empty wilderness, whereas the land actually had been depopulated by the infectious diseases brought to the continent by explorers and invaders during the previous 200 years.

One rather direct way of putting it is that the soldiers based at Fort Robinson were involved in finishing the job through the Indian Wars of the late 1800s, reducing the number of Indigenous People in North American to fewer than 250,000. I had read that Hitler had studied America's wars against Native Americans when he planned the extermination of the Jews in Europe.[3] He had also been motivated by the writings of Madison Grant, one of the original American white nationalists of the 1900s, who proposed the concept of a superior Nordic people in his book, *The Passing of the Great Race.*[4]

Lakota Sioux Warriors, Old Eagle and He Dog. *Photos taken with permission of the Nebraska State Historical Society*

Today, Fort Robinson is a military museum. I drove around acres of well-manicured lawns and stately buildings, then visited the main museum to see how history was portrayed there. As I entered, I prepared myself for whitewashed presentations, hiding the facts of much mayhem. The displays avoided grizzly scenes, but I could picture what had happened here. The photographic portraits of Lakota Sioux leaders like "Old Eagle" and "He Dog" attracted me most—noble faces with penetrating stares or wry smiles.

I left the museum and crossed a road to what appeared to be a sports field or military parade ground. Small log cabins stood on one side. They looked like quaint western settlers' homes, but when I read the descriptions on display boards, I understood them to be replicas of prisons that once held Sioux captives. I walked to a small monument for Crazy Horse, a Lakota Sioux leader, who, in the 1860s, began his fight against the encroachment of white American settlers onto Sioux reservations, as designated in treaties formerly signed with the US Government.

Monument at Crazy Horse's place of death

In June 1876, Crazy Horse participated with the Northern Cheyenne and Arapaho tribes in the Battle of Little Bighorn in Montana—General George Custer's last stand. Sitting Bull was the other great Lakota Sioux leader who inspired this battle. About 3,000 warriors attacked and killed Custer and many men in his 7th Cavalry Regiment. But the Native American victory was short lived.[5] Thousands more soldiers soon poured into Fort Robinson and other Western outposts to do battle with Native Americans. The US Army captured Crazy Horse, and he met his end on September 5, 1877, on the very field where I walked. A soldier bayoneted him for allegedly resisting arrest.[6]

I stayed in a hotel in nearby Chadron overnight, and in the morning headed for Rushville to attend an 11 a.m. service at the United Methodist Church, where my grandfather, John Addison Neill, had been the pastor. I had phoned the current pastor to make sure he would welcome me, and I found him to be very helpful. He mentioned people I should talk to, since he had only recently been posted to the church and didn't know much about its history. I had left a message on his cell phone on Saturday, and when he called me back in the evening, he told me he'd been busy all day with a "roundup." I didn't ask him what he meant by that, thinking he may have been rounding up souls.

When I approached the church, however, his meaning became clear. I saw this guy wearing a "ten-gallon hat" drive up in a huge pickup. When he stepped out of the truck, he greeted me warmly, saying, "You must be the guy I talked to on the phone, looking for info on your grandfather."

"That's me. You're the pastor?"

As Pastor Paul Smith introduced himself, I found his hand-shake firm, almost crushing. I guessed him to be in his early 60s. He stood over six feet, even without the hat. He also wore other Western apparel: blue jeans, brown cowboy boots, a light-blue cowboy shirt with pearl buttons, and a belt with a large silver buckle. He sported a gray panhandle mustache. His matching gray tie appeared to be the only thing out of character. I wanted to replace it with a bolo—a Western string necktie and medal-lion—the true sign of a cowboy. He sure spoke like one.

"Yes-sir-ee. Come on in and meet the folks. Service starts soon."

"You mentioned you were at a round up yesterday?"

"Sure was. I help out on a large ranch nearby. Keeps me in shape bringin' in the cattle for market and preparin' for winter."

"Your hobby?"

"I used to work as a cowboy. It's been a big part of my life."

I wondered what I had gotten myself into. Another hour of ranting by a conservative gun-loving preacher? As we entered the church, Pastor Paul introduced me to some of the other people he told me I should talk to regarding the church's history, while he went off to prepare for the service. A new church building had been completed in 1937, replacing the old one in which my grandfather had preached. None of the parishioners knew much about the earlier period when my grandparents had lived here. I estimated they had arrived in the fall of 1904 because their son, Ralph, was born in Rushville in January 1905. As usual, they didn't stay long. I had already found records of them in Wyoming by mid-1905.

To my surprise, Pastor Paul began his sermon by proclaim-ing, "Ninety percent of the most effective Christian ministers sometimes feel inadequate or unworthy." He went on to explain, "It takes introspection to be a true leader who serves others.

Choose humility over pride. Don't live with inner conflicts; recognize them and take the right path."

Pastor Cowboy Paul preached a much more enlightened message than the militaristic sermon I had sat through in Cadott, Wisconsin, the year before. He did mention me and my interest in church history to the small congregation, but for some unknown reason he didn't talk about the fact that my grandfather had once preached here. Maybe he thought I didn't have sufficient proof.

After the service, everyone departed quickly, including the good pastor. He headed off to a celebration at another church. I went to the church hall next door, following directions I'd been given. Inside and to the right, a glass case held photos of former clergy with dates of service. I looked for my grandfather's face but couldn't find it. On the top right I could make out the names of pre-1920 pastors on small gold-colored metal strips, some nearly falling off the display board. There he was, "J. A. Neill, 1904-05"—physical proof that he had been here.

Rushville's main street

I left the church and went to a bowling alley that housed the only restaurant in town. It served a pretty basic buffet, each dish fortunately covered with individual nets. Barn flies filled the room—a normal pestilence during summers on the prairie.

I had made a 2 p.m. appointment with the curator of the Sheridan County Historical Society, Jerry Wellnetz, and had time to kill, so after lunch I drove around town to take photos. On a wide Western-style main street leading to the railway tracks, I saw an old hotel and saloon with a faded sign. I mused that the setting would have been a perfect place for a gunfight.

The neighborhood next to the train tracks appeared run-down, with junk lying all around. I had read that Rushville's population of 890 in 2010 was about 74 percent white and 22 percent Native American, so I jumped to the conclusion that the poorer housing belonged to the latter group.

When I met Jerry at his museum, he corrected my assumption. He told me that over the years the town had become largely integrated—a bit of a surprise and a lesson for me not to think stereotypically.

Jerry allowed me to photograph anything in the museum—a congenial guy, as I had found all museum curators and local historians to be on my travels. It was thoughtful of him to let me see the collection on a Sunday instead of making me hang around until the morning. On the contrary, he had driven five miles from his son's place in the country to meet me.

I found some old unpublished documents on Rushville's Methodist church history in the museum, but didn't discover any mention of my grandfather. The week before, I'd made calls to other churches where he most likely also had duties, but these enquiries had drawn a blank. The account in the museum did mention that churches in town had served as shelters for settlers in the area during the "Indian scares" of 1890-91, fueled by the massacre at Wounded Knee. Sadly, by the time my grandfather and his family arrived, most of the Great Plains Indians and their culture had been decimated. This included the herds of bison (mistakenly called "buffalo" by many), on which they depended for meat, clothing, and shelter. I don't know if my grandfather grasped the extent of that tragedy, but I like to think he did.

I had recently read Dee Brown's *Bury My Heart at Wounded Knee*,[7] which is told from the point of view of various Indigenous People—witnesses to their near total genocide by white men. My brief account below of the Lakota Sioux before, during, and after the Wounded Knee massacre is adapted from that source.

The great struggle continued after the death of Crazy Horse. Many surrendered, but not Sitting Bull. He and his men resisted the invading American settlers and the US Army. However, in May 1877, they took refuge in Canada's North-West Territory, which included present-day Alberta, where he met a platoon of North-West Mounted Police, a force established in 1873. These lawmen were the forerunners of today's Royal Canadian Mounted Police. They dressed in red uniforms—symbolic of the British Crown and the Rule of Law. One of their main jobs involved tracking down and jailing American outlaws and whiskey traders, or driving them back over the border into the hands of elected judges, sheriffs, and free-lance bounty hunters. Although most Canadians of my generation loved watching the antics of these outlaws and lawmen in Western movies, many of us perceived them as part of the lunatic fringe. To us, the US version of law and order was an alien concept. How could a legal system function fairly when the people elected judges and sheriffs, who were often aligned with the designs of corrupt politicians and political parties?

The police and the territorial authorities allowed Sitting Bull and his people to settle in Canada for some time, but after four years of exile they found life too hard. The bison herds had greatly diminished there as well, and his people began to starve. Besides, Sitting Bull's presence near the US border increased tension between the two countries.

In 1881, he led his band back over the border to surrender, and the government eventually allowed them to return to Standing Rock Reservation, their home in Dakota Territory. Due to all the stories about Sitting Bull, he had gained much fame and managed to escape imprisonment for his leadership in the war against General Custer and his US Army troops. He had become the stuff of folklore.

Americans love their frontier heroes. Sitting Bull was one of them. He met Annie Oakley and participated in Buffalo Bill Cody's Wild West Shows, which began around 1870 in North Platte, Nebraska. He joined these traveling vaudeville performances as they toured throughout the US and Canada. Buffalo Bill's productions depicted romanticized versions of the American West—stereotypes of cowboys, Plains Indians, prostitutes, outlaws, the US President, and the US Army. Sitting Bull became a willing participant in this sensationalistic exploitation of his people.

After Sitting Bull's return to Standing Rock, tension grew between him and US Government's Indian agents. The Sioux protested against the reduction of beef rations by Congress, which had sustained them as the bison disappeared—one of many injustices that also included attempts to swindle them out of portions of their reservations. Government agents tried to divide their lands and offer parcels for sale to white settlers and established ranchers.

What happened next set off a series of disasters. A Northern

Paiute Native American shaman named Wovoka had a mystic vision during the solar eclipse of January 1, 1889, igniting a religious movement called "Ghost Dances." His message spread from Nevada eastward across the prairies. Surprisingly, the ritual involved the belief that Jesus Christ would return in 1892 to lead Native Americans, resurrect deceased relatives, banish all evil from the world—including white men from the Great Plains—and bring back the bison. Ghost Dancers believed their traditional way of life would be revived.

When the movement reached Standing Rock, Sitting Bull allowed the dancers onto his land. Although he didn't take part in the ritual, the US Government viewed him as a key instigator because of his welcoming gesture. Nearby white settlers grew alarmed as the Sioux added a new feature to the myths involved in the dance—"ghost shirts," which they believed to be bullet-proof.

On December 15, 1890, Indian police working with the US Cavalry shot and killed Sitting Bull while arresting him. Chief Big Foot, now in command of the Standing Rock Sioux, fled with his people and the remaining Ghost Dancers. They had hoped to reach Pine Ridge Reservation and then escape into the Black Hills to the west, but Chief Big Foot—sick with pneumonia—surrendered when the cavalry caught up to them. The soldiers escorted his band of around 106 armed warriors and 250 women and children to Wounded Knee on Pine Ridge. On December 28, they allowed the Sioux to camp beside Wounded Knee Creek, encircling them on the hills all around, guns at the ready.

The massacre took place the following morning. Unfortunately, a medicine man by the name of Yellow Bird had encouraged some braves to do the Ghost Dance, claiming their shirts would protect them against the soldiers' bullets. When the soldiers tried to disarm the Sioux warriors, a man by the name of Black Coyote protested giving up his precious rifle, and a shot rang out. All hell broke loose as the soldiers fired their Hotchkiss machine guns from the hills. People scattered and bullets mowed down many.

When the madness ended, the soldiers counted and buried the bodies of Chief Big Foot and 153 of his people, but many of the wounded had crawled away to die. One estimate placed the final death toll at nearly 300 of the original 356 men, women, and children. The soldiers lost 25 men and 39 were wounded, most of them struck by their own bullets and shrapnel. An official US Army investigation not only exonerated the 7th Cavalry, Medals of Honor were awarded to 20 soldiers. Perhaps they thought it to be retribution for the Army's previous defeat at the Battle of Little Bighorn.

When the Lakota Sioux embraced a prediction about the return of Christ within their own cultural context, it led to their final defeat. I find this ironic, especially considering that Grandfather Neill had come to this land to preach Christ's "good news" only 14 years after the massacre. How much did he know about this recent bloody history of the area he had entered? Did it concern him?

Lakota Sioux in Rushville Nebraska, "Getting Ready to Join Buffalo Bill's Wild West Show, 1901." *Photo taken courtesy of Sheridan County Historical Society*

I didn't realize how much the Lakota Sioux had been indoctrinated into the white man's view of reality until I saw a telling photo in Rushville's museum—a large group of Lakota Sioux participating in Buffalo Bill Cody's Wild West Show in Rushville, itself. They had followed the path of Sitting Bull, in spite of the fact that his fame gained through this route contributed to his death at the hands of the US Cavalry.

At Rushville, as usual, Grandpa Neill had a "three-point charge," meaning he had ministerial duties with two other congregations besides the one in which he lived. One Sunday morning in winter, he preached in Rushville and then left for these other churches. Since there are no records of him in the area other than those revealed by Methodist archivists, the Neill family Bible, and the small brass plaque I had found, I wondered if these other churches involved a ministry to Lakota Sioux people. A family story mentioned that these other congregations were located about 20 miles (32 km) from Rushville. An account passed on by Uncle Millard had become part of family lore:

*The Prince Albert Suit Coat, 1905:* My grandpa Neill, a Methodist pastor, preached one Sunday morning in Rushville, Nebraska, then left for his other churches, 20 miles away. Warmed by a buffalo coat, he drove his sleigh pulled by Indian ponies through drifting snow, arriving in time for evensong. Realizing he'd forgotten his Prince Albert suit-coat, with two more sermons to preach on Monday, back he and his ponies went in the cold calm moonlight. Opening the door, he found the house so still, his family breathing in deadly vapors. Grandma had dampened down the coal stove too soon. But Grandpa pulled her and their four children out-side—all saved by love for that coat, his mysterious pride.

This family story made me realize how slim a chance we have of being born. One forgetful moment or decision by an ancestor involving emotions, pride, preference, or self-image could have determined whether we were ever to become at all.

From Rushville, I drove north that afternoon over a wide plain, observing its transition into undulating brown hills scorched by a summer drought. I headed for a place called "Extension Community Chapel." Jerry, the curator at Rushville's museum, had suggested that maybe my grandfather had taken the sleigh to this place that Sunday afternoon, and perhaps it had been a Methodist Church outreach post for the settlers in the area. It happened to be exactly 20 miles from Rushville. I imagined Grandpa Neill driving his team of ponies over these hills in blowing snow. The land appeared desolate enough to me in September 2018, so how would it have been for him in the dead of winter in 1905?

When I arrived at the chapel, I walked around trying to find out what denomination it could be. The freshly painted sign on the road didn't mention that, but it did announce times for Sunday school, Sunday service, and Bible study. I surveyed the small graveyard and found typical Anglo-Saxon names. Had my grandfather ministered to these people? With no available records, his destination that day seemed mysterious—almost like a ghost story.

The mystery remained with me for some time, but I had noted the telephone number on the church's sign and I left a voice mail with Pastor Larry Miller. He sent me an email a few weeks later, giving a source for the history of the place.[8] Early white settlers in the area were first serviced by Circuit Riders—preachers on horseback or with a team of horses, traveling through the wilderness for religious revivals. But with the Indian uprising during 1890-91, catalyzed by the massacre at Wounded Knee, the area was put under the Indian Department, and all settlers were removed. In 1904, the land was reopened for settlement and called the "Extension Community." Church services began again during 1904-05 in a dugout building. My grandfather had arrived in Nebraska in the fall of 1904 and stayed until mid-1905, so Larry Miller thought it was quite possible that he was the one to restart services in the area.

Perhaps my grandfather thought of his uncle Jacob Neill, who left Ontario to become a Circuit Rider in Indiana, Kentucky, and Tennessee, finally settling in Kansas (Chapter 4). This seemed like the kind of romantic image that would have appealed to him. What eventually transpired with the resettlement of white folks in the area, at least in the nearby small town of Whiteclay, is not something that he would have appealed to him.

From the chapel, I drove to Whiteclay, where, in 2010, beer sales totaled 4,900,000 cans—13,000 per day—for annual gross sales of $3,000,000.[9] Until 2016, it had been a legal source of alcohol for the inhabitants of Pine Ridge Reservation. After a lawsuit by the Oglala Sioux, the subtribe of the Lakota Sioux in this area, alcohol sales were terminated. The liquor and beer outlets had been boarded up. As I passed a number of uninhabited houses, I wondered how soon it would be before this place turned into a ghost town.

I kept heading farther north across the South Dakota border. After passing through the town of Pine Ridge, I drove east through Pine Ridge Sioux Reservation, an area of 3,468

Commercial oilseed sunflowers, along with one uninvited cousin

square miles (8,982 km²), the eighth-largest reserve for Native Americans in the United States. The land appears expansive and promising to the untrained eye, but only a small portion is said to be suitable for agriculture. I stopped to inspect a field of huge sunflowers ready for harvest, all heads bowed to the east, like faithful worshippers.

In about half an hour, I arrived at a large red sign, giving details of the Wounded Knee massacre. I parked by some make-shift roadside stands with people behind them, selling souvenirs and maps. I walked up to a Sioux man to ask him for the exact location of Wounded Knee. He waved his arm in a circle and said, "This whole valley is Wounded Knee."

"Got it," I said. I looked down at his table to see an array of products. A shy Sioux woman standing at the next bench had her own display, and they appeared to be working together. "What are you selling?" I asked.

The man picked up one of the larger pieces made of metal hoops wound with red, white, and blue leather, and dyed beads. "This will ward off all evil spirits," he said.

"Really? How much?"

"Fifty dollars cash," he replied with confidence.

I smiled and said, "That's not much for keeping all evil away. But I don't have that much cash on me." Due to the positive message of Rev. Paul's sermon, I'd given an offering of more money than I should have that morning. I noticed a smaller ornament on the table directly in front of the woman. It consisted of a light-blue hoop with a brown woven web in the middle. Strands made of blue, silver, and black beads, leather strips, and horsehair hung from the hoop.

"What's this?" I asked the woman, assuming she was the creator.

The man replied instead, "A dream catcher."

I became intrigued, "How does it work?"

"You can read this," he said, handing me a small brochure. The description read:

> The hoop represents the circle of life. The four colors are the four races of man, the four directions, and the four virtues of the Lakota Sioux people: courage, generosity, fortitude, and wisdom. The horse hair represents the western power of thunder and lightning. The feathers are the messengers to the almighty creator....*Mitakuye Oyasinx*!

I pointed to that final Sioux phrase, and the man translated it as "All are related." I could see no feathers on the piece, so I assumed the leather strips had been used in their place. The brochure went on to describe the object's utility:

> Dream catcher is a symbol of good luck to the Lakota *Oyate* (Nation). It is hung by a person's bed or window when they

are sleeping. As they sleep, their dreams are sifted throughout the night. As they are sifted, the good dreams are caught in the web, and the bad dreams are passed through the hole in the center of the web. The good of the dreams are then carried with you throughout the rest of your life. May you always have good dreams.

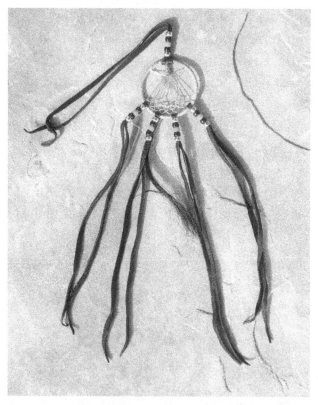

"The dream catcher" purchased at Wounded Knee

I much preferred this artifact of modest claims and delicate beauty to the more expensive one, so I asked, "How much?"

"Twenty," he replied.

I took out my last remaining 20-dollar bill and bought the piece. Then, I asked him about the hill across the road.

"It's the cemetery," he said. "Many of our people are buried there. It's a memorial to the massacre. You can drive up there. It's free of charge. If they ask you for money to enter, don't pay."

I thanked the man and bid him and the quiet woman good-bye. Their brochure identified them with the surname "Elk" and included a telephone number and email address in case I wanted to order more dream catchers. I took my car to the top of the hill, a more difficult lane than I had expected, due to the deep ruts for which my low-hanging Prius had not been designed. At the entrance, I saw a young Sioux man engaged with some visitors. I walked past him because the people below had told me there would be no admission fee.

I could see some tombstones and a small monument with inscribed names of the Sioux who had died in the 1890 massacre—not very impressive at all. Compared to the military museum at Fort Robinson, this placed looked like a pitiful attempt at remembering what had happened here. I photographed a number

Wounded Knee Monument

of tombstones with the surname "Elk"—the same name as the people from whom I had bought my dream catcher. According to the memorials, some of the men buried here fought in World War II and Vietnam.

I walked back to talk to the young Sioux man at the entrance. He had long shiny black hair and wore a sleeveless shirt, blue jeans, and sandals. Had he been mounted on a horse, he would have looked no different from many Sioux warriors I'd seen in Western movies—except for the denims. He didn't smile, just nodded at me. He was engaged in a conversation with some German travelers, a long-haired man and a woman in a plain ankle-length skirt—kind of hippie-looking—but they drove a new rental car. I had seen them down below and recognized their accents. I knew from German friends that many people in their country have a fascination with American Indian culture and people. They even join clubs and go camping, Indian-style, all dressed up in expensive costumes with feathers, an appropriation of indigenous culture that a growing number of people now judge as inappropriate, even offensive.

The Germans were discussing the meaning of the young man's creations. Probably they had been made by someone else, I thought. He was only a middle man. After they had completed their exchange, the young Sioux man turned to me, motioning that it was now my turn to buy from him. With no more cash on hand, I took control of the conversation, "Do you know the history of the place?'

"Yes, everything. My 9th great-grandfather is buried here."

"Wow. Were your people at the Wounded Knee massacre?" I asked.

"Yes, he survived."

I did a quick calculation in my head and concluded the survivor of the massacre must have been his great-grandfather or 2nd great-grandfather, not his 9th, who would have lived in the late

1600s or early 1700s. It didn't make sense, but I didn't contradict him. He continued with the whole history of the place and the massacre, appearing to be very well-versed in the matter.

I asked his name and he gave me his Anglo name. I knew he probably had a Sioux name so I asked him for that too. He spit out some unpronounceable words, but I didn't want to take notes in case he got suspicious of my intentions.

"How far did you go in school?" I hoped he didn't think I was too snoopy. The Germans just listened.

"I finished high school. But there's nothing to do here. There's 40,000 of us and 90 percent unemployment."

"But I saw huge fields of sunflower crops on my way here."

"Those belong to outside commercial companies," he said. "Some people rent out their land to them." It sounded to me like he thought these people were "sell-outs."

"Do you or your family have a farm?" I asked.

"Our land is no good. It's not far from here. It's been difficult since Wounded Knee Two." The young man went on to describe the 1973 siege. I had forgotten about this incident because I had been living overseas at the time and had only seen a short article on it. He had memorized all the actions by some Sioux and the American Indian Movement versus the FBI, backed by tribal police.

The young Sioux man continued, gesturing with his hands, "White people had taken over the land. There was a trading post down there that cheated us, and some cabins for visitors to rent. Missionaries built churches over there and there," he said, as he pointed to places on the other side of the valley. But my mind drifted as he continued—this more recent battle was beyond the scope of my research.

As he spoke, I thought about the tragedy of this place. I woke up from my daydream when he stopped talking and asked, "Do you want to buy one of my ornaments?"

I finally told him, "I bought a piece down there and don't have any more cash." But I don't think he believed me.

"The ones down there are bad people. That family was part of the tribal policemen who killed and wounded good people in 1973." I marveled that in 2018, this young man, who had not yet been born at the time, carried on such hatred over the incident.

"Sorry," I said. "Do you have an email address?" I handed him one of my business cards. I wanted to help him somehow.

"Yes, I have email." He said this like he found me insulting for inferring that he might not.

"Write me. I'll order one of your pieces." The young man was silent. The Germans, witnesses to all this, didn't voice an opinion either. Perhaps I appeared too cheap to help this young guy in distress. I bade him goodbye and he said nothing, still sulking. I never did receive an email from him. Perhaps he lost my card, but more likely he didn't have reliable email access or any faith in visitors like me.

In any case, my interaction with him felt like a wounding incident at Wounded Knee. By coming here, had I only contributed to his feelings of long-standing exploitation? What had my grandfather felt about the Lakota Sioux people he met? Did he harbor any white man's guilt? Or did he see himself as an outsider, a Canadian who treats Indigenous Canadians differently? But did we really? Maybe we learned to be more subtle about our exploitation. I recalled our apartheid-like reserve system that stripped Indigenous People of many human rights, and remembered the boarding schools set up to try to stop future generations from learning their own languages and cultures, making them convert to Christianity, but also victims of sexual abuse. Discriminatory policies and actions by Canadian police and others continue to this day. In all that, we are no different from the US.

I got into my car to return to my hotel in Chadron. I planned to drive through the Black Hills the next day—the hoped-for refuge of the people who died in the massacre of 1890 at Wounded Knee. As I made my way through the rolling plains of South Dakota and back into Nebraska, the young man's conflicted, disappointed, and bitter face occupied my thoughts.

I decided I would need to use my new dream catcher that night.

# 7

---

# MY GRANDPARENTS'
# WYOMING SOJOURN
# *and* RETREAT

Wild bison in the Black Hills of South Dakota

THE NEXT MORNING, I LEFT NEBRASKA FOR WYOMING, traveling northwest through the Black Hills of South Dakota, advertised in a tourist brochure I'd picked up as "a genuine oasis in a sea of prairie." But in a dry September, much of the barren hills looked as brown as the prairie to me. At least I saw wild bison. The brochure claimed that the name "Black Hills" comes from the Lakota Sioux words, *Pahá Sápa*, and that at a distance the hills are supposed to have a dark appearance, but I couldn't see what the Sioux people saw when they named them. Perhaps the darkness in their name foreshadowed the acts of treachery and deceit they would endure over their claim to this land.

The Lakota Sioux gradually gained control of the northern plains in the late 1700s and early 1800s. They developed a unique culture based on the abundant bison herds of that era. The Fort Laramie Treaty of 1868 guaranteed the Lakota people owner-ship of the Black Hills.[1] In the 1800s, when mining companies and the US Government realized the value of these mineral-rich hills, especially their gold deposits, they began taking them back, starting with mining rights. Since the Sioux didn't mine the earth, what would they care? But miners need houses, stores, restaurants, bars, and land for growing food crops. Settlements began to spring up. Enter Crazy Horse and his warriors in the Great Sioux War of 1876-77—a concerted attempt to drive out the settlers, and an objective that failed.

I turned west down State Highway 16, Mount Rushmore Road. I purposely didn't take the road in the direction toward Mount Rushmore monument, laboriously chiseled out of rock to create the countenances of George Washington, Thomas Jefferson, Theodore Roosevelt, and Abraham Lincoln. I also avoided the smaller road north that leads to the monument in memory of Crazy Horse—carving his head destroyed another natural hilltop. When I had viewed these memorials on the Internet the night before, they all seemed pretentious to me. Nations love to oversimplify history and glorify personalities, while overlooking their defects. Crazy Horse's people naturally had the inclination to oversimplify and glorify as well.

The Sioux had fought first against white settlement in Minnesota and escaped westward, colonizing the lands of other

Indigenous People, taking more and more territory.[2] In fact, the name "Sioux" is derived from a Chippewa word, *nadowe-is-iw*, meaning "adder" (snake) or "enemy." The Great Sioux Nation is composed of three main dialect groups: the Nakota, the Dakota, and the Lakota. The Lakota Sioux, who reached farthest west, fought their way against settled nations such as the Pawnee and Arikara, as well as nomadic groups like the Arapaho. When the Lakota Sioux came to the forested slopes and meadows of the Black Hills, they began to displace the Cheyenne and Kiowa people, who had previously enjoyed the region's abundant forests, water, fish, and game. Crazy Horse, who had met his death while a prisoner at Fort Robinson (Chapter 6), cut his teeth on engaging in conflict with other tribes.[3]

As I drove down Highway 16, slowly winding out of the forested hills towards eastern Wyoming, my thoughts turned away from tribal history and back to my family's genealogy. I aimed to reach my Neill grandparents' one-time home in Newcastle, a small railway town nestled between the Black Hills and the

Newcastle, Wyoming

rolling plains. Newcastle is higher in elevation than Rushville, with more rain. My grandparents thought the climate would be better for their asthmatic daughter, Eleanor. But I don't think they anticipated the socio-political climate they encountered in their new home.

Newcastle, Wyoming had been named after Newcastle, England—a centuries-old coal mining center. A large deposit of coal was discovered in the nearby Black Hills, where the Cambria Fuel Company established a mine in 1887. They called the small settlement that grew around it "Cambria." The mine supplied much of the fuel needed for the westward push of the railway.

In mid-May 1905, Grandfather Neill arrived in Newcastle by train to check out the place, and then went back to Rushville to collect his family, returning to Newcastle with Effie Jane and their four children on Friday, June 2, 1905. I found such details thanks to an electronic collection of the *Newcastle News-Journal* in the Anna Miller Museum, a well-run place named after the daughter of a pioneer family. She was the widow of Sheriff Billy Miller, who had been killed in what was reported to have been the last incident of the Indian Wars, The Battle of Lightning Creek.[4] The skirmish took place on October 23, 1903, less than three years before my grandparents arrived. A group of Lakota Sioux from the Pine Ridge Reservation in South Dakota had been given a pass from the Indian Agent to enter Wyoming in search of their runaway ponies and to harvest plants for herbal medicines. Assuming them to be illegal hunters, Sheriff Miller and his posse fired first, killing five Sioux. This violent news was reported next to social events in the newspaper at the time.

The *Newcastle News-Journal*, then a single-page broadsheet, contained many short reports of Grandpa Neill's activities as the Methodist pastor in town: mainly weddings, funerals, and trips to places like Cambria or Pine Grove, to hold services and minister to the needy. A memoir by a doctor who lived in Cambria listed the settlement's population by nationality at the turn of the 20th century: Polish, Austrian, Yugoslav, Macedonian, Russian, Bulgarian, Hungarian, German, Greek, Montenegrin, French, Belgian, Finnish, Swedish, Danish, Irish, Welsh, English, Scots, and Bohemian.[5]

A short history of Cambria,[6] which I found in the museum, listed many deaths. Mining accidents comprised the majority: explosions, limbs caught in machinery, runaway rail cars, rock slides, sudden illnesses, but also shootings and stabbings. Most likely, Grandfather Neill had to provide comfort to many families due to such horrific incidents or accidents in the area. On June 23, 1905, right after his arrival with his family, the newspaper reported that a man was thrown from his horse, but one of his feet got caught in a stirrup. His horse dragged him to death over rocky ground.

My grandparents had entered a true Wild West frontier town, complete with saloons, dance halls, gambling dens, prostitutes, and gun-packing cowboys. During 1896-1900, Butch Cassidy and the Sundance Kid began their famous careers in Wyoming and other western states and territories. They staged spectacular train robberies before hightailing it to Argentina and later to Bolivia, where they finally met their deaths in a shootout with the Bolivian Army.[7] The town of Sundance is situated only 47 miles to the north of Newcastle, where after breaking out of jail in October 1897, Harry Longabaugh came to be known as "the Sundance Kid." He hid for a few days in Newcastle's newspaper office under the local sheriff's nose. (Possibly he had made a deal—a temporary hiding place for an interview.)

There were plenty of stories to collect in this Wild West town. I heard some of them from Leonard Cash. I'd called him from Albuquerque on the advice of someone at the local newspaper.

He and his wife, Linda, run a ceramics and pet supply business, Cashbox Ceramics, on the corner just a few doors away from the Methodist church where my grandfather once preached.

I spent the morning with Leonard and Linda, listening to their stories. Leonard had made it his mission to record the history of Newcastle and the area. His grandfather had been the first in the family to move here and, except for a stint in the US Navy in the Pacific during the Korean War, Leonard had been a resident of the place all his life. These days, semi-retired, he spends many hours in the local library studying historical records, while Linda takes care of the shop, making and selling white ceramic ornaments for lawn and household decoration. Before I arrived, Leonard had taken the trouble to write out, in longhand, every single mention of my grandparents' presence recorded in the *Newcastle News-Journal,* including Grandma Neill's meetings with the Ladies' Aid Society.

Leonard and Linda Cash by their ceramics shop

I walked with Leonard, a distant relative of Johnny Cash, so he told me, from their shop to the Methodist Church, now quite an imposing, well-maintained structure with an extension. He showed me where the parsonage had once stood. I had found a line drawing of the house and church together in a museum publication.

Leonard said, "It's quite a beautiful old place, as you can see. That side part was added some years ago."

"So, lots of people still attend church here?"

"I guess, but they've got plenty of competition," he replied.

We walked on until he stopped and said, "I want to point out something else. Just down the street on the other side, the Star Hotel once stood. A ladies' hotel."

"What do you mean, a ladies hotel?" I asked.

Leonard grinned, "A palace of pleasure for men."

I pointed, "You mean right there was a brothel, so close to the church?"

"Yes sir, a two-story cathouse, bigger than the church and parsonage together. I've got a picture of it in my shop. You can take a photo if you like."

"Sure will. You mean the brothel customers went right by my grandparents' door on their way to and from the place?"

"I'm sure they did. I read that some of the richer customers parked their horses and buggies behind the place. A lot of men would have come from the sheriff's saloon just around the corner on main street."

"What do you mean the sheriff's saloon?"

"The sheriff back then, Johnny Owens, built and ran 'The Castle,' a saloon and dance hall just up the street from our shop. It became known as 'The House of Blazes.'"

"Did Sheriff Owens own the brothel too?"

"No, by all accounts he was a law-abiding man. But maybe he just looked the other way." Leonard said.

United Methodist Church, Newcastle, 2018

Methodist Episcopalian Church and Parsonage, circa 1900

The Star Hotel, Newcastle, circa 1900

"He employed dance hall girls?" I asked.

"Yep, and married one too. Quite a fellow. Had a long history before he came to Newcastle. I think there's a story about him in the museum, and probably some photos too."

"I saw it. I think I'll have to go back and take a better look," I said.

What an amazing find, I thought, as we walked back to look at the building that now sat on the lot where the saloon once stood. At the time, Johnny Owens was the main agent of law and order in Newcastle, besides his deputy, the judge, and a posse he could assemble when needed.

I returned to the museum in the afternoon to photograph every page of *The House of Blazes: The Story of Johnny Owens.*[8] The Castle had burned down in 1933 in one last glorious blaze. When I had a chance to read through the short biography, some happenings in my grandparents' world of 1905-06 in Newcastle came alive. I derived his story from that short local publication.

Johnny was born in Texas in 1843 and moved to Missouri with his family. During the Civil War, he joined a squad of the Confederate Cavalry in the Missouri Militia, a state with divided loyalty. He didn't spend long in the militia and somehow ended up escorting supply trains in Dakota Territory. After the war, he stayed out West where he fought Indians during the 1876-77 struggle for territorial control. Before he arrived in Newcastle, he also occupied himself in many other ways. He captured horse thieves, owned a hog ranch, drove a stage coach, gambled, raced horses, and more.[9]

I found plenty of stories about Johnny Owens in *The House of Blazes*, including one about how he beat Wild Bill Hickok in a shooting match. He gunned down outlaws in bars or on the streets of the towns where he acted as a lawman. Apparently, he had 20 notches on his pistol handle, one for every man he had killed.

Sheriff John Owens

One of 14 saloons in Newcastle's early days

Despite this reputation, Owens tried to operate within the law. People said he neither drank nor smoked, ran his businesses well, and was a devoted husband and admired father. They described him as "handsome, soft-spoken, etc., endowed with steady gray eyes, and slender in build."[10] These qualities countered some of the gossip about his reputation as a killer.

Owens arrived in Newcastle during the summer of 1889, bought land, and built himself a new saloon with attached theater and music hall. This establishment became the talk of the town. He hired entertainers such as the Allen Sisters from Denver and also more sensational performers like "Diablo, the fire fiend," who drank flaming liquids and could be seen for 25 cents admission. On the one hand, Johnny Owens became a popular man in town, but on the other hand, someone to be feared: "Though he was not a violent man, his business had exposed him to violent characters and situations. He did not allow himself to be forced into a 'kill or be killed' spot but, if confronted, it was Johnny who stayed alive."[11]

In 1892, Johnny's friends urged him to run for County Sheriff. He did so and won by a large majority, despite being a southern Democrat in a Republican county. After he took the oath of office, he became the stereotypical Old West lawman most of us know from Western movies and television shows: a cool, controlled "Wyatt Earp." The big difference was that Johnny Owens continued to own and operate his saloon while in office.

I can only imagine my grandfather Neill watching the parade of drunken men walking to and from The Castle and the Star Hotel and quickly catching on. I wonder if he even discussed the matter with my grandmother, who probably remained an innocent soul. Surely there would have been a lot of commotion at night, while the family tried to sleep. At any rate, how would a 35-year-old preacher complain to a 62-year-old lawman who was well-regarded by most of the citizenry? At six-foot three, my grandfather had a three-inch advantage over Owens, but who could argue with a man who had 20 notches on his gun?

According to *The House of Blazes*, in February of 1906, Owens went into the hills to the northeast to bring back a 19-year-old horse thief by the name of Logan Blissard. He had been arrested before, but escaped. After his recapture, he was sentenced to five years in the penitentiary at Rawlins, and Owens intended to take him there by train. Owens handcuffed Blissard and fitted him with leg irons, but the train derailed and they had to take another one. Blissard complained he'd hurt his leg in the accident. Owens removed his leg irons, and then his handcuffs, when Blissard said he had to go to the toilet. Blissard slammed and locked the door, and escaped through the washroom window, even though the train was speeding along at 40 miles an hour. Although he managed to steal a rifle and a horse and take refuge in a nearby ranch, Johnny Owens tracked him down.

I can visualize my grandfather reading what happened next in the local paper. Blissard had had plenty of time to think, not only on the train but during his ride across the snowy plains looking for shelter. From inside his hiding place, he told Johnny he would rather be dead than go to prison, "If you shoot, for God's sake, shoot straight and don't cripple me!" Blissard suddenly burst out, and Johnny put a bullet in the middle of his forehead. According to the newspaper account, by then Johnny no longer had his original great physical strength, whereas Blissard stood six-foot one and weighed 175 pounds. He had not been handicapped at all by his ordeal of leaping out of the moving train.[12]

After the coroner's inquest report ran in the newspaper, the townspeople naturally began to speculate whether the killing was really justified. Why didn't Owens shoot the youth in the leg and then overpower him? Did he have to follow Blissard's request for instant death? Eventually, as the story goes, the court cleared Owens of all wrongdoing, for the kid had clearly resisted arrest, but a cloud hung over Johnny Owens' reputation for the rest of his career. In all likelihood, I thought, he never made that 21st notch on his pistol.

It's speculation on my part, but this "freelance" method of keeping law and order—electing a sheriff who owned and ran a saloon and turned a blind eye to the nearby illegal brothel—was probably so alien to my grandfather's sense of how a society should be run, that he told my grandmother they would be returning east. In addition, they found Wyoming winters colder and wetter than anticipated. The relocation had not brought about any marked improvement in their daughter's health.

The departure of the Neill family from Newcastle appeared in the *Newcastle News-Journal* on April 27, 1906. Surprisingly, these were the only words I found on how any congregation received them at their many postings:

> Rev. J. A. Neill who has been pastor of the M. E. church at Newcastle and Cambria for the last year, left with his family Tuesday for Latimer, Iowa, where he has accepted a pastorate. Rev. Neill is an earnest capable man who has made many warm and sincere friends during his short residence here. Genial and pleasant, always commanding the respect of all as a thorough Christian gentleman, tasteful and faithful in his pastoral duties....Mrs. Neill also by her quiet though pleasant manners and her high sense of faith, won her way to the hearts of those with whom she was brought in contact and few families have formed closer ties in the

course of the year than have Rev. and Mrs. Neill. May they prosper in their new home.

Before leaving Newcastle myself, I went to the Methodist Church to meet the current pastor. I didn't know what to expect, given my previous meetings with the Methodist cowboy in Nebraska and the fiery conservative in Wisconsin. Much to my surprise, I met a middle-aged woman with long curly red hair, Reverend Brenda Torrie, a native of Montreal. She had been born a Catholic but converted to the United Church of Canada and settled with her family in southern California. She experienced a mid-career calling to the ministry, and Newcastle was her first posting where she played the leading role.

I told her about my grandparents' year in Newcastle and some of the stories I'd gathered during my brief stay. Although new to the place, she expressed no surprise about the saloon-owning sheriff or the brothel that once stood across the road from her church. In her short tenure, she'd experienced a very independent people with a Libertarian streak. She talked about the difficulty of keeping Methodist ministers in Newcastle for long. There'd been a rapid turnover in recent years, but she hoped to stay for some time. People had responded well to her presence. My ears perked up when she told me that she remained a Canadian citizen only—like me.

I mentioned my grandparents' retreat to Iowa. We'll never know what had been in my grandfather's mind, for he never kept a diary—at least not one that was handed down in the family. So, it is difficult to guess the thoughts and sentiments that lay in his heart as their train pulled out of Newcastle. Did he have warm feelings for those he had met during the past year? Or did he simply feel overwhelming relief in escaping the Wild West? His wife was pregnant again, and I believe they wanted to settle

One of my grandparents' trunks

in Latimer, Iowa, while she could still travel. My uncle Merrill, their fourth surviving son, was born there in October 1906.

True to form, they only stayed in Iowa a few more months. In mid-1907, Grandpa took his American-born family to his home in Canada. They told a story of hiring a freight car with trunks and household goods at one end, a cow and horse at the other, while the family slept in between. Most likely, their train journey took them through Chicago and Detroit to southern Ontario— an 800-mile (1287 km) endurance course. He had lined up a Methodist pastorate in Ontario, but his American pension couldn't be transferred to Canada, so his years of service didn't count. They must have been desperate to get out of the US if they had to leave over a decade of retirement money behind.

In Ontario, Grandpa Neill accepted two different Methodist

charges near Georgian Bay, the eastern flank of Lake Huron. First, they lived in Keppel, where I found their former church and home—no longer a parsonage. In spite of that, the owner was friendly and invited me in for tea—such a warm feeling to sit in the kitchen where my grandparents once sat!

Between 1909 and 1912, my grandparents were stationed at the small settlement of Colpoy's Bay—their longest posting anywhere. Was this because Grandpa Neill had an opportunity to address some of the inequities he had seen in the American West? At Colpoy's Bay Methodist Church, he had a regular white congregation, but also ministered to the Ojibway people, a branch of the Algonquian tribe who lived at nearby Cape Croker. At the time, it took Grandpa a whole day to drive his horse and buggy, or sleigh in the winter, to their reserve, where he stayed with an Ojibway family. There's a family story that he helped to translate the Methodist hymnal to phonetic Ojibway, and Grandpa, with his booming voice, led the singing in that language.

In mid-April 2017, at the beginning of my "Epic Journey," I paid a visit to Colpoy's Bay where the old church had been torn down a decade earlier. I could see the same thing here as in Wisconsin—aging congregations and few new members. The United Church of Canada, which had been formed by a Methodist-Presbyterian-Congregationalist union in 1925, had grown too liberal for many and not liberal enough for others.

I drove to the Ojibway reserve on Cape Croker, traveling the 20 miles (32 km) Grandpa Neill had driven with his horses. The wind whipped in from Georgian Bay—a cold and rainy day. No one answered my telephone calls to the number for the church where he once preached, but I decided to give it a try. I meandered around the reserve and found it, but the building was locked. I asked a grocery store attendant if she knew anyone who worked at the church. This also led to a dead end. I found out later that the only church employee had recently been laid off, due to a lack of funding.

On the reservation, I could detect little economic activity. All services appeared to be provided by the government. I saw a school bus dropping off children at their homes—the only movement I witnessed besides a couple of guys in a pickup truck who stopped to ask me if I needed directions. Honestly, the whole settlement depressed me. In retrospect, it appeared to be much like what I saw at Pine Ridge Reservation in South Dakota.

The 1996 report of Canada's Royal Commission on Aboriginal Peoples stated that many of the 1876 Indian Act's measures were oppressive, and noted that "recognition as 'Indian' in Canadian law often had little to do with whether a person was actually of Indian ancestry." Indeed, the administration of Indian status became a tool of assimilation and cultural destruction. A First Nations person lost indigenous status if he or she graduated from university, became a Christian minister, or achieved professional designation as a doctor or lawyer. For nearly a century, it was effectively illegal to be a First Nations person in a traditional sense, while interacting with non-indigenous society in any meaningful way, without losing aboriginal status.[13]

Apparently, Grandpa Neill wanted to take his growing family to the more peaceful and less gun-happy land of Ontario, even if it had economic consequences. Although he did contribute to a Canadian pension, his salary remained very low. At one church in 1918, a special meeting was held to decide that the minister's salary should be set at Canadian $1,100 per year, with $100 for "horse keep," a term that indicated they still depended on a horse and buggy for getting around rather than a motorcar. In a reported incident, a member of one congregation gave the family a chicken for some holiday or occasion, so the church committee docked its value from his pay.

In Ontario, my grandparents continued moving from post to post. By the time retirement arrived, I calculated they had lived in at least 25 different parsonages in the US and Canada. They never owned a home of their own. They raised ten children and adopted one in her teens. My mother was the last child, born in 1920. Her birth occurred two years after their daughter Eleanor died in 1918 at the age of 16 of the "Spanish Flu." That pandemic infected an estimated 500 million people and killed approximately 50 million globally, including over 700 thousand in North America.

Eleanor was vulnerable because of a "weak constitution," as they said in those days, due to her asthma attacks since childhood. With no understanding of the virus 100 years ago, and few medical resources, my grandparents probably could only pray as they witnessed their daughter's last weak attempts to fill her lungs with air. (In the process of putting the finishing touches on this book during the raging Covid-19 pandemic in early 2020, when I saw an elderly lady on television in Italy, gasping for breath while other pedestrians wearing masks tried to help her, I felt a chill go down my spine for the hopelessness my grandparents must have experienced.)

My grandparents were devastated by the loss of their daughter, whom they had cared for through so many difficult moves across the American West and Ontario. But I'm sure they felt that God had paid them back when my mother arrived, although Grandma Neill was 45 years old by then, a risky age to have children, even today.

On an August day in 1948, when marching in an Orange Parade, Grandfather Neill collapsed with a stroke and died shortly afterwards, at 77 years of age. His membership in the Orange Order surprised me, given his interest in service to Indigenous People and other social causes. This movement, founded in 1795 in County Armagh, Ulster, during a period of great conflict between Protestants and Catholics, is a semi-secret fraternity that once

Rev. John Addison Neill and Effie Jane (Haskins) Neill in their 70s

advocated for Protestant ascendancy over Catholics. But by 1948, the Orange Order evidently had morphed into a community service club of sorts, at least for helping poor Protestants.

Regardless of his Orange Order connection, I thought of my grandfather Neill as a godly man. He died when I was a toddler, so I never knew him like I knew my grandmother Neill, who lived with us from the mid-50s until she died in 1966. I had personal experience with her "godliness" and appreciated, from a young age, that she had come from Wisconsin and had lived in America's Wild West during the time of the cowboys, outlaws, and sheriffs I followed in the movies and on television.

In my search for more on the "guns and gods in my genes," I decided that on my American side, Grandma Neill's family, the Haskins, probably had many more relevant stories to be discovered, especially on guns and wars.

# 8

## THE HASKINS FAMILY
### *and the* CIVIL WAR

Civil War Cannon, Brawner's Farm National Park, Virginia

ON MY "EPIC JOURNEY OF 2017," I STOPPED IN MISSOURI to see a distant Haskins cousin, Tamara Jorstad, whose DNA matched mine on *Ancestry.com*. We had begun correspondence by email. She was a great-granddaughter of Catherine Alma Haskins, my grandmother Effie Jane Neill's younger sister, whom we called "Aunt Kittie"—a lady I remember from her visits to our home in Ontario when I was a kid. But since my grandmother's

death in May 1966 and Aunt Kittie's passing in December of
the same year, the families had lost connection. Tamara gave
me copies of the Civil War records of our mutual ancestor,
Lafayette Haskins, Kittie and Effie Jane's father. Lafayette was
my great-grandfather and Tamara's 2nd great-grandfather.

A couple of weeks later, records in hand, I drove southwest
from Washington, DC into Virginia to investigate. I headed for a
place in the countryside where Lafayette Haskins, at 18 years of
age, had fought in 1862. I navigated my car to Brawner Farm, location of the Second Battle of Bull Run (a.k.a., the Battle of Second
Manassas), fought on August 28-30, 1862. There, I joined a small
group of tourists led by a park guide who gave us a brief preview.
He quickly understood by my questions that I had something to
say. I proudly announced, "My great-grandfather fought with the
7th Wisconsin Regiment here."

"Wow! He was with the Union's Iron Brigade," our guide
replied. "I can show you where they fought."

Lafayette Haskins as a young man

The Hardee Hat[1]

The group remained quiet for a moment, everyone impressed with our exchange. Then one guy in the back asked, "Did he survive?"

"I'm here, aren't I?" I answered with a big smile. The whole group laughed. "Somehow, he wasn't even wounded," I added.

"Against great odds," our guide said.

I had already read about the Iron Brigade, an infantry group in the Union Army. The brigade was noted for its fighting ability and the iron dispositions of its men, as well as for its unique uniform—especially the distinctive "Hardee Hat" designed by William J. Hardee, who later became a Confederate Lt. General. The term "Iron Brigade" was applied formally or informally to a number of units in the Civil War and in later conflicts.[2]

The guide led us a few hundred feet across the battlefield to the ground where the 2nd Wisconsin Regiment had stood at the opening of the fight. Once everyone had caught up, he pointed to a place about 500 feet (152 meters) away where Confederate forces had formed their line. He said, "The soldiers on both sides spread out almost a mile through the fields, down the hill there and into the woods. Major General Thomas J. 'Stonewall' Jackson commanded the Confederate troops and Major General John Pope oversaw all Union soldiers."

Our guide continued as if he had memorized a brochure, "Both sides stood tall in the field in ordered lines and went through a repeated process of loading their rifles, stepping forward to fire, and then stepping back to reload as the next line came forward."

The guide was speaking too fast for me to catch all of his talk, but it went something like this: "Reloading took most of a minute. Each soldier had to 1. remove a cartridge from his cartridge box, 2. bite off the end of the paper wrapping, 3. pour the gunpowder down the barrel, 4. remove the bullet from the paper and place it in the muzzle, 5. take out the ramrod and use it to push the bullet on top of the charge, 6. take a percussion cap from his pouch and place it in the nipple, and finally, after moving to the front line, 7. yank the hammer to full cock and pull the trigger on command."

I'd read that both sides in the war started with smoothbore muzzle-loading long guns, but had converted from flintlock to percussion cap gradually, starting in 1862. The old long guns were replaced with models such as the Enfield 1853 and the Springfield Model 1861. These weapons were bored out and rifled to .58 caliber to fit a standard Minié-ball, a conical-shaped bullet that spun as it exited the barrel, making it accurate up to at least 500 yards (457 meters) and lethal up to over 1,000 yards (914 meters).[3]

The guide told us that no one was allowed to take shelter, except as they reloaded behind the line of men who were aiming and firing. In only 90 minutes of action, casualties on both sides amounted to about 2,000 dead, wounded, captured, or missing. No ground was gained by either side—a total stalemate. The next day the tactics turned to cannon fire, killing and maiming many more.

I didn't hear our guide say anything about the 7th Wisconsin, so I asked him, "Did the 7th Wisconsin Infantry fire from here as well?"

"I believe so."

"There's no plaque for them," I said.

"You're right, not sure why."

I wondered if our guide might be new to the place, which would account for his memorization of the facts—perhaps trying to impress us with what he did know. After he completed his talk, I left the group and walked down the hill where I found the place Great-grandfather Lafayette Haskins and his comrades had stood. A small sign for the 7th Wisconsin Infantry marked the line. I read the plaque and recognized the name of the officer in charge, Colonel William W. Robinson. I had him in my notes as a cousin of Lafayette's mother, Clarfira (Robinson) Haskins. (Her given name was also spelled "Clarphyra" or "Clafira" in various records.) I would later learn the importance of this Robinson line in my American genealogy. (See Chapters 9, 10, 14, 15, and 16.)

Both Clarfira and William Robinson had been born in Vermont, where William had attended Castleton Grammar School, Rutland Academy, and finally Norwich Military Academy, before serving in the Mexican-American War. He was a man of action who, in 1852, joined the California Gold Rush— the sort of figure to be remembered as a legend in his family. In 1858, he moved to Sparta, Wisconsin, becoming a farmer and a colonel in the state militia.[4]

Was it pressure from this famous cousin or from his parents that led Lafayette Haskins to sign up voluntarily for military service? He enlisted in the 7th Wisconsin Regiment on September 2, 1861, at the age of 17, and served as a Private in Company A. The Haskins were poor Wisconsin farmers, and Lafayette—the youngest of nine children including four other sons—could not depend on inheriting land. Somehow, I doubt if his parents would have pushed him to make this decision. But did they anticipate the dangers that lay ahead for their youngest son?

I calculated that Lafayette's chances of survival had been very slim on the afternoon and evening of August 28th. This battle was probably his first direct engagement with the enemy, and I could imagine him shaking as he stood with his rifle, seeing his comrades dropping around him, groaning and bleeding to death in agony before being carried away by stretcher bearers. What went through Lafayette Haskins' mind as he looked up at the slight hill from which other young men his age fired down on him? Their bullets of soft lead could penetrate a body and do much internal damage. They could decapitate a man, or take off an arm or a leg if they hit the bone directly. Did he sicken at the sight of flying body parts and spurting blood all around him?

Union soldiers were outnumbered and outgunned by Confederates that day. But Georgian troops who tried to move on the Union lines "met stiff opposition from the 7th Wisconsin... blue-coated foot soldiers who stood their ground, keeping the southerners from moving forward, although the two forces remained but 100 yards apart."[5]

As a rule, officers ordered regular troops not to help the wounded. They had to keep to the task of loading and discharging their rifles. As Lafayette and other survivors retreated, they likely had to step over corpses of their comrades, left where they'd fallen. Other wounded men moaned all around them, some calling out for help while their blood soaked the ground.

The battle raged for two more bloody days. Stonewall Jackson and his Confederate soldiers claimed victory. Estimates vary but the total casualties for the battle topped 22,000, with Union losses numbering 13,824 dead and wounded out of 70,000 engaged, and Confederate casualties (killed, wounded, or missing) amounting to about 8,353 out of 55,000[6]—a five percent higher rate on the Union side.

I explored the old farmhouse and the grounds of the nearby site of the First Battle of Bull Run, which took place on July 21, 1861. The amount of money and resources Americans put into preserving the sites of these battles is impressive, as are the sites themselves—hundreds of acres of well-manicured farmland, old log cabins, and modern buildings with multimedia exhibits, books, CDs, and souvenirs available for purchase.

In a video re-enactment of the two battles, I saw many faces of young men the age of Lafayette at the time. In the portion on the 1861 battle, spectators—including women and children—spread tablecloths on surrounding hills for picnics, while observing the conflict below. Some came from as far away as Washington, DC, thinking it would be the one and only battle of the Civil War in Virginia. I guess it didn't look like much, at least at first.

Gradually, the horror became clear as casualties mounted. The Union Army of 28,450 suffered 460 killed and 1,124 wounded, while over 1,300 were listed as missing or captured. The Confederate forces, composed of 32,230 men, lost 387 killed and 1,582 wounded, with only 13 reported missing or captured[7]—an outcome of four percent more Union casualties.

This distant mayhem probably didn't seem real to the picknickers until a nearby farmhouse suddenly exploded in cannon fire with an old woman trapped inside. The picnics ended and the spectators fled.

From Manassas, I drove south to Fredericksburg, Virginia and checked into a hotel. In the morning, I easily found the road to various scenes of the Battle of the Wilderness where Lafayette Haskins fought on May 5, 1864. Between his first battle and this one, his military record includes many periods of illness:

He fell sick with a diarrheal disease on September 11, 1862 and remained in hospital or too ill to fight, missing the Battle of South Mountain and the Battle of Antietam in Maryland. He may have fought in the First Battle of Fredericksburg in Virginia from December 11 to 13, 1862, but fell sick again and missed the Battle of Gettysburg in Pennsylvania from July 1 to 3, 1863—another close escape for my genetic heritage and future life. In August of 1863, he came down with a fever and, after recovering, was furloughed for the month of November. He missed two more key battles but returned to duty on December 1, 1863. Lafayette's reoccurring illnesses probably saved him from death in action. His records mention "diarrhea," another malady they called "remittent fever," or just "sick in hospital."

Only luck can account for his survival through all these bouts of illness, for military doctors at the time had little concept of germ theory or appropriate treatments. Instead of rehydration for diarrheal diseases and other ailments, physicians employed bloodletting, purging, and blistering, or all three at once, supposedly to "rebalance body humors." Out of an estimated 700,000 soldiers who died during the Civil War, about 400,000 died of dysentery, typhoid fever, pneumonia, mumps, measles, or tuberculosis. They were easy targets for such diseases because of their weakness from marching, battle fatigue, unsanitary conditions, and poor diets.[8]

I stopped at a Civil War tourist post to watch a movie and buy a book about the Battle of the Wilderness, May 5-6, 1864. The lady behind the counter offered to look up my great-grandfather on her computerized list of those who had fought. "Lafayette Haskins, 7th Wisconsin Regiment" popped up immediately, and she offered to sell me a special certificate with his name on it. Then she realized she had run out of Union certificates.

"Would you like his name on a Confederate certificate?" she asked.

"No ma'am." I forced a polite smile. "He fought for the 7th Wisconsin Infantry, the Iron Brigade, on the Union side." I knew I stood on former Confederate soil, but my great-grandfather would not have accepted her reconciliatory gesture. She didn't make the offer in a humorous or sarcastic way. Was she just being kind? Did she not know the animosity between the two sides, some of which still lingers, especially in southern states?

I drove on to Saunders Field and walked along a hillcrest overlooking the cleared area, which had been part of a farm at the time. I noticed shallow ditches along the top of the hill. A

Remains of Confederate trenches above Saunders Field

description on a sign clarified that these depressions were the remains of Confederate trenches from which Virginian and North Carolinian troops fired on my great-grandfather and his 7th Wisconsin Regiment on May 5, 1864, as well as other units.

After consulting the battle map I'd picked up at the tourist post, I walked downhill and into the woods to the right of the field, where the 7th Wisconsin and other units had advanced on the Confederates. The place seemed spooky. In spite of the usual artistic depiction of a valiant battle in an ancient forest, a good deal of the fighting took place in tangled brush because most of the larger trees in the area had been harvested for iron smelting. As a survivor recorded afterwards, "It was a blind and bloody hunt to the death in bewildering thickets, rather than a battle."[9]

I could imagine the terror and confusion that must have come over Lafayette. He was a man of 20 by then, and probably pretty thin due to all his bouts of dysentery or typhoid. I visualized the Confederate bullet whistling through the brush and striking his upper right leg. Most likely, he fell immediately, writhing in pain, but had to wait until his commander called for a retreat before stretcher bearers could apply a tourniquet to help stop the bleeding and carry him to a nearby field hospital. There, he was probably administered chloroform or laudanum—the morphine syrup then used to relieve acute pain—until doctors could attend to him.

Meanwhile, General Grant and General Lee commanded their forces at nearby temporary headquarters. Grant had miscalculated that Lee and his men couldn't reach the Wilderness until late in the day. Acting on this false assumption, the Union Army failed to adequately patrol the roads leading into the area. The Confederates surprised the Union forces by their sudden buildup on higher positions. However, the two days of action ended inconclusively, neither side gaining ground. The fighting became so fierce that, for the first time in its history, the Iron Brigade broke and retreated, bumping into the reserve troops behind them.[10]

During the two-day battle, the Union side suffered an estimated total of 17,666 casualties: 2,246 killed, 12,037 wounded, and 3,383 captured. This may be a lower estimate than the true numbers because the Union Army did not want to demoralize public support for their efforts. The Confederates also suffered an estimated 11,000 casualties.[11]

Corpses remained in the woods for many days before being buried. Wounded men like Lafayette were likely transferred to Fredericksburg before being sent to hospitals in Washington, DC and Maryland. He was one of the lucky ones to survive without an amputation. But Lafayette's injury must have been serious, for he didn't receive an honorable discharge until September 5,

1864, exactly four months after he was wounded. He had taken part in at least two major battles, both of them a loss for the Union side. As he lay on his hospital bed, I wonder if his thoughts about becoming a famous soldier like his cousin, Col. William Robinson, vanished from his mind, if he ever had any such aspirations at all.

A book titled *The War of the Common Soldier,* by Peter S. Carmichael,[12] provides a vivid picture of the lives of soldiers on both sides of the fight. Though various degrees of literacy are revealed in letters home to their families, I have summarized the general content and tone below:

*Letters Home, 1862-65:* Noble sentiments are expressed in the early days: just cause, duty, honor, gallantry, the role of "Providence"—God's intervention in the lives of men. Then the letters become transformed by accounts and descriptions of sores and lice, rancid meat and moldy bread, ceaseless drumming preventing sleep, men urinating and defecating anywhere, polluted streams, nowhere to wash, ragged gloves and boots, torn and dirty uniforms. In battle, heads, arms, and legs fly off, some soldiers hide behind trees, waiting for any chance to flee. When silence returns, hungry dogs eat corpses. Shirkers, malingerers, and marauders roam behind the lines. With capture comes quick judgment and bullets from firing squads. Commanders speak of the need for death with dignity, but where is Divine Providence now? Their eyes have not seen the glory of the coming of the Lord.

On the Saturday of Memorial Day weekend in May 2017, I visited the Veterans Home at King, Wisconsin. It's a huge complex covering many acres beside a lake. When I entered the main nursing home, I didn't see anyone in the reception area except a veteran in a wheelchair, watching television. It seemed like a sad and lonely activity to be doing on a weekend established to remember those who fought in and some who died in America's many wars.

Arriving at the nurses' station, I approached the first nurse I saw and said, "I'm here to track down my great-grandfather and his wife. He was a veteran of the Civil War and I have records of their burial sites in that huge cemetery across the road. I even have the section and lot numbers, but how can I get a map of the cemetery?"

"Not here," she said. "You might try the recreation center." She gave me directions.

I asked, "Do you think they'd be buried side by side?"

"Well I couldn't tell you about that," she laughed. "My parents are buried over there and there are two other women between them. My mom wasn't much of a talker and the family joke is that he's being entertained by those other two."

I added, "My great-grandparents were separated for 20 years before they came here to die. I wonder if they're still arguing."

The nurse and I continued our humorous interchange for a few minutes before I headed to the recreation center. I had to ask several people for directions before locating it.

A volunteer took me to an on-going Bingo game, so I could ask directions from a staff member who was helping three disabled vets play. I said, "Do you know where I can locate a map of the veterans' cemetery?" I felt like a real cad because she immediately interrupted her assistance to the vets to take me to a gift shop for help. The gift shop lady in turn directed me to an emergency station housing police and fire departments. *This is really getting serious*, I thought.

At the station, a friendly policewoman pulled out a copy of the missing map saying, "I have what you're looking for, but there's no staff at the cemetery today."

What a struggle I had finding this map on a Memorial Day weekend. The cemetery opened in 1888 and is the final resting place of vets from the Civil War, Indian Wars, the Spanish-American War, World Wars I and II, Korea, Vietnam, the Gulf War, and possibly the more recent conflicts in Iraq and Afghanistan. I read that over 6,600 veterans and spouses are buried here.[13] You'd think there would be plenty of visitors on such a weekend, but I found this not to be the case. For most of the time, I was alone in my search.

Even with the map, it was difficult to locate my great-grandparents' tombstones because the cemetery has no signs with section and lot numbers to match the map. Too ugly for this

Neill McKee at the tombstones of Lafayette and Sarah Haskins, Central Wisconsin Veterans Memorial Cemetery, King, Wisconsin

well-manicured place? Finally, after a half-hour I found them. They had been buried next to each other.

Exhausted, I lay down between their tombstones and thought about how the Civil War had affected Lafayette and therefore their marriage. Perhaps their long separation was the reason why Grandmother Neill never said much about her parents—to shameful to speak about in those days.

I fell asleep on the grass in the warm spring sun. Waking up with a bit of a sunburn, I took photos from various angles, then I set up my tripod and took a "selfie" with me between their tombstones. *What a perfectly self-centered 21st century gesture,* I thought on leaving.

Before my journey, I had discovered some information on Lafayette Haskins' early life. He was born in 1844 in the town of Almond, Allegany County, New York, the youngest son of David Haskins (ca. 1803-73) and Clarfira Robinson (ca. 1807-67). David married Clarfira sometime around 1829 in Allegany County. (See Table 4)

I don't know why they called their youngest son "Lafayette," other than the fact it was fashionable at the time. The Frenchman, Gilbert du Motier, Marquis de Lafayette, had been a popular Revolutionary figure who fought on the American side, and his name remains on hundreds of American cities, towns, counties, rivers, and monuments to this day.

According to a brief biography by Lafayette's brother, Martin, the Haskins family moved from western New York to Wisconsin around 1847, living first at Beaver Dam. But the 1850 US Census, locates them in Leroy, Dodge County, where they bought land, making them some of the first pioneers in the area. They helped build the first schoolhouse there, and Lafayette and his siblings attended primary classes. By 1856, the family had moved close to Jackson in Adams County, about 67 miles west of Leroy. David Haskins purchased 120 acres of land near Davis Corners Post Office. The 1860 US Census lists Lafayette as 16 years old at the time, and attending school in Jackson.

On July 26, 1868, after he had returned from the Civil War, Lafayette married Sarah Alma Catherine Thomas in Jackson. She was born in Indiana in 1847, but the family moved to Wisconsin. Sarah and Lafayette lived with her parents at first and started a family. Their oldest child, Willis, was born on December 16, 1869, in Jackson.

Lafayette had a farm near Sarah's parents in 1869, but by 1875 he had given up that occupation and moved the family to Chippewa County, Wisconsin. My grandmother, Effie Jane (Haskins) Neill, was born in Cadott on February 23, 1876. I found the family with six children in the 1880 US Census, then living in Chippewa Falls, the county seat. My grandmother was listed as age four.

From a cousin, I had received a family photo taken around 1887. Their attire, and the fact that they could have a photo taken at all, indicates they were not poor. Effie Jane was about 11 years of age at the time. Lafayette applied for a veteran's pension and was listed on the Surviving Soldiers Special Census of 1890. He claimed his disability as "rheumatism." At some point, the family moved back to Cadott, which I visited (Chapter 5). It's located "half-way between the Equator and the North Pole," according to a sign in the town park. Jean Baptiste Cadotte, the son of a French-Canadian fur trader, started the settlement as a trading post. The railroad reached Cadott in 1880 and, due to power from the Yellow River, it spurred the development of a large hub-and-spoke factory, sawmills, a barrel mill, a shingle mill, and a cheese

Lafayette and Sarah with children, ca. 1887 (top row from left: probably Eli 16, Willis 18, Vernon 15, Sarah 40; middle row: Catharine Alma [Weston] Thomas 68 - mother of Sarah, Harvey 8, Lafayette 43; bottom row: Ralph 4, Effie Jane 11)

box factory. A family story has it that Lafayette owned a lumber business, but he was listed in the 1880 US Census as working in a wagon shop.

Lafayette is noted in various records as a blacksmith and wagon maker, a carpenter, a school supplies and grocery salesman, and a house builder. However, as mentioned above, Lafayette and Sarah were separated between 1905 and 1924. Sarah lived with some of their children in Wisconsin and California, while Lafayette moved for a spell to Lorriane, Dickie County, North Dakota, where he bought some land, probably with an old house that needed renovation, near his son Vernon's place. There's a 1906 record of his purchase: 160 acres in Dickey County, North Dakota. The family called it "Haskins Folly," probably because he

Lafayette and Sara Haskins in their later years

had made a bad financial decision. During that era, Wisconsinites moved west to the Dakotas because of the promise of prairie farmland but many failed at farming, often due to the lack of rain.

In May 1924, Lafayette was admitted to the Veterans Home in King, where he died of prostate and stomach cancer on May 19, 1925 at the age of 81. He had fallen and fractured his hip two months earlier. In July 1924, Sarah was also admitted to the Veterans Home and died on August 22, 1931 at the age of 84, while visiting their son Harvey in Clintonville, Wisconsin.

Lafayette was not the only one in his family to fight in the Civil War. His four older brothers (Nathaniel, Enos, Martin, and Charles), also served in various Wisconsin infantries. I received their complete military records from my cousin in Missouri.

Nathaniel, born in 1832, joined General Sherman's march through Georgia in the Battle of Resaca, the Battle of Dallas, and the Battle of Kennesaw Mountain. Then they moved on to Atlanta where the Confederates captured him and sent him to the infamous Andersonville Prison in Georgia on July 22, 1864. Somehow, he survived that hellish place and, after release through a prisoner exchange, he fought again in the Battle of Decatur in Alabama. The Union Army transferred him to Company D of the 12th Wisconsin on June 2, 1865, five days before his first wife died, leaving three children to be looked after by the family. He was finally mustered out of service on July 16 in Louisville, Kentucky, at the age of 33. He returned to Wisconsin, remarried in 1866 and had another son, but died in 1868 of unrecorded causes.

Enos, born in 1835, and Martin in 1837, fought in various battles: the Battle of Chaplin Hill (Perryville), Kentucky; the Battle of Stones River (a.k.a., Second Battle of Murfreesboro) in Tennessee, where Enos contracted lung disease; the Tullahoma Campaign; and the Battle of Hoover's Gap on June 24-26, 1863, when the Union Army drove the Confederates out of Central Tennessee by feigned moves and surprise attacks. For the first time in the Civil War, soldiers like my great-grand uncles held the Spencer Rifle in this battle, an American-made, manually operated, lever-action, seven-shot repeater, making killing even more efficient.

On September 20th, 1863, the two brothers also fought in the Battle of Chickamauga, the second advance on Chattanooga, Tennessee. But there, Martin's luck ran out when he received a gunshot wound which fractured both bones in his right arm. He was taken prisoner and later exchanged. Martin ended up at a hospital in Annapolis, Maryland, and then was transferred to Baltimore, where he recovered until July 27, 1864, when he was honorably discharged at the age of 27. He returned to Wisconsin and married twice (his first wife died young) and raised a family. His right arm remained useless, qualifying him to receive an invalid's pension. He died in 1921 at the age of 84.

Enos suffered from lung disease and severe diarrhea through-out the war. He came down with lumbago and other ailments but recovered enough to return to duty briefly in September 1864. He was finally mustered out at Point Lookout, Maryland on October 5, 1864, at the age of 29. He returned to Wisconsin to marry and raise a family. His lung disease continued to bother him and, in 1905 at the age of 43, the family said he "looked like a skeleton." He moved to California but struggled with his health for the rest of his life, kidney disease and rheumatism adding to his suffering. His first wife died in 1874, and he remarried later in the same year. Despite his poor health, he died in 1928 at the age of 92—a testament to his will to live.

Charles, born in 1842, enlisted and was wounded in both legs in the Battle of Antietam, Maryland, on September 17, 1862. The bullet went through his left thigh, lodged in his right thigh, and the doctors cut it out three days later. He spent time in hospital in Smokestown, Maryland and then in Baltimore. The Union Army released him on October 31, 1863 and transferred him to an Invalid's or Veteran's Reserve Corps, until his honor-able discharge on June 30, 1864 at the age of 22. He returned to Wisconsin, married, and raised a family. The government gave him a meager pension of about $2.65 a month. He received an increase to $8.00 per month in 1887, and then $14.00 in 1888—small compensation for the pain he suffered the rest of his life, mostly due to his gunshot wounds. His first wife also died young. He remarried and had more children, and passed away in Wisconsin, in 1912, at the age of 70.

These detailed accounts had been preserved in records by the Haskins family and pieced together by my cousin, Tamara. I considered it to be a near miracle that these five brothers all vol-untarily enlisted, survived the Civil War, and left the army with honors. All but one lived to a relatively old age, working in various semi-skilled occupations, while fighting for invalid and pension benefits. Somehow, they made it through those trials. But it is evident that the war took a great toll on them and affected their quality of life for the remainder of their days.

When I was growing up after World War II, my father described some veterans as "shell shocked," a condition now recognized officially as post-traumatic stress disorder, a mental health ailment that's triggered by experiencing or witnessing a terrifying event or series of events. Few people were inclined to talk about it in the past, for it was often viewed as a sign of cowardice, but it is addressed more openly and fairly now.

Maybe my great-grandfather and his brothers had nightmares and often woke up in a sweat. Did they hear dying young men crying out for their mothers? They had fought for a good cause, freeing the slaves and keeping the American states together. But as I read the descriptions of their lives, Lafayette and his brothers seemed a lot like the "lost Vietnam generation" of veterans, in spite of the fact that, unlike in Vietnam, their side had won. Did they talk about any of this at all with their parents or spouses? I wondered if my grandma Neill heard some of her father's war stories. Was that the reason she was so against guns?

I wanted to delve deeper into the history of the Haskins family in America, their religious beliefs and the battles they fought in. What about the War of 1812, the American Revolution, and the French and Indian War? I thought, perhaps, I'd find some answers in Allegany County, New York, where Lafayette Haskins was born.

# 9

## ALLEGANY COUNTY, NEW YORK: ANCESTRAL CONNECTING POINT

Whitney Valley, Allegany County, New York

ON A SUNNY DAY IN THE SPRING OF 2017, I DROVE southeast from Buffalo, New York, to Allegany County and its Whitney Valley. I passed through the town of Almond and on to the Allegany County Museum in Andover to meet Ron Taylor, President of the Allegany County Historical Society. This gentleman showed me his newly rebuilt establishment, funded with the help of a local business. For the next five or six hours, we talked about the history of his county, as he showed me through the museum and drove me around, trying to find physical traces of my Haskins ancestors. His interest and helpful attitude amazed me. We had corresponded by email for a few weeks and he had done some research and printed out family records he'd located.

We headed back towards Almond where my great-grandfather Lafayette Haskins was born on February 10, 1844. Ron told me he'd come across a number of Haskins families still living in the area. Lafayette's great-grandfather, Micah Nathan Haskins Sr., is my oldest ancestor to have settled here—around 1800—accompanied by three of his sons: Roswell, Micah Jr., and David. Another son, Lafayette's grandfather, Nathaniel (my 3rd great-grandfather), had died around 1805 in Brookfield, Madison County, New York, and sometime between 1805 and 1807, the Haskins brothers brought Nathaniel's widow, Lydia Haskins née Stevens, to the area, along with her two children: David (Lafayette's father) and his brother, Eri. By this point in my research, I had a good idea about the lineage of the Haskins and had verified the names of two of the women my ancestors had married: Lydia Stevens and Clarfira Robinson. Clarfira, first mentioned in Chapter 8, met and married David Haskins here. Both of these women came from families I discovered to be important parts of my American genealogy. Western New York had been a connecting point for my ancestors. (See Table 4.)

Most of western New York had been the territory of the Seneca, one of the tribes of the Iroquois Confederacy. The French were the first to explore the area in the 1700s, and they developed peaceful relations with the Seneca nation. But by the time the Haskins entered the land, it was relatively unpopulated because diseases brought by the early explorers had already taken a toll. An 1896 publication by the Allegany Historical Society stated:

Although the owners of these lands made strenuous efforts to attract settlers, distrust of titles, the density of the forest, the presence of bears, wolves and panthers, and of roving bands of Indians, greatly retarded settlement until after the War of 1812.[1]

The Haskins probably carried a number of old muskets to defend themselves and to hunt for game, their major source of protein, especially before they could raise cattle, sheep, and poultry. In the same historical publication, I found a poem which captures the sentiment of my ancestors' time in this place:

Where the dark green pines and hemlocks grow,
Where the fountains of height from rock sources flow,
Where the Red Man's foot had scarce ceased to roam,
Our fathers established their pioneer home.

'Tis the "top of the world," 'tis the land where we see
The waters flow all ways to get to the sea;
To the north, to the south, to the east, to the west,
The crystal streams spring to the broad ocean's breast.
—W. A. Fergusson[2]

By appearances, the tall hills and thick forests continued to hide this land from the 21st century. I couldn't see what made up the county's economic base in 2017. The farms were small and some of the houses looked rundown. When we drove through the town of Alfred, I finally saw signs of thriving modern life—students, coffee shops, and traffic. This place hosts Alfred University and Alfred State College of Technology, two of the main employers left in the county. Ron had worked in the college much of his career.

Ron explained, "Yes, without these colleges, there isn't much work in the area. Things really went downhill during the 2007-08 recession. Many people lost their houses and had to start over. We're also seeing a lot of drug use here—heroin and meth. Not a good scene."

"Are there any Native Americans left in the area?" I asked.

"Sure, and they're doing pretty well by contrast. To the west of here there's the Seneca Allegany Resort and Casino."

I had seen the signs for Seneca Casinos in Niagara Falls and Buffalo. By establishing such popular businesses, Native Americans could win back a part of what was taken from them, even if it meant taxing poorer people in the American population—especially those addicted to gambling from paycheck to paycheck. Those casinos, I decided, were a kind of retribution for past deeds of the white man.

Ron took me to the well-kept Woodlawn Cemetery in Almond. He went to the top of its hill while I searched around the bottom. It wasn't long before Ron shouted for me. He had found the tombstone of Eri Haskins and his third wife, Caroline. (His first two wives died prematurely.) Eri was the brother of my 2nd great-grandfather, David Haskins. So, I found proof, set in stone, that my Haskins ancestors had lived here—better than only census records. Other Haskins had been buried in the cemetery, according to the list Ron gave me, but they were not directly related to my line, so we didn't investigate further. Besides, it would have taken hours to locate them without a cemetery map, and I knew I was taking up a lot of Ron's time.

I was disappointed not to find traces of Micah Haskins Sr., my 4th great-grandfather. I had found his will online, made on May 5, 1818. He left all his property to his son and namesake, Micah Haskins Jr.

The history of Allegany County, cited above, records dozens

Eri and Caroline Haskins' tombstone, Allegany County, New York

of taverns throughout the county. Some sources (unverified) report that Micah Jr. must have been acquainted with a large share of the early settlers because he kept a tavern for nearly a quarter of a century.

To counter such influences, the people of Allegany built many churches—especially "seventh-day Baptists" and Methodists. I read about this age of religious revivalism in Daniel Walker Howe's great work, *What Hath God Wrought: The Transformation of America, 1815-1848*.[3] With little or no ecclesiastic authority to oversee congregations, preachers having only rudimentary knowledge of theology and history came forth to capture the popular imagination, especially during the early 1700s and early 1800s. During the "Second Great Awakening" of the 1830s and 1840s, self-proclaimed saviors traveled from town-to-town preaching that only their religion held the key to salvation and eternal life in the New Millennium, when Jesus Christ would come again and reign over the whole Earth. Thousands of people attended religious events lasting many days, listening to preachers—some perched in trees as they spouted forth sermons on sin and redemption. The movement emphasized emotions and an appeal to the supernatural, while rejecting the deism of the Enlightenment and its rationalism. Put simply, deists believe in God, or a Creator, who doesn't intervene in the universe, and certainly not in human affairs, which should be governed by empirical observation, knowledge, and reason, rather than religion and emotions.

I found no such "hot-headed" ministers among my Haskins ancestors in the generations from Lafayette Haskins to Micah Haskins Sr. I would like to think of them as moderate people who wouldn't listen to feverish preachers working up crowds with their talk of hell and damnation. Eri Haskins had not ordered any religious symbols or verses on his tombstone. Micah Haskins Sr. died sometime before June 1820, around the age of 85. While researching him, I discovered that my Haskins line goes back to the 1600s in Connecticut, and I planned to visit the places where they lived later in the trip (Chapter 13).

Micah Haskins Sr., 41 years old when the American Revolution began, did not join the fight. I had some information at the time that he was a veteran of the French and Indian War (Chapter 12), so perhaps he was considered to be too old. Besides, someone had to supply food for the would-be nation. I had hoped to find war records of the involvement of my 3rd great-grandfather, Nathaniel, but he and all his brothers were born between 1766 and 1779, so that generation of Haskins missed the conflict.

I knew that many family histories ignore the female line. By following my maternal grandmother, Effie Jane Neill, who was born a Haskins in Wisconsin, I had found the stories of her father and his brothers in the Civil War. Before I started my trip, I also had begun to study the genealogy of Lydia (Stevens) Haskins' father, Joseph Stevens, one of my 4th great-grandfathers. I found some records on *Ancestry.com* of his involvement in the American Revolution in New York State. I also discovered that Clarfira (Robinson) Haskins' father, Abel Robinson, a 3rd great-grandfather of mine, had been a Revolutionary War soldier in Connecticut and New York.

Allegany County, New York was a connecting point for many of my American genes. My short time there proved to be very productive. Working gradually backwards chronologically, I decided I had to visit the Hudson highlands to check out Abel Robinson's role in the Revolutionary War.

# 10

## ABEL ROBINSON *in the* HUDSON HIGHLANDS *and* VERMONT

Hudson River from Stony Point Battlefield, New York

ABEL ROBINSON, MY 3RD GREAT-GRANDFATHER, WAS born on September 15, 1761 in Scotland, Windham County, Connecticut. On May 17, 1777, although not yet 16, he managed to enlist in the 3rd Connecticut Regiment, Connecticut Line, a unit within the Continental Army during the American Revolution. He served for eight months and was discharged, but re-enlisted on January 1, 1778 and completed his time in the military on December 20, 1780. After an extensive search, I found his enrollment records online in an old volume on the subject.[1]

Throughout much of his time in the army, Abel served in Captain cum Major Wills Clift's Company. Clift, in turn, answered to Colonel Samuel Wyllis (also spelled "Wyllys" in old records). From January 1, 1777 to January 1, 1781, Colonel Wyllis led the 3rd Connecticut Regiment.[2] Little information came up in my online searches about exactly what his regiment had done for the war effort. I could see in the records that Abel Robinson had remained a private, only a foot soldier. It wasn't until I reached the Hudson highlands north of New York City that his military duties came to life.

I visited West Point, the famous military academy located on a strategic bend of the Hudson River. This is a majestic part of New York State that I had never visited before. In many places, steep hills rise on both sides of the Hudson, pushing the water into a narrow gushing torrent. I visited West Point Museum and took an official tour of the place. Earlier, I had discovered online, the ruins of Fort Wyllis within the compound of the academy, which the 3rd Connecticut Regiment had helped to construct. It was named after the regiment's Samuel Wyllis, who eventually rose to the rank of Major General.

I found it frustrating that I couldn't gain access to these ruins. The area had been restricted since the 9/11 terrorist attacks. But I had an idea. After several attempts, the museum operator put me through to Paul Ackermann, a Museum Specialist/Conservator in charge of the historic ruins within West Point. I told him, "I traveled from New Mexico, hoping to see Fort Wyllis. I'm a writer doing a book on places where my 3rd great-grandfather was stationed in the Revolutionary War. He was under Samuel Wyllis."

Ackermann replied, "Where are you now?'

"Just outside the museum."

"Can you meet me downstairs at the reception in five minutes. Ask them to page me."

"Sure can; see you there."

I spent the next hour in Ackermann's office. He went over, in detail, why he thought that the so-called Fort Wyllis was never a fort at all, but a "redoubt"—a supplementary fortification, typically square or polygonal, on which cannons were mounted—in this case to defend against British forces trying to advance up the Hudson River. The details of his investigations intrigued me, mainly for the fact that, after many years of study, he had concluded that earlier archaeological research—even the information given out on tours of West Point— lacked accuracy. He also shared with me a paper he had written, opining that calling the whole place "Fortress West Point" is actually a misnomer since a fortress, in military terms, is a fortified structure usually encircling a town, whereas West Point was built in phases with no clear overall strategic design. It had been constructed as a complex network of forts and redoubts designed by a succession of engineers, the most famous being Thaddeus Kosciuszko, a Polish man who arrived on the job in March 1778.

Remains of Redoubt Wyllis, inside West Point, overlooking the Hudson River. *Photo by Paul Ackermann*

I became encouraged by this conversation because Ackermann assured me that if Abel Robinson served with the 3rd Connecticut under Samuel Wyllis, there was a good chance his hands had helped to put in place those old stones of Redoubt Wyllis. He promised to take photos of the ruins for my book.

I left the museum greatly satisfied with the information from Ackermann, and traveled south to Stony Point Battlefield to see other fortifications raised there during the Revolutionary War. Today, all that remains is a few stones and a lighthouse. I asked the young student at the museum's welcome desk if he knew which rebel army units had built the place. He didn't know, but went outside to call in Michael Sheehan, an enthusiastic young historian and New York State employee wearing a colonial rebel uniform.

I asked Sheehan, "Do you know if the 3rd Connecticut Regiment was ever based here? My 3rd great-grandfather was with that regiment in the Revolutionary War."

"I don't think so," he said, "but come into my office and we'll find out."

For the next half-hour, we searched together until he offered a book titled *The Sinews of Independence* by Charles Lesser.[3] I found this to be a breakthrough moment. The publication listed the locations of most of the regiments of Washington's Continental Army from 1777 to the 1780s. It provided further evidence that Abel Robinson briefly worked on Redoubt Wyllis, and also recorded that by April 1778 the 3rd Connecticut had been posted to a supply depot at Fishkill, across the river, a place with a small museum that I later visited. In the summer of 1778, the 3rd Connecticut shifted to White Plains, New York, trying to goad the British forces based in New York City into a fight. Then they wintered at Redding, Connecticut.

In the spring of 1779, the 3rd Connecticut returned to the Hudson highlands. According to *The Sinews of Independence*, the regiment spent most of its time on the eastern side of the river, involved in some back and forth skirmishes. I concluded that more than likely my ancestor had been a laborer involved in tasks such as hauling materiel of war here and there, raising tents, baking thousands of loaves of bread, or helping to operate a forge to make bayonets, knives, and swords. Perhaps he also saw some direct action.

The 3rd Connecticut spent the winter of 1779-80 at the Morristown Encampment in New Jersey. It was one of the coldest winters of the 1700s, but the Continental Army was much better prepared than at Valley Forge, where many had died of exposure and diseases during the previous winter. The worst enemy for Abel and his comrades was surely boredom—being far from their families, spending long days and freezing nights crammed into small log cabins, tending the fire and cooking, playing cards, drinking their rations of rum, and venturing outdoors for supplies of firewood. Probably, they were forced to regularly drill in the snow to keep in shape.

My ancestor labored near George Washington throughout much of his time in the Army, but likely only saw him from afar. When I read that in August and September 1780 his regiment was based at Tappan, New York, and may have been deployed to reinforce rebel forces at West Point, his rather boring record became more interesting. I had read *The Notorious Benedict Arnold* by Steve Sheinkin,[4] a well-written account of a man Americans have labeled as the worst traitor of all time. The historical parts of my summary below are derived from that book, except where otherwise cited.

In Tappan, a British spy, John André, was imprisoned, tried, and hung on October 2, 1780, for conspiring with Benedict Arnold, the commander of West Point. Sheinkin's account states that

The tavern where John André was tried and sentenced to death

they didn't even afford André proper gallows. They tied a rope to a tree branch, put the noose around his neck, and made him stand at the end of a wagon. When they whipped the horses, causing them to lunge forward, quite likely his neck didn't break as he fell off. His death would have been a slow and agonizing one. I can picture his body kicking and convulsing just above the ground for some minutes before he expired, unlike most of the similar hangings we see in movies, which I classify in the general category of "Hollywood deaths."

I had dinner in the old tavern where John André had been tried. I walked on the original uneven floor boards and admired its rustic furnishings. At the trial, André had requested a firing squad, but Washington didn't allow such an honorable means of death for a spy. He had to experience the ignominious death of a thief. Many people, including Washington himself, felt sorry for this otherwise honorable soldier, poet, and sometimes play-wright, who had become caught up in this affair with the traitor, Arnold. General Lafayette, who, it is said, witnessed the proceed-ings, wept. Perhaps he had read André's poem on a raid by the rebel leader, Anthony Wayne, who had been a tanner in civilian life. It ends in a prophetic manner:

**The Cow Chase**[5] (an excerpt):
His daring words from all the crowd such great applause did gain
That every man declared aloud for serious work with Wayne,
And now the foe began to lead his forces to the attack,
Balls whistling unto balls succeed and make the blockhouse crack.

The firmer as the Rebels pressed, the loyal heroes stand,
Virtue had nerved each honest breast and industry each hand,
And as the fight was further fought and balls began to thicken,
The fray assumed, the generals thought, the color of a lickin'.

Yet undismayed the chiefs command, and to redeem the day,
Cry, "Soldiers, charge!" They hear, they stand, they turn and run away.
And now I've closed my epic strain, I tremble as I show it,
Lest this same warrior-drover, Wayne, should ever catch— this poet.

If Abel Robinson ever saw John André or Benedict Arnold at West Point, it would have been from a distance. Possibly he spotted Arnold on his way to and from his headquarters across the Hudson River, where he held a fatal rendezvous with André. This dramatic spy story had to be the talk of the troops all along the Hudson highlands.

The American Revolution had so many chances of failure, in this case due to the divided loyalty of one man. Three years of my ancestor's labor in fort construction, materiel handling, and marching up and down the banks of the Hudson with a musket over his shoulder could have been for nothing had Benedict Arnold and John André's scheme succeeded. According to my new historian friend at West Point, the plans they stole were not "Kosciuszko's plans" at all, but rather an inventory of all the fortifications' weaknesses, drawn from the designs of others, and written in Benedict Arnold's hand.

I must admit that as I read Sheinkin's book I gained a certain sympathy for Benedict Arnold. The book portrays a true patriot to the American cause who was treated badly by the Continental Army establishment. In early 1775, before the formal declaration of war, Arnold, with authority from the Massachusetts Committee of Safety, helped to seize Fort Ticonderoga on Lake Champlain from the British. They wanted to capture the heavy cannons there to bring to Boston, where the rebels hoped to blast the British Navy out of the harbor. Arnold took action without the approval of the Continental Congress, but it helped force their hand to declare independence. Arnold had teamed up with Ethan Allen and his Green Mountain Boys of Vermont to take Ticonderoga, but most of the credit went to them, in spite of the fact that Arnold had been the only one with formal orders in his pocket.

In the fall of 1775, after being passed over to lead the main invasion force against the British in Canada, Arnold proposed to Washington that he take a second invasion force through the wilderness of Maine to attack the Fortress of Quebec—a mad scheme that failed completely. About 300 men turned back and another 200 died en route. The remaining small force could not penetrate the walls of the fortress, and they barely survived the winter. But this romantic charge captured the American population's rebellious imagination and Arnold became a kind of folk hero—a David attempting to battle the giant British military machine.

In his retreat from Canada, in 1776, Arnold received all the blame from the higher-ups for allowing his men to loot the property of merchants in Montreal—an inability to maintain proper discipline in his troops by someone who was supposed to be a gentleman commander.

In the same year, on the shore of Lake Champlain, Arnold ordered the building and launching of a fleet of small ships to do battle with the stronger British fleet in a surprise attack at Valcour Island, thereby delaying the British from taking back Fort Ticonderoga. He succeeded, but the rebel generals blamed him for the loss of most of his fleet in the battle, rather than praising him for driving the British north to their winter quarters.

Wherever he went, Arnold seemed to take extreme chances and make enemies among the growing "old boys" network in the Continental Army, many of whom had served together in the French and Indian War, 1754-63. They denied him the rank he thought he deserved. In 1777, he returned to the Hudson Valley where General Gates had taken over the American forces at Saratoga, New York. The two men clashed in style and temperament. Gates held back many of his troops during the first battle in September, while Arnold pushed him to attack. The results of the combat were inconclusive, and Gates and Arnold continued to argue.

Gates removed Arnold's authority over any troops. But during the second battle in October, while Gates sat in his camp receiving periodic reports, Arnold grew so frustrated that he charged with his horse into the clashing armies to rally and direct the rebel troops. His actions helped defeat British General Burgoyne, who surrendered on October 17, 1777. This second battle is said to have been the "turning point" in the American Revolution. The defeat of the British forces impressed the French military and brought them in on the American side.

Arnold, however, was severely wounded in the leg and had to lie in a traction box for almost six months. Due to Arnold's bravery at Saratoga, Congress restored his command seniority, but Arnold scoffed at this token of appreciation. He suspected they were only showing pity on him. Due to his wound and treatment, his left leg became two inches (five cm) shorter than the right, and he had to wear a special high sole and heel for the rest of his life. As he lay there recovering, he probably mulled over his situation. His first wife had died in 1775, and he had also lost a great deal of his wealth due to neglect of his businesses while away on military service.

When he recovered, Arnold traveled to Valley Forge in Pennsylvania, where Washington and his troops had been stationed throughout the winter of 1777-78. When the British abandoned Philadelphia in June 1778, Washington offered Arnold the post of Military Governor of the city, which would be restored as the capital of the recently declared independent country. There, Arnold's final downfall began when, in an attempt to regain some of his wealth, he used his new position to order government transport to carry goods he had purchased for sale at a profit. He also met Margaret (Peggy) Shippen, a woman who had befriended John André during the time the British had occupied Philadelphia. Arnold and Peggy married in 1779.

The Continental Army charged Arnold with a number of offenses concerning use of his military office for private gain. He demanded a trial in Congress, which was delayed but finally began in May 1779. In December, Congress found him not guilty of most charges, but the tribunal demanded that George Washington reprimand him. Washington finally did so, but in a mild manner. Meanwhile, Arnold had concocted a scheme with his new wife to gain back his wealth by convincing Washington to put him in charge of West Point, rather than an army unit, using his infirmity as the main reason.

Once Arnold took over this strategic post, through intermediaries, he and Peggy sent messages to the British, indicating they would sell them the plans of West Point. To clinch the deal, John André traveled from British headquarters in New York City to Arnold's headquarters across the Hudson from West Point. However, to make a long story short, they bungled the secrecy of this liaison and rebel militia detained André on his retreat. He was dressed in plain clothes with the plans hidden in his boots. Without a British uniform, he could be tried as a spy according to military code. On hearing of André's arrest, Arnold escaped down the river to New York, and André was taken across the river to Washington's headquarters at Tappan to be tried and hung.

Arnold fought on the British side for the rest of the war. Afterwards, he attempted to settle in Nova Scotia but returned to Britain, trying to regain his station in life. English society regarded him as a man of questionable character and Americans knew him as an absolute traitor for the remainder of his life. He died in London in 1801. Peggy bore him five children and died in London in 1804.

During his time at Valley Forge with Washington, Arnold was among a number of officers who had taken the first Oath of Allegiance to the United States, which went like this:

> I, Benedict Arnold do acknowledge the UNITED STATES of AMERICA to be Free, Independent and Sovereign States, and declare that the people thereof owe no allegiance or obedience to George the Third, King of Great Britain; and I renounce, refuse and abjure any allegiance or obedience to him; and I do Swear that I will, to the utmost

of my power, support, maintain and defend the said United States against the said King George the Third, his heirs and successors, and his or their abettors, assistants, and adherents, and will serve the said United States in the office of _____ which I now hold, with fidelity, according to the best of my skill and understanding.[6]

Swearing this oath made Arnold a formal traitor, rather than just a man who could not decide between loyalty to the Crown and the rebel cause, which appeared to be losing up until the last few months of the American Revolution. Throughout the war, many people could not decide which side to take and many Loyalists moved back to England, to Canada, or to Britain's Caribbean colonies.

The reason the story of Benedict Arnold became so important to me is that, while I researched my American roots, I too was trying to decide whether to become a US citizen, in addition to my Canadian citizenship. Queen Elizabeth II remains the head of state of Canada and the Governor General of Canada represents her. (The position was held by upperclass men sent from Britain until 1952. Since then, only Canadians have been appointed—eight men and four women.) I learned from the story of Benedict Arnold that oaths have consequences. (More on this in Chapter 17.)

So, the story I can now tell is that my 3rd great-grandfather, Abel Robinson, helped to build West Point, which was almost sold out to the British by an American patriot turned traitor. I wonder what Abel thought about this after Arnold fled to New York City, and I question whether he and his compatriots ever had similar doubts about where their loyalty lay during those freezing winters in military camps, when it looked like the British would prevail.

Abel Robinson left the Continental Army at the end of 1780 and returned to his home in Connecticut. His father and mother were still alive at the time and he probably helped on the family farm. But around 1785, he joined his brothers Ephraim and Richard, who had also fought in the American Revolution, in seeking their fortunes in "New Connecticut." The territory declared independence in 1777 and decided on the name "Vermont," a translation from French, meaning "green mountain." It became a state on March 4, 1791.

Abel and his brothers settled and farmed near Pawlet, a small village in Rutland County, in the southwestern portion of Vermont. I traveled to Pawlet in search of their stories. There I met Stephen Williams, President of the Pawlet Historical Society. He is a transplanted Welshman who made his home in America and settled in Pawlet after retirement. He introduced me to the lady who kept the records of Old Pawlet Cemetery, and took me to visit the place, but most of the Robinson tombstones were so overgrown with moss that they were illegible. Besides, there were no records indicating Abel or his family were buried in this graveyard, except perhaps one son who died in his infancy in 1794.

Williams introduced me to the town clerk, who let me look through tattered binders containing records that are not on the Internet. I found this to be a time consuming and mainly fruitless endeavor. I did find one land purchase by Abel, but no sales, marriage registration, or records of the births of his children. I had more luck with the land transactions and other records of his brothers, Ephraim and Richard. I also found a Robinson Hill Road in Pawlet, with a number of homes, which may be located on the original Robinson farms.

It took me a long time and quite a lot of expense to track down the story of Abel Robinson's final days. Abel's first wife, Rhoda (her maiden name was possibly "Ormsby"), died in Pawlet in the early 1790s. He married Eunice Woodward, probably in March 1795. By his two wives, he had at least eight surviving children, including my 2nd great-grandmother, Clarfira Robinson, born in 1806.

Abel applied for a Revolutionary War pension on April 20, 1818 and was paid eight dollars per month.[7] I commissioned further research by the New England Historical Genealogy Society (NEHGS), which led to proof that in 1830 Abel transferred his veteran's pension from Vermont to New York.[8] By then he had moved with Eunice and at least one daughter, Clarifa, to Allegany County in order to live with or near their married daughter, Alzina (Robinson) Howell. That's where Clarfira met and married David Haskins, my 2nd great-grandfather, around 1829. Abel's pension payments ceased after his death, around 1835. No other death or burial records remain.

My 2nd great-grandparents, David and Clarfira Haskins, with their six children, including Lafayette, left Allegany County around 1847 and headed to Wisconsin (Chapter 8). They also took along Clarfira's mother, Eunice, who appears with them in the 1850 Wisconsin census—but with the mistaken age of 18, when she should have been recorded as age 78. Her age was written in a column for people over 20 years of age, so 18 made no sense. This slip of the pen by the census taker had caused a lot of confusion by Haskins family genealogical enthusiasts, which the NEHGS researchers settled for me. This finding became one of the most important factors for proof of much of my New England ancestry and *Mayflower* connection.

Abel Robinson left little trace of his last days in Allegany County, except his pension record—and almost nothing in

Vermont, where he lived most of his adult life. The hilly land there involved a tremendous amount of labor to clear and manage in order to feed his growing family. Perhaps, after his youthful adventures on the Hudson highlands, serving near the great George Washington, everything else was an anticlimax.

# 11

## JOSEPH STEVENS *in the* AMERICAN REVOLUTION

Saratoga Battlefield, New York

FROM PAWLET, VERMONT TO SARATOGA NATIONAL Historical Park in upstate New York, it's about a two-hour drive on winding roads through verdant rolling hills. In 1777, British General Burgoyne had hoped to divide New England from the southern American Colonies. He and his forces headed south from Canada to capture Fort Ticonderoga—rather easy to do since the fort had been stripped of its cannons in 1775 by the Green Mountain Boys and Benedict Arnold. Burgoyne had expected other British forces to come from the south and west, but they never arrived. This battle was the first big victory for the rebel army in the Revolution, and it captured the attention of the French and Spanish, who then decided to formally enter the war on the American side, the so-called "turning point" in the Revolution, as mentioned in the previous chapter.

Saratoga Park is a huge piece of real estate crisscrossed by roads and trails for hiking and picnicking. It had rained heavily during the night before my visit, so the land was soaked. I parked my vehicle and walked for at least three miles in the spring sun, reading some of the signs commemorating skirmishes between the opposing forces. About 1,000 British troops and 500 rebel Americans were killed or wounded during the two major encounters here. I had come to Saratoga to check out the involvement of my 4th great-grandfather, Joseph Stevens Sr. in these historic battles, according to records I found on *Ancestry.com*. Another record mentioned that he fought in the War of 1812.

Earlier on my trip, I had stopped at the Village of Bath, Steuben County, New York, to the east of Allegany County. I wanted to find traces of Joseph Stevens Sr., the father of my 3rd great-grandmother, Lydia (Stevens) Haskins. He was born in Sheffield, Massachusetts, on June 14, 1752, and died around 1830. Bath hosts the Steuben County Historical Society, and the people I met there let me make copies of any records I wanted. Once again, the friendliness and facilitating nature of such local historians impressed me. They also gave me directions to Hillside Cemetery near the small town of Campbell on the Cohocton River. Joseph Stevens Sr. and family had settled there around 1805, after moving from Sangerfield, New York.

I walked up the lane into the cemetery and spent an hour or so on its steep slope, searching for Joseph and his second wife, Desire. His first wife, Naomi Mathews (born ca. 1754 - died 1778) was Lydia's mother. I didn't really expect to find Joseph Stevens Sr.'s tombstone since I had found no proven record of death. I did see a mention in one Stevens family tree on *Ancestry. com* that he had died in 1830 in Wheeler, New York, a village a few miles to the north.

Walking around the cemetery, I soon found the tombstone of Joseph Sr.'s eldest son, Joseph Jr., who had been a farmer and also an artist in Campbell. He was born in 1771 in Stillwater, New York, and died in 1843. Someone had placed a veteran's medal and flag beside his tombstone. The medal commemorated his participation in the War of 1812, between America and Britain and their respective allies in North America, from June 1812 to February 1815. This made more sense than his father's involvement in that war because, by then, Joseph Sr. would have been around 41 years old and a busy father and farmer. Joseph Jr. wasn't a direct ancestor of mine, but I had to digest the fact that he, the eldest brother

Tombstone of Joseph Stevens Jr. and medal of service, War of 1812

of my 3rd great-grandmother, Lydia Stevens, fought the British in the War of 1812. It felt a little strange to me, as a Canadian, that I'd had a relative on the opposite side. In my school days in Ontario, our teachers taught us how the Canadian and British forces valiantly defeated the Americans in many battles during the War of 1812, thereby making sure Canada remained under British rule until it was granted independence in 1867. We were always proud of this fact.

As a teenager, I had visited the site of the Battle of Queenston Heights, where, on October 13, 1812, the British-Canadian forces, with help from allied native tribes, successfully fought off the Americans on the Canadian side of the Niagara River, even though Major General Isaac Brock, "the hero of Upper Canada," was killed in action.

From 2001 to 2008, I worked as an international media producer at Johns Hopkins University in Baltimore, Maryland, where I often visited Federal Hill across the harbor from my office. There, a gigantic American flag commemorates the place where Frances Scott Key wrote the poem that became the lyrics for the "Star Spangled Banner." Key was inspired when he saw an American flag flying after he'd witnessed the bombardment by the British Navy of Fort McHenry on September 14, 1814. As kids in Canada, we made fun of the American national anthem, and American-style nationalism in general, by substituting the opening lyrics with:

> José can you see any bed bugs on me?
> If you do, pick a few, 'cause I got 'em from you!

As Canadians, we were taught to emphasize our independence from both the United States and Britain.

Now, as I looked down from Hillside Cemetery onto the land

my Stevens ancestors once farmed, I wondered in which battles Joseph Stevens Jr. had fought and what he thought about that war. Had he been caught up in such nationalism? I'd read that the War of 1812 had really been a part of the Napoleonic War in Europe and that it was all about Britain's intention to maintain control of the seas. The US fought the British over its maritime policies: restricting US trade with Napoleon and his allies, and accosting American ships to press both British and American merchant seamen into the Royal Navy. Multiple attacks by the Americans on Canadian-based forces were mainly attempts to change Britain's maritime policies, and when these invasions failed, Canada remained part of the British Empire, while the British defeated Napoleon at Waterloo, and maintained dominance of the seas for years to come.[1]

As I left the graveyard, ruminating on the sentiments at the time on both sides of the war, and what the descendants of Joseph Stevens Jr. knew about it, I saw a lady emerge from a little yellow house across the road. I approached her and asked, "Hello, are you from here? I was looking for the tombstones of my Stevens ancestors in the cemetery. Do you know anyone by the name of Stevens around here?"

The lady appeared to be a little surprised by my question but answered, "No, but if there's anyone who'll know around here, it's my aunt. Come on into the house."

I found her aunt busily cooking lunch in the kitchen, and she never stopped as I put the same question to her. She was matter of fact in her answer, as if people dropped in all the time to ask her about their ancestors, "You just head down Highway 415 about a mile and make a right on McNutt Run. There's a lady up there who's got a beauty parlor. Her maiden name is Stevens."

I thanked her, explaining that the Stevens descendant I wanted to find probably cleared her land in the early 1800s. She didn't seem too impressed at that notion—just looked up at me nonplussed as she fried her bacon.

There was more I could have told her. I'd read a description of the early settlement at the Historical Society in Bath—log cabins along the Cohocton River with a few Indians huts remaining in place. The settlers sowed fields of flax, which they harvested to make linen cloth for summer wear. They raised sheep and spun and wove wool for winter clothes and blankets. They had to guard their sheep against wolves, which could be heard howling in the forested hills all around, a chilling sound during the night. Fortunately, there were plenty of deer for both man and beast.

I drove on and turned right on McNutt Run Road. After a half mile, I saw a lady with her hair all perfectly done up, saying goodbye to customers in front of her beauty salon. I parked in her driveway and introduced myself and my purpose.

"Yes, I'm a Stephens," she said, "but my father is the one who knows all about the history of our family and he's away. He should be back by evening if you want to see him. I'll give you his phone number."

I was about to give excuses, since I thought it would be a longshot, when she continued, "But just a minute. Is it a Stephens with a 'ph' or a 'v' you're asking about?"

"A 'v' Stevens," I replied. I knew about the two spellings of the surname. Although they came from the same ancestors in England, some family branches had changed the spelling, especially in America.

"Oh, too bad. We're 'ph' Stephens. But if you go down Highway 415 about a mile and turn right on Wolf Run, you'll find a place on the left where a man grows and sells flowers. He's a Stevens with a 'v' and I think his family has been in these parts a long time."

I thanked her and followed her directions, turning up Wolf Run Road. There, I quickly spotted a small bungalow with a sign out front telling customers to enter the gate and go around to the back. I found the farmer putting on his boots with the help of his wife, ready to start work after lunch. I guessed him to be about 80 years of age and spoke up as I introduced myself, "I'm a 4th great-grandson of Joseph Stevens Sr., who moved to Campbell in the early 1800s. I just came from Hillside Cemetery looking for his tombstone. I understand you're a Stevens with a 'v' and wonder if we might be related."

Mr. Stevens looked at me with wide eyes, "I'm Ralph V. Stevens and Joseph Stevens was my 4th great-grandfather too! You got time to come in and talk?"

For the next magical hour, Ralph Stevens took me through his genealogy, a binder three inches thick. He knew it all. He descended from Joseph Stevens Jr.'s son, Jonas (1803-87). This branch of the family stayed put in Campbell and surrounds for over two centuries. Ralph had done a genealogy project with a local educator around 25 years ago and had given copies of his binder to all his children so their family history wouldn't be lost.

He also showed me his own story—well-documented with photos. He had only finished high school, but said he'd been interested in history ever since his youth. He had signed up for military duty at the time of the Korean War. He didn't want to kill people, so he asked to join the medical corps. To his surprise, the US Army granted him his wish and he ended up serving in Germany. Afterwards, he returned to marry his high school sweetheart. They have two acres and grow flowers and cacti for sale.

Ralph explained that he had checked all the cemeteries in the vicinity, including at Wheeler. He had concluded that our mutual 4th great-grandfather was buried there, but he never could locate his tombstone or any kind of precise records. Much later, I finally found a record of Joseph Stevens Sr.'s death at the age of 77 in early 1830, in Wheeler.[2]

Ralph's records mentioned that Joseph Stevens Sr. had been with George Washington at Valley Forge and also that he fought in the Battle of Saratoga. The amazing thing about his binder, however, is that he had researched and documented the Stevens family in America and in England, through 30 generations. The Stevens/Stephens genealogy, which I also later looked up on the Internet, has many claims to fame throughout the history of England—Members of Parliament, Lords of Eastington in Gloucestershire, barons, knights with castles, and high sheriffs. The first Stephens to arrive in England from Normandy, France, was Airard Fitz-Stephen (1036- 85), who landed with William the Conqueror. He commanded a ship called "Mora" during the Norman invasion of England and fought in the Battle of Hastings, 1066. Some sources claim that the first of the family to arrive in America was Nicholas Stevens, who fought alongside Oliver Cromwell in the English Civil War. (See Table 5.)

At any rate, all this majestic lineage seemed a bit much for me, a person of humble Canadian Scots-Irish descent, who could only trace his Neill and McKee ancestors back five or six generations. I had read a little about Viking history and had been watching the television series "Vikings" on the History Channel. It covered the exploits of Viking King Ragnar Lothbrok and his first queen, Lagertha. The earlier episodes interested me most: their invasions along the coasts of Ireland and Scotland beginning in 793, their battles and interactions with Anglo-Saxon kingdoms, and how they rowed down the Seine River and raided Paris. These "Norse" or "Northmen" made a deal with the King of the France in 911, and settled in northwest France in an area that came to be called "Normandy." I stopped watching when the series became too violent and repetitive.

Before I began my genealogical search, I had no idea that my genetic make-up included these Viking adventurers and marauders. When I had my DNA tested through *Ancestry.com*, I found the evidence: Most of my DNA comes from Northern Ireland, Lowland Scotland, England Wales, and northwest Europe, with about 10 percent from Sweden. (I was disappointed not to find a trace of Jewish, African, Asian, or Native American origin in my genetic makeup.) Besides Sweden, my Viking DNA likely shows up in just about all of it—probably the reason why sometimes I am impatient and want to knock stupid people on the head! Fortunately, the peaceful Celtic farmer and weaver genes in me cancel out some of those tendencies. After all, I don't have much use for guns. Neither did my newly-found Stevens cousin in New York, when he refused to carry a gun in the Korean War. But he mentioned to me that he kept a couple of rifles for deer hunting in the fall.

After walking all around the former Saratoga Battlefield in upstate New York, I returned to park headquarters to buy a book on the battles and to search in their computerized index for Joseph Stevens Sr. He wasn't listed there. At first, I thought this is just the kind of frustration one has to get used to in such searches into history because records were often poorly kept. Later, I went back to the record on *Ancestry.com* that I had seen before, an application by some descendants of Joseph Stevens for membership in the "Michigan Society of Sons of the American Revolution" dated November 25, 1912. On more careful reading, I realized that the document didn't stipulate that Joseph had fought at the Battle of Saratoga nor that he had been with George Washington's Continental Army at Valley Forge, but rather that his regiment, the 13th Albany Militia, had been engaged in these historic events. (I had passed through Valley Forge earlier on my travels and found no trace of him or his regiment in their database.) Eventually, I discovered the records for Joseph Stevens Sr., which stipulated that his time of service in the 13th Albany Militia was during 1779-81, after these famous events. He fought under Colonel Cornelius Van Veghten.[3]

Joseph Stevens Sr. had first moved from Canaan, Connecticut to Stillwater, New York, which is located very close to the Saratoga battlefield. Joseph's daughter, my 3rd great-grandmother, Lydia Stevens, was born in Stillwater on August 27, 1778, the year when Joseph's first wife Naomi Mathews died, possibly while giving birth to Lydia. After the American Revolution, Joseph and his family continued to live in Stillwater, where he appears in the 1790 census as a farmer. Lydia Stevens and my 3rd great-grandfather, Nathaniel Haskins, married around 1800, probably in Stillwater. (See Table 5.)

A number of Stevens' family trees and stories I found on the Internet and other old records repeat those claims to fame about Valley Forge and the Battle of Saratoga, possibly taken from a less than careful reading of that 1912 Sons of the American Revolution application, mentioned above, or from other family trees. This is a lesson for genealogy enthusiasts—all such claims need careful inspection and verification through various sources.

After I left Saratoga, I found the right person to finally settle the question. I contacted Eric Schnitzer, Park Ranger and Military Historian at the Saratoga. He looked up the records and confirmed my suspicion in an email: "According to *New York in the Revolution as Colony and State*, as well as the information you provided, records show that your ancestor served in various companies as an NCO [non-commissioned officer] at various times in Colonel Van Veghten's battalion, i.e., the 13th Regiment Albany County Militia. This is significant, because Colonel Van Veghten became colonel of the regiment later in the war (post

1777), and so your ancestor would have served at that time, as you mentioned. In other words, it appears that your ancestor only served after the Battles of Saratoga. Indeed, as you point out, he could not have been at Valley Forge, since at no time were NY militia deployed there."

Eric Schnitzer also advised me to read Theodore Corbett's, *No Turning Point: The Saratoga Campaign in Perspective*.[4] When I delved into this scholarly work, I also uncovered an even greater myth—the Second Battle of Saratoga, won by the rebels, was not so clearly a "turning point" in the American Revolution, as many historians have repeated down through the years. Setting the battle in its social and political context, Corbett examines the aftermath. After Burgoyne's defeat, British forces continued to invade from Canada, entering Lake Champlain and the Hudson River Valley. The exact military actions Joseph Stevens Sr. took part in during that time, remain unclear. In 1911, many historical war and genealogical records burned in a fire at the New York State Library in Albany.[5]

It's likely that Joseph Stevens found himself marching with his comrades to and from the forts in the Hudson River-Lake Champlain Valley, such as Ticonderoga, which the British destroyed and abandoned in November 1777. He probably helped to guard against more British advances and to keep peace among landowners, tenant farmers, townspeople, and Native Americans, many with different political views and divided loyalties. Some remained Loyalists and migrated to Canada before and after the final British defeat.

In Ontario, I grew up knowing certain families who proudly identified themselves as "United Empire Loyalists"—people who escaped the chaos of the American Revolution and its aftermath for the stability of British rule. They sang songs like the last stanza of the one below, to a bawdy tavern tune, *Black Joke*:

An historic cannon guarding Lake Champlain at Fort Ticonderoga

> Come take up you glasses, each true loyal heart,
> And may every rebel meet his due dessert,
> With his hunting shirt and rifle gun.
> May Congress, Conventions, those damned inquisitions,
> Be fed with hot Sulphur from Lucifer's kitchens,
> May commerce and peace again be restored,
> And Americans own their true sovereign lord,
> Then oblivion to shirts and rifle guns.
> GOD SAVE THE KING![6]

Many loyalists settled along the northern shore of Lake Ontario and the southern part of Quebec. In northern New York, strife between settlers of various ethnic, linguistic, and religious backgrounds had begun long before the Declaration of

Independence and continued long after the Battle of Saratoga. The British managed to maintain control of the northern portion of the area, enlisting Loyalists and Native American allies to continue raids on their behalf. In the short term, at least, the American victory at Saratoga actually resolved very little.

I had explored some of the landscape where my Stevens ancestor served—no great battles, no clear villains or good guys. It's a messy view of history that is often glossed over with declarations such as "Saratoga was the turning point."

# 12

# MY ANCESTORS *in the*
# FRENCH *and* INDIAN WAR

Re-enactment of firing a musket used by colonial militia, mid-1700s

AFTER FINDING THAT ABEL ROBINSON AND JOSEPH Stevens Sr. were soldiers in the American Revolution on the winning side, I decided to investigate the earlier conflict, the French and Indian War—the North American theater of the Seven Years War. In my database searches, I found a notation that Joseph Stevens' father, Samuel, had been killed by Indians on September 1, 1754, either in Stockbridge or Lennox, Massachusetts. I could find no exact record, but there's a possibility he met his end when a group of marauding Indians attacked Stockbridge settlers then.[1] At the time, most of the settlement's friendly local Christian Mohicans had left to join the British in a type of special forces unit, preparing for the fight against French invasions from Canada. Samuel Stevens had probably been a civilian, caught up in the early repercussions of the overall conflict. He died before full-scale fighting between the British and the French broke out.

Samuel Stevens was born March 6, 1714 or 1715, in Plainfield, Connecticut. Samuel's father was Thomas Stevens, born in Stonington, Connecticut on December 14, 1678. Thomas married a woman by the name of Mary Hall and they had seven sons, Samuel being their sixth. Most likely, Samuel went to northwest Massachusetts because he had no prospects for inheriting or buying land in crowded Connecticut. His father, Thomas, died in Canaan, Connecticut, and is buried in the old cemetery south of the town. The inscription, below, on his tombstone was recorded before it became too eroded to read.

Here lies the body of Thomas Stevens
who died Sept 7, 1750 in the
72nd year of his age.

All ye who dwell below the sun,
Prepare to die to judgement come,
Though here my body lies in dust,
Seven sons I had, I went the first,
And they soon must follow me.

Thomas Stevens' tombstone,
Old Canaan Cemetery[2]

When I read this poem, I thought how right Thomas had been, at least regarding his son, Samuel. He died at the age of 40, only four years after his father. He'd been seeking a new life in less crowded western Massachusetts, but met a sudden death by musket fire or tomahawk due to dynamic political forces beyond his control.

I also found evidence of the involvement in the French and Indian War by my 4th great-grandfather, Micah Nathan Haskins Sr.—the old man who died in Allegany County, New York (Chapter 9). (The spelling of the original family name "Hoskins" evolved, and the "o" became an "a" and even a "u" or "e" in different branches of the family, often depending on the spelling tastes and abilities of clerks and census takers in various towns and villages.) Micah Nathan, the fourth son of Anthony Hoskins III, was born on a farm near Harwinton in Litchfield County, Connecticut, on May, 10, 1735. At the time, Micah's surname was spelled "Hoskins," which I will use here and for generations before him. Also, in some records he is referred to by his middle name, "Nathan."

Like Samuel Stevens, Micah Nathan Hoskins, didn't stay in Connecticut, probably because he had five brothers (Table 6), and had little chance of acquiring land. He may have been seeking adventure as well. His name appears along with those of his brothers Anthony IV and Daniel on a deed in Alford, Berkshire, Massachusetts, dated October 29, 1756. Perhaps Micah intended only to farm, but he understood his duty, and in 1755, at the age of 20, he signed up with the Massachusetts militia to fight in the French and Indian War, which had recently broken out in upstate New York.

For a better understanding of the historical antecedents to the French and Indian War in New York, I drove north through the Hudson River-Lake Champlain Valley to Crown Point. There, I gazed northwards on Lake Champlain, toward Canada. The

Looking north on Lake Champlain from Crown Point, New York

lake had been named after an historic figure familiar to me as a Canadian—Samuel de Champlain. He was the Frenchman who founded the first French settlement of Quebec, as well as the Acadian settlements of present-day Nova Scotia and New Brunswick. I read the book, *Champlain's Dream: The European Founding of North America*, by David Hackett Fischer,[3] from which this brief account is derived.

Farther up Lake Champlain on its western shore, Samuel de Champlain, with his soldiers and native allies—Montagnais, Algonquin, and Huron—encountered a Mohawk war party on July 30, 1609, and fired their old muskets called "arquebuses" at them, as depicted in an often-printed illustration of that moment. Champlain remained hidden by his Native American friends until they were ready to attack. Suddenly, he appeared in shiny steel armor, arquebus aimed at the enemy, loaded with four balls. I preferred Champlain's handsome and kind-looking portrait, known to me since childhood, which was an invention of an artist, not an exact likeness, for no portrait of him survived.

Champlain actually fired a wheel-lock arquebus, an alternative to the simple but problematic matchlock musket that requires the user to keep a mounted fuse smoldering, which swings down into a pan containing gunpowder when the trigger-lever is pulled. The wheel-lock version involves a spring-activated steel wheel which spins against a piece of iron pyrite to produce sparks required to fire a charge of powder. With his first volley, Champlain killed two very surprised Mohawk chiefs. Champlain's men also fired their arquebuses, and arrows flew from both sides. The surviving enemy were overpowered and fled. This incident signaled the beginning of more than 150 years of enmity between some of the Mohawk and the French.

The action by Champlain and his native allies served as retribution for attacks by New York based Mohawk on their settlements in the St. Lawrence River Valley. Otherwise, Champlain took a very different approach in his dealings with the natives

Champlain in armor, firing an arquebus[4]

Portrait of Samuel de Champlain[5]

of North America. As a young man of 15, he had been a stow-away on a ship bound for Mexico, where he witnessed how badly the Spaniards treated the natives of that land. During his early voyages to North America during 1604-06 (he made at least 27 Atlantic crossings during his lifetime), he also witnessed how the English fishermen and traders mistreated Indians on the coast of what would become New England.

On the contrary, Champlain sent young *coureurs de bois* and *voyageurs* into the wilderness to explore and to exchange various European goods for furs with Native Americans. He hoped to establish peaceful coexistence with them. He encouraged these young Frenchmen to learn native languages and even to inter-marry with Indians. The French eventually traveled through and mapped a good deal of North America. This early explora-tion provided the start for opening up the land to Catholic mis-sionaries and French soldiers who built forts. Gradually, they gained control over most of the Great Lakes region, the Ohio and Mississippi valleys, and even farther west. Along with their com-paratively peaceful approach, however, the French-Canadians brought diseases such as smallpox to Native Americans, greatly reducing their numbers.

The Mohawk of the Hudson River-Lake Champlain Valley, with whom Samuel de Champlain battled, later formed a union of five Iroquois-language group nations: the Mohawk, Oneida, Onondaga, Cayuga, and Seneca. In 1722, the Tuscarora tribe joined to form the Six Nations Iroquois Confederacy. They inhabited the lands of upstate New York from Lake Ontario, east to Lake Champlain and Lake George, as well as to the southern bank of the St. Lawrence River.

The Iroquois, led by the dominant Mohawk, originally acquired firearms from Dutch traders in New York, which they used to subdue the Algonquin, Huron (a.k.a., Northern Iroquois or Wyandot), and other French-backed tribes. Their goal was to control the fur trade in the Great Lakes region and farther south into New York, Pennsylvania, and along the borders of New England. These so-called "Beaver Wars" were brutal and bloody, and the Iroquois eventually decimated several large tribal confederacies, including the Mohican, Huron, Erie, and Susquehannock.

In preparation for understanding the war that my 4th great-grandfather fought in, I also read Fred Anderson's book, *The War that Made America: A Short History of the French and Indian War*,[6] from which the historical parts of the account below is derived, except where otherwise noted.

The French and Indian War (1754-63) started two years before the Seven Years War (1756-63) and became part of this much wider conflict fought in Europe and North America, as well as in the Caribbean. Many historians choose to characterize it as "the first world war" because of the complicated issues and number of nations involved, but Anderson's treatment brings alive the reason Americans included "Indian" in the name of the struggle. The Indigenous People of North America played a crucial role throughout the war, and they greatly determined its outcome. That's something I never learned during my Ontario schooldays.

When the Iroquois lost their Dutch allies in New York State and the western part of New England, as the English took over, the French attempted to make the Iroquois an ally against English encroachment. However, the Iroquois became trading partners with the British and colonial American settlers. They also partnered with the passivist Pennsylvanian Colony by acting as their military force, controlling the Delaware, Susquehannock, and other native groups. They were even allowed to travel south through Virginia to carry out raids on the Cherokee. This alliance was a crucial component of both Pennsylvania's and Virginia's ambitions of western expansion into the vast lands of the Ohio Valley, where they met opposition from the French and their Indian allies, many of whom had been driven westward by Pennsylvania and Virginia settlers and their enforcers, the Iroquois. Eventually, the Iroquois learned how to incite French-English conflict, playing one side against the other, and thereby extending their influence throughout the land, both north and south of the Great Lakes.

The French and Indian War began on May 28, 1754, when an inexperienced 22-year-old major of the Virginia Militia, George Washington, watched in surprise and alarm, as the unpredictable part-Iroquois "half-king" Tanaghrisson drove a tomahawk into the skull of the French soldier-diplomat, Joseph Coulon de Villiers de Jumonville. Tanaghrisson had been guiding Washington and his militia on a mission to determine how Virginia could gain control over the Ohio Valley.

Perhaps Washington learned a lesson from this incident. To a great extent, success or failure in future battles depended on the leadership of European men who understood the cultures and psychology of North America's Indigenous People, and who could predict their behavior and military moves. That awareness included cultivating alliances and friendships with them through gifts, allowing them to continue using their tactics of the Beaver Wars, which most Europeans regarded as brutal and uncivilized acts of guerrilla warfare. The French called it *la guerre sauvage*. But in French, "sauvage" means "wild" or "things which live in the forest," different than the English word "savage," which has a sinister and judgmental connotation.[7]

The tactics of Native Americans included ambushing and killing non-combatants, scalping the dead and wounded, brutally torturing to death captured enemy, and sometimes eating their body parts in victory rituals. They took women and children captive for ransom, or to help replenish their own dwindling numbers, due to warfare casualties. Except when Native Americans kidnapped European women and children, French and British military leaders and their colonial allies learned to look the other way, calculating that the end justified the means.

As in the American Revolution, the Hudson River-Lake Champlain Valley provided one of the major battlegrounds of the French and Indian War. This lake and river corridor offered a natural channel for quick attacks and retreats by the French in Canada and the British in the American colonies, along with colonial militia and native allies on both sides.

On a sunny afternoon in May 2017, I found myself totally alone at the historic fort of Crown Point. That made it a perfect opportunity for photography without the intrusion of other tourists in my shots, though being by myself also induced an eerie feeling. I could sense the ghosts of the men who fought and died here. The fort is set on the western shore of the Crown Point Peninsula, which almost cuts Lake Champlain in two. The French built the first structure near this place between 1734 and 1737. They named it "Fort St. Frédéric" and used it as a base for raids on settlements in New York and New England.

It wasn't until 1759 that British and American colonial troops succeeded in taking it, although the French destroyed much of their creation before retreating north. British regulars with New England and New York militia then constructed new

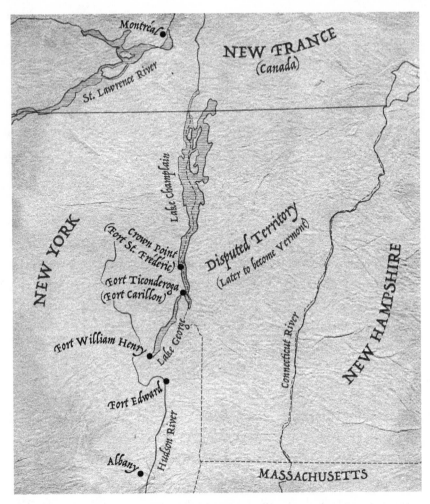

Map of Upper Hudson and Lake Champlain Valley in 1750s

fortifications, the ruins of which can be seen today. They named the new complex "His Majesty's Fort of Crown Point."

After an hour or so at Crown Point, I traveled south a few miles to Fort Ticonderoga, which the French first built and named "Fort Carillon." This site was of strategic importance because it controlled a portage point between Lake Champlain and Lake George. The French had designed it to assist in their competition with the British for control of the whole watershed.

Crown Point Historic Park, Essex County, New York

By contrast with bucolic Crown Point, I found Carillon/ Ticonderoga abuzz with activity. Summer employees, mainly history students, busied themselves with the activities of French soldiers and civilian staff at the time they built the fort between October 1755 and 1757. I had a long discussion with a young man dressed like a French cobbler about the period of history they were re-enacting. He mentioned that he had been wounded in 1755 during the Battle at Lake George to the south and could no longer fight. He looked too young and able for the role he was playing, but his tale was entertaining.

I focused most of my research interest on the years 1755-56, when my 4th great-grandfather, Micah Nathan Hoskins, fought in the war. I also wanted to confirm whether he fought in 1757. Available records are sparse because many were incinerated during the previously-mentioned 1911 fire at New York State Library in Albany (Chapter 11). The one record I did find located him at Fort Edward in 1755 in Joseph Dwight's Regiment.[8] (This was later confirmed by professional genealogical researchers at NEHGS.)

Actor-educators re-enacting activities of French soldiers stationed at Fort Carillion (Ticonderoga) during 1756-58

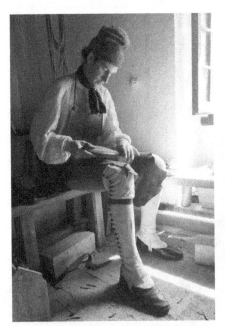
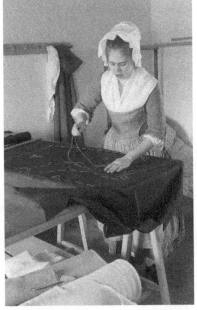

Actor-educators re-enacting civilian life inside Fort Carillion (Ticonderoga) during 1756-58

The regiment in which Micah served was under the overall command of Colonel William Johnson, who also acted as the British agent for the Iroquois. Col. Johnson ordered construction of the fortification and storehouse on the Hudson River, later named "Fort Edward," to act as a principal guard post against attacks on Albany and other settlements farther south. At this place, the Hudson curves northwest upstream toward its tumultuous source, where canoes encounter rapids and waterfalls. The natives called the location "the Great Carrying Place" because, to continue up the Hudson River-Lake Champlain Valley, they had to carry their *bateaux* and canoes about 20 miles north to what the French called *Lac du Saint Sacrament*, which Johnson renamed "Lake George."

Today, Fort Edward is just a normal small town that I visited to photograph any remnants I could find of the old fort my ancestor probably helped to build. I went to a restaurant called "The Anvil Inn," which claimed in its online advertisement to be located where an outer wall of the former fort once stood. The restaurant building had been constructed as a blacksmith shop in the 1840s. I entered and approached the woman bartender.

"Is this the location of Old Fort Edward?" I asked.

She looked at me with a blank face, "Don't have a clue what you're talking about."

"The fort built here in 1755 during the French and Indian War."

She seemed a bit annoyed, "What war?" She looked at her colleague, who shrugged.

"Is there anything on your walls about it?" I asked.

"Don't know. You're welcome to take a look around."

Her colleague weighed in, "Why don't you try the museum? It's about a quarter mile down the road."

"Thanks. I'll do that," I said. I looked around, as suggested, but saw nothing of interest on the walls. Neither of these women had a clue about their town's founding and apparently couldn't care less.

I left the restaurant and drove down to the local museum, hoping to find the usual helpful people, but it had closed for the day. Frustrated but not defeated, I drove down a small road beside The Anvil Inn and soon came to a branch of the Hudson. I saw a sign by the riverside and walked down to take a look. Sure enough, Fort Edward had once stood on this place, about 100 yards (91 meters) from the restaurant. Not only that, when I returned to The Anvil Inn for dinner, I noticed a sign about Fort Edward right outside by the sidewalk. As usual, I'd missed something staring me right in the face.

When I passed the bar to enter the restaurant, I mentioned my two finds to the ladies I'd spoken to earlier. One of them shrugged and the other said, "Would you like a drink then?"

"Thanks, I said. I'll have some wine with my meal." I had to remind myself, as I ate their fish dish and drank a glass of *Pinot Grigio,* that most people go about daily life with little or no clue or care about the world that came before them.

I stayed overnight at a nearby motel and headed north the next day, following the path of Col. Johnson in 1755. He commanded about 3,500 colonial militia from New York and Massachusetts, plus 200 Mohawk scouts and warriors, taking some of them north to the southern tip of Lake George to build another fort. I don't know if Micah Hoskins stayed behind to work on Fort Edward or advanced northwards to help build what Johnson called "Fort William Henry," using the given names of two British princes combined. Col. Johnson wanted a base from which he could

Location of former Fort Edward on a canal of the Hudson River

Fort Edward sign by The Anvil Inn

advance farther north to attack France's Fort St. Frédéric. I did find the name of Micah Hoskins' commander, Joseph Dwight, in one chronicle of the war,[9] listing him as one who advanced north, so there is a possibility that Micah Hoskins went with him.

Johnson marched his troops north with the hope of preventing France's southward thrust. Meanwhile, the French commander at Fort St. Frédéric, Jean Erdman, the Baron Dieskau, was heading in Johnson's direction with a force of 200 French regulars, 600 French-Canadian militiamen, and 700 Algonquin and Catholic Mohawk warriors. They planned to reach the southern tip of Lake George, where Johnson's troops and the Mohawk had begun construction of the new fort.

In early September 1755, the opposing forces engaged in three bloody battles that would be named collectively as the "Battle of Lake George." These included an ambush by French forces, later named "The Bloody Morning Scout," a head-on charge by French regulars into Johnson's incomplete fort, and a struggle in the woods between French forces and a relief column of New England militia moving up from Fort Edward, later called "The Battle of Bloody Pond." After this skirmish, the bodies of French-Canadian militia and their Indian allies were thrown into a pool, which bears the name "Bloody Pond" to this day.

In the Battle of Lake George, each side lost around 300 men. British Col. Ephraim Williams and Mohawk Chief Hendrick also perished. The French commander, Baron Dieskau, was wounded and captured. Johnson received a wound in the leg but claimed victory because the French forces retreated north to Fort St. Frédéric, and then built Fort Carillon, 15 miles (24 km) to the south, as protection against the northward advancement of the British colonial troops.

To me, the most interesting lesson of this battle was a clash of cultures. Baron Dieskau was new to North American warfare, and although he had been briefed on what to expect and even to encourage the use of native tactics (*la guerre sauvage*), he did not predict that his Catholic Mohawks from the St. Lawrence River Valley would refuse to attack their blood brethren, Johnson's Mohawks from New York and Massachusetts. In fact, the Catholic Mohawks warned their cousins before the first engagement.

Secondly, the French-Canadian militia and their native allies would not obey orders to charge headlong into Johnson's rudimentary barricade under construction. They perceived such action as suicidal and ludicrous. In addition, Johnson's New York Mohawks realized that further involvement in the war would mean doing battle with their Canadian-based Mohawk cousins, and many of them departed, choosing neutrality. In spite of all this confusion, for his so-called victory, Johnson was given the title of Baron in England, and made the sole Superintendent of Indian Affairs for the northern colonies.

By visiting and studying these three forts and reading Fred Anderson's book, I could better understand the times through which Micah Hoskins had lived, even if I still had to guess about his exact role. He may have been only a laborer, helping to build the forts, but even if so, who can argue that such work had not been essential to the outcome?

When I arrived at Fort William Henry, I found enthusiastic history buffs engaged in re-enacting life at the fort after its completion in 1757. A cousin who had conducted considerable investigations before me on the French and Indian War, claimed that Micah Hoskins re-enlisted in 1757, but, even with the help of NEHGS researchers, I could find no records of this. If he did re-enlist, I wondered if he was ever located at Fort William Henry during that year. If so, he barely escaped an early death, for the French returned with a vengeance, commanded by General Marquis Louis-Joseph de Montcalm with a force of about 6,500 French troops, French-Canadian militia, and Indian allies from the Great Lakes region and even farther west, all sworn enemies of the Mohawk.

Re-enactment of cannon fire, Fort William Henry, mid-1700s

Like Baron Dieskau, General Montcalm was new to North America, and he had great distain for the ungentlemanly tactics of *la guerre sauvage*. He carried out a four-day siege on the fort's thick log walls following standard European warfare protocol, and eventually blasting large breaches with his cannons. Many on the British side had fallen sick with smallpox before the attack, and Lieutenant-Colonel George Monro finally asked for a truce. General Montcalm agreed to let Munro and his forces retreat with their muskets, colors, and full honors, due to their valiant attempt at defending the fort. I looked at the replica of the table setting where they dined together and even toasted with wine—quintessential gentlemen warriors of the day. Meanwhile, Montcalm's native allies waited impatiently outside, ready to loot the fort for treasure and captives.

The next day, Montcalm's Indian forces attacked the fort to take their expected prizes. They also ambushed Munro with his defeated troops and civilians, as they retreated to Fort Edward. In all, they managed to kill about 200 mainly Massachusetts militia and take some of the retreating people prisoner. (This disastrous battle and massacre became the basis for *Last of the Mohicans: A Narrative of 1757*,[10] an historical novel written by James Fenimore Cooper in 1826, centered on the story of Mohican heroes gallantly rescuing Munro's beautiful daughters—who were never actually present—from their capture by vicious Hurons.) A more disastrous but less dramatic and romantic outcome followed, namely the slow deaths of thousands of Great Lakes Indigenous People, when the warriors returned home with captives and their belongings, infected and infested with smallpox.

Abandoned by most of his native allies, Montcalm decided not to march his troops farther south to attack Fort Edward. He retreated north to Fort Carillon and Fort St. Frédéric, reflecting on the horrific massacre he had inadvertently caused. His name was so blackened in British eyes that he became a marked man who would no longer be dealt with in honorable terms.

In 1758, Montcalm, with 4,000 French soldiers and militia, managed to repel an attack by 16,000 British and their colonial militia in and around Fort Carillon. At least 500 British regulars and colonial militia were killed and more than 1,300 wounded in the ill-planned operation. But in 1759, the British and colonial forces returned and drove a token French garrison from the fort after a couple days of fighting. They then advanced north on Crown Point Peninsula and took Fort St. Frédéric too, while Montcalm and his troops destroyed most of it before retreating north to Quebec.

In my school days in Ontario, we always called the French and Indian War the "Seven Years War," as it would not have been politically correct to emphasize the conflict as a British war against French-Canadians, who remain a large percentage of the Canadian population. This war helped to determine Canada's future because it led to the September 1759 defeat of French forces under General Montcalm by British General James Wolfe on the Plains of Abraham, located below the walls of Fortress Quebec. I recall words of a song from my childhood: "The Maple Leaf Forever," which we had to sing over and over in school:

> In days of yore, from Britain's shore,
> Wolfe, the dauntless hero came,
> And planted firm Britannia's flag,
> On Canada's fair domain.
> Here may it wave, our boast, our pride,
> And joined in love together,
> The thistle, shamrock, rose entwine,
> The Maple Leaf forever![11]

The lyrics of this pro Scottish-Irish-English song were thrown onto the trash heap of history when the Quebec nationalist and separatist movement gained strength in the 1960s. No one wanted to inflame passions further.

After Montcalm's defeat, the French gradually lost much influence over the Indigenous People of North America and lost control of their military forts throughout the Great Lakes region and the Ohio and Mississippi valleys. American settlers pushed westwards, with even greater malice in their hearts towards Native Americans because of all the death and destruction they had suffered during the French and Indian War. This set the stage for the further displacement of Indigenous People in the American Revolution and the Indian Wars of the 1800s.

A young Mohawk man, Joseph Brant, observed some of the battles of the French and Indian War from the British side. He was the half-brother of Col. William Johnson's consort, Molly Brant, with whom Johnson had eight children. As a young man, Joseph Brant lived with them in Johnson Hall, Col. Johnson's mansion in upstate New York. Johnson sponsored Joseph's education. This relationship further wedded the Six Nations Iroquois Confederacy to the British and eventually led to their downfall. In 1777, the Iroquois abandoned their neutrality and backed the British during the American Revolution. When the American rebels won, Joseph Brant and some of his followers fled to Canada.[12]

In high school, I learned about these Canadian-based Iroquois. On my research travels in Ontario, in 2017, I decided to visit the Six Nations Reserve southeast of Hamilton, granted by the British to Joseph Brant and the Iroquois for their help in fighting against the rebels in the American Revolution. I drove to the town office in the bustling business center called "Ohsweken," where I saw well-maintained shops and houses, new cars and trucks—quite a contrast to other Indigenous Peoples' reserves I had visited.

I asked for directions to a museum, and a clerk suggested I go to the visitors' center. There, I found a beautiful young Iroquois woman, Alysha Longboat. She had graduated with a major in children's welfare and a minor in aboriginal studies. She had returned to the reserve to work for her people. Alysha briefed me on the whole history of the Iroquois in Canada and the US, explaining, "Iroquois means 'people of the longhouse.'" She claimed their federation had been very advanced in political terms, for the time. This I had read about, but wanted to know what she would say. She explained the meaning of *wampum* beads on display in a glass case. They symbolize the various treaties made with the white man, all broken.

I found my conversation with Alysha enchanting until she handed me a glossy, well-formulated brochure, which gave me a bit of a shock. Today, the Six Nations Iroquois continue to claim ownership of their original land grant, the Grand River Valley—a long swath of land six miles (9.65 km) wide on both sides of the river, amounting to 950,000 acres (384,451 hectares), reaching through the heart of the most densely populated part of southern Ontario, including my hometown, Elmira! Their brochure documents that in the Haldimand Treaty of October 25, 1784, the Iroquois people were granted this land "which Them and Their Posterity are to enjoy forever."[13]

In 1796, the Iroquois agreed to share four blocks of land, including that on which Elmira sits, with white settlers "on condition that a continual revenue stream be derived from these lands for 999 years to be dedicated for Six Nations perpetual care and maintenance." Other agreements for use of land by settlers were made, but disputes followed. Although the Iroquois received some cash payments, no continual revenue stream materialized. Today, the Six Nations claim they are owed billions of dollars in compensation and they have appealed to the United Kingdom and the United Nations. Needless to say, negotiations with Canada remain at a stalemate.

The Iroquois, consummate diplomats and fierce warriors in the history I read, had played both sides in the colonial wars of North America. In their strategic moves, they also had dominated and destroyed other native nations. As I left the flourishing town of Ohsweken, I felt relieved—at least here—that some Indigenous People had ended up in a relatively good place. But I must say, I felt ambivalent about their claim to my hometown.

Returning to the search for my roots in colonial America, at this point in my journey, I had found some pieces of the stories of two American ancestors who had fought in the Hudson River-Lake Champlain Valley. I began to think of this land and its waterways as a valley of historical conflict, which foretold the position of future borders and the politics of both the United States and Canada. I wondered what my ancestors had told their grandchildren about their adventures, as they sat by the fireplace in the evenings after they came home. Or had they been silent about the events they witnessed? Did my ancestor have some kind of religious faith that saw them through such trials? What kind of people raised and nurtured them?

With these questions in mind, I wanted to dig deeper into the history of the Hoskins family in Connecticut.

# 13

DISCOVERING *a* "ROWDY"
ANCESTOR *in* CONNECTICUT

The Hoskins house in Windsor, Connecticut and sign on Hoskins House

I DROVE TO THE HISTORICAL SOCIETY MUSEUM IN
Windsor, Connecticut, where I located records, received directions to important landmarks, and purchased an original settlers'
map—so much useful information. Once again, this meeting
with Americans who care about their history encouraged me.

From the museum, I followed their map to a large white colo-
nial-style house. I immediately spotted a sign which read, "Built
by John Hoskins in 1750." I searched for the plaque I had seen on

## WINDSOR PILGRIMS

Original homestead of John and Thomas Hoskins, father and son, who arrived on the *Mary and John* from England in 1630. They were members of the Dorcester party that settled Windsor north of the Rivulet in 1632. Goodman John Hoskins served as a delegate to Connecticut's General Court in 1637. John married Ann Filer, raised four children here, and passed away in 1648. Thomas married Elizabeth Gaylord Birge, raised one child, and passed away in 1666. John's great grandson built the present house prior to the American Revolution in 1750. The farm was passed down through the generations and stayed in the Hoskins family until 1822.

Hoskins family historical plaque, Windsor, Connecticut

the Internet and easily found it on the lawn—concrete proof I'd reached the land on which John Hoskins settled around 1632. The builder of the house was a later John Hoskins, one of his great-grandsons.

I took a few photos of the brass plaque and the house and knocked on the front door several times. No one answered. As I turned to leave, I saw a woman with two small dogs in a four-wheel-drive utility vehicle speeding across the property toward some sheds, where she cut her engine. She looked Hispanic to me. I walked over to greet her.

"What could I do for you?" she asked.

"I am an 8th great-grandson of John Hoskins who settled on this land around 1632."

The woman studied me for a moment before holding out her hand, "Really! I'm Magda."

I showed her my binder of ancestor research findings—credentials I used sometimes—and opened it to the Hoskins section.

"That's fantastic," she said. "Jump in and I'll show you around."

Her dogs, Bee and Thunder, eyed me as I displaced them on the seat beside her. Bee, especially, appeared to be a little distrustful of me—an intruder. Magda started the engine and we barreled down the hill behind the house. At the bottom she stopped beside her husband, Bob, who was chopping away at an old tree trunk like my ancestors must have done when they settled on this land over 370 years ago. He greeted me in an equally friendly way, surprised to hear about my connection with their place.

Magda called to their three goats, Jay-Jay, Gaby, and Emily, who ran down the hill inside a fenced-in area. I didn't know goats would obey commands like dogs.

For the next hour, Magda, Bee, Thunder, and I toured the property. The lower parcel of land held a surprising variety of trees, thorn bushes, wild roses, and small marshes, all of which Magda pointed out in great detail. She explained that she had an engineering degree and had moved to the US from Brazil about 25 years ago. Her business card read, "A Full Service, Licensed, Female Contractor." I quickly appraised her as a mission-driven mover and shaker. Besides her professional work, they were in the process of restoring the old Hoskins property to its original condition—their retirement dream home purchased a few years earlier.

We drove on small dirt lanes over the river flats, now a sod farm owned by someone else. At one time, all this land belonged to the Hoskins family, she explained. We drove down a bumpy path to the Connecticut River. Magda told me she often came to this tree-lined bank to admire the view. Because of a very wet spring throughout the northeast that year, the river rushed briskly towards the Atlantic Ocean. She said it often flooded, bringing water levels to the bottom of the hill on which their house stood.

As she explained how the annual spring floods revitalized the soil, I imagined my ancestors clearing this land for growing grain and pasturing animals.

Magda also gave me a tour of the old Hoskins house. They had renovated parts of it, trying to bring it back to its 18th century condition. They had stripped the floors down to the original boards and peeled away part of a wall, discovering in the process, an historic fireplace—clearly her pride and joy. She told me a story about the kitchen, "Right here, under the floor below the table, we found a small room. I was told it was a place to temporarily hide runaway slaves—part of the underground railway to Canada."

I had heard that there were a lot of unproven claims like this about colonial buildings in New England, but didn't want to question her. If it was true, the Hoskins had participated in a worthy cause.

Next, Magda led me up a steep staircase to show me their bedrooms. In the first room, she stopped to tell me another story: "I was deep asleep one night after we moved in when something in the room woke me up. I felt and then saw a woman rubbing my ankles—soothing them actually. The lady wore a long pink dress and she smiled at me. She seemed to be very happy that I was taking good care of the old place. In fact, a few months later, she also visited Bob's granddaughter one night when she was staying with us."

I had to agree with the ghost that Magda and Bob were exactly the right people to own the house now. I invited them to dinner, and promised to send them the completed Haskins family history and a copy of my book, when completed.

Later, I searched for the story of John Hoskins IV, who built this house. He was one of a long line of family members who had remained in Windsor over the years. He was born on December 1, 1701, and fought in the French and Indian War in 1758. He died in

View of the Connecticut River by the former Hoskins property

Magda with her restored fireplace

1765, about 15 years after he completed the house. His well-preserved tombstone is in the town's pioneer Palisedo Cemetery across the road from the Historical Society I had visited.

I also found a record of his wife, Catherine Viets from New York. She lived until November 8, 1776.[1] I wondered whether Catherine was the lady in pink who had visited Magda and her step-granddaughter at night.

I found the name "John Hoskins" etched into a statue near the Windsor Historical Society, along with all the other founders

Tombstone of John Hoskins, Great-grandson of John Hoskins IV[2]

of Windsor. The elder John Hoskins was born in England, probably around 1585. The Hoskins family hailed from Beaminster, Dorset County, in southern England. They had lived there for hundreds of years after migrating from the border area between Herefordshire and south Wales. This region was once called "Ergyng," the name of an old Welsh kingdom that later became an English administrative center. An online site claimed that

Founders of Windsor monument, Windsor, Connecticut

Inscription of John Hoskins on the monument

the genetic haplogroup of the Hoskins is not Welsh, but rather came from southern Denmark around 6,000 years ago. DNA evidence cited by this same source links the Hoskins to the Jutland Peninsula as far back as the year 500. Here was even more evidence of my "Viking" blood![3]

In 1630, John Hoskins, a 45-year-old widower from Dorset, sailed to New England aboard a ship called the *Mary and John* with his son Thomas, born in England around 1610. John and Thomas are among the "A-List," which includes the most certain passengers on this ship—part of the Winthrop Fleet that transported approximately about 1,000 Puritans to the Massachusetts Bay Colony that year. Also, on the same passenger list was Ann Filer (sometimes spelled "Fyler"), probably a widow of about 40 years of age.[4, 5] The Hoskins and the Filers first settled in Dorchester, Massachusetts, now part of Boston. It is believed that soon after their arrival in New England, John Hoskins and Ann Filer married.

These Puritans, led by John Winthrop, had not completely broken from the established Church of England. They were non-separating Congregationalists, unlike the Separatist Pilgrim Puritans who landed at Plymouth in 1620 (Chapter 15). Winthrop and his followers aimed to establish a home in America where they hoped to reform the Church of England from within. They had been granted a charter for settlement, and had chosen a location near the Charles River. The settlers sought security and freedom for their religious and political beliefs—the right of self-government and individual responsibility under Divine Law.[6] They believed that they should be treated as citizens. On May 18, 1631, John Hoskins took the oath to become a freeman[7] i.e., a person who is not a slave or serf and is entitled to full political and civil rights.

John Hoskins was granted land in Dorchester, but he and others soon grew discontented with John Winthrop, the Governor of Massachusetts Bay Colony. To them, Winthrop and his group of magistrates and clergymen were authoritarians who resisted attempts at widening church membership, voting rights, and codifying laws by which magistrates should be bound. These men did not believe in the strict separation of church and state. Many, including John Hoskins, felt that in Dorchester they continued to be dominated by a small group of men with aristocratic tendencies—one of the main reasons they had fled England. They sought a place where they could live without being subjugated by people who saw themselves as "lords of the manors."

John Hoskins sold his four acres in Dorchester and, together with other families, departed for Connecticut around 1632 with Ann and his son Thomas. *The History and Genealogies of Ancient Windsor, Connecticut* records that they brought two new children with them—Anthony and Rebecca—presumably born in Dorchester in 1632 and 1634, respectively.[8] (Anthony, as it turned out, was my 7th great-grandfather.) John Hoskins and his family, along with other adventurers, had to travel over 100 miles (160 kilometers) to the southwest—an arduous and dangerous trek through forests inhabited by wolves and bears, and potentially hostile Indians.

In the Windsor land inventory of November 16, 1640, we find: "John Hoskins the father and Tho[mas] Hoskins the son have granted from the plantation an homelot with the additions whereon the dwelling house stands eighteen acres," seventeen acres in the Meade, "over the Great River next the said river in breadth eighteen rods in length, to the east three miles,... towards Pine Meadow twenty-seven acres" and "in the Pine Meade fourteen acres."[9] Reading over this inventory, I wondered how they understood what land they owned by that rather confusing description.

In 1637, after the Hoskins family had settled in Windsor, war broke out between the Pequot Indians of southern Connecticut and the Puritans of Massachusetts Bay Colony. Prior to this time, there had been incidents between the Pequots and New England settlers with some loss of life, largely due to English efforts to break Dutch-Pequot control of the fur and *wampum* trade (i.e., seashells used as currency by Native Americans). In the summer of 1634, John Stone—a trader, smuggler, and privateer—and his men were attacked and murdered by Niantic Indians, western tributary clients of the Pequots. (The Dutch had murdered the Pequot leader, Tatobem, so the attack on Stone was retribution.) Tension grew and in 1636 another trader, John Oldham, was murdered by the Manissean tribe, Narragansett-allied Indians, who sought to discourage English settlers from trading with their Pequot rivals. The English of Massachusetts Bay decided they had to act, leading to attacks and counterattacks.[10]

After deliberations, the Connecticut settlers decided to join the war against the Pequots. On May 26, 1637, the English attacked the Pequot fortress at Mystic, Connecticut, where they set the place on fire and shot and hacked to death around 400 Pequot men, women, and children.[11] The Pequot War ended in 1638, when the English finally won, but it continued to have lasting effects on relations between the English and Native Americans. (See Chapter 16 for more discussion on this point.) John Hoskins had been excused from military duty on account of his ill health. Given the massacre he might have taken part in, I was glad to learn this.

On May 3 or 5, 1648, John Hoskins died at the age of 50. It's believed he was buried in Palisedo Cemetery in Windsor, although his tombstone is not visible today. In his will, he set terms for the freedom of his indentured servant, Samuel Rockwell, paid off all his debts, and gave his goods, houses, and lands to his wife, Ann, and his son Thomas. Curiously, John and Ann's children, Anthony and Rebecca, were not included in his will.[12] Ann died March 6, 1662, also leaving her portion of the estate to her stepson Thomas and his children. Neither Anthony nor Rebecca are mentioned in her will either.[13] Rebecca married in 1659, and was probably well taken care of when Ann made her will in 1660. But it is odd that neither of these supposed full children of Ann were mentioned in her will. There remains much confusion over who the true children of Ann were, both from her first marriage and her marriage to John.

After my 2017 visit to Windsor, I discovered some write-ups on genealogical research that disputed the claim that Anthony was the son of John and Ann Hoskins. These researchers focused on Anthony and Rebecca's exclusion from their supposed parents' wills. They argued that such an exclusion would have been very unusual if they were biological children. The authors suggested that Anthony might have been a nephew or cousin under their care.[14] There is DNA evidence that Anthony was a true Hoskins.[15]

I commissioned more investigation by NEHGS researchers, but they never were able to come up with any answers to this dilemma. They offered further research into Anthony's parentage that would have involved going back into old records in England, a task which I estimated would be time consuming and expensive, and beyond the scope of my book. I concluded that even if Anthony was not a biological son of John, in all likelihood he grew up on the land I had visited, for no other Hoskins families were recorded in the Old Windsor records I consulted.

According to a primary source, *The History and Genealogies of Ancient Windsor,* Anthony married Isabel Browne on July 16, 1656, and they had nine children.[16] This source mentions that, in the year of his marriage, Anthony received a land grant of his own and that he also bought more properties in 1660 and 1672. It seems, despite his lack of inheritance, he was a resourceful man, capable of taking care of himself. I respect that possibility. My own father and his eight siblings received no such inheritance (Chapter 2). Even Uncle John, the son who remained on the McKee family farm, had to purchase it from his widowed mother.

My known Hoskins ancestors are listed in Table 4 and Table 6. These connections, with the exception of John Hoskins, were confirmed by professional genealogists at NEHGS through a deep analysis of Connecticut, Massachusetts, New York, and Wisconsin records. I assumed that I would not find anything more interesting than the dispute over Anthony's lack of inheritance in my Hoskins genealogy in Connecticut. Anthony Hoskins begat Anthony II, who begat Anthony III, who begat Micah Nathan, who fought in the French and Indian War (Chapter 12). The three Anthony Hopkinses born in Windsor, Connecticut, were farmers and family men. Farmers are wed to the land and must rigidly adhere to clock and calendar, following mundane routines: feeding and caring for animals, ploughing, planting, weeding, harvesting, storing, and using or selling the output of their labor. What else besides such boring details would I find about their lives?

My assumption was wrong. I found an interesting account of the first Anthony Hoskins' tumultuous life, as described in the "Anthony Hoskins Project," which contains a description of his days, taken from old Windsor court records.[17] These records, written in 17th century English, include words and phrases with a seeming lack of logic to the modern ear and inconsistencies in spelling, so I have taken the liberty of summarizing them below in a more digestible form.

### The Rowdy Man of Windsor

In March of 1663, Anthony Hoskins was ordered by the magistrate,
"Pay ten pounds bond to ensure henceforth you'll go straight."
In spite of this, Constable Thomas Dible soon complained of him,
"He offered violence against me, threatened to strike my limb."
Anthony had to give forty shillings to the treasury,
And ten more to Thomas Dible for his treachery.
But soon his bond was dropped for good behavior,
He even joined the dragoons to curry favor.

For a while all seemed to go well in Anthony's life,
Three daughters and a son born to his good wife.
In October of 1669, the town made him a freeman,
But such an honor awoke in him an inner demon.
Joseph Fitch complained Anthony neglected his fence,
The argument between them became so intense.
Anthony had to pay court costs and damages for all despoiled,
Including twelve bushels of corn to an Indian "squaw" for her toil.

As Anthony became older, he also became bolder.
Townspeople avoided him, giving the cold-shoulder.
Daniel Clarke accused him of trespassing and slander,
Claiming Anthony was a man who lacked all candor.
The argument continued, Clarke fearing for his safety.
Then Anthony apologized, saying he'd been too hasty.
But he had to post one hundred pounds in bond,
The magistrate must have feared he might abscond.

Soon Anthony was accused of another infraction:
Notoriously defaming, reproaching, and other action
Against Captain Newberry who worked in country service.
With bursts of anger, Anthony made people very nervous.

The magistrate charged him with breach of peace
For using foul language, so he was ordered to cease.
Then due to continued altercations with neighbors,
Anthony was disenfranchised and began to quaver.

But instead of reforming, he dug in his heels,
Amid complaints for unpaid debt and other ordeals.
John Wolcott accused him of felling a tree,
And stealing all the fruit from it with great glee.
In 1684, Anthony became even more rowdy,
Overcharged with drink and shouting loudly,
So, twenty shillings he was ordered to pay,
And another warning to go not astray.

Next Wolcott claimed Anthony mistreated his swine.
Then, fearing he'd become more entwined,
He withdrew the charge out of sheer fatigue.
Further engagement would only lead to added intrigue.
There was no way to win against this rowdy man.

The Puritans believed in predestination. Stated in a simplistic manner, this meant that God would save only a tiny minority of sinners and send the rest to hell. Since all humans were corrupt, nothing people did could affect their fate. Only God's grace was saving. The good works or misdeeds mortals performed during their lifetime had nothing to do with going to heaven. But many Puritans believed that God's grace showed itself by the good works of those already sanctified; people who set an example for the community.[18]

What Anthony Hoskins believed on such weighty matters I do not know, but perhaps he thought his "goose was cooked" long ago, so why bother trying to be good? I can't help but speculate that he also fought with John and Thomas, starting as a young man. Could this be one of the reasons why he was cut out of John and Ann Hoskins' wills? I wonder.

As mentioned in my poem above, Anthony did enlist in the local militia—perhaps a move that redeemed him somewhat in the eyes of his community, at least for a while. As noted by Henry R. Stiles in *The History of Ancient Windsor*, the old Windsor *Book of Rates* contains a record of his registration in the dragoons (cavalry) during King Philip's War (1675-78).[19] Philip was a Native American *sachem* (chief or leader), who adopted the name "Philip." He was mockingly dubbed "King Philip" by the English settlers because he made it clear that he thought himself equal to King Charles II of England.[20] After a number of provocations, some involving Philip himself, war broke out between the English and most of the Native American tribes of New England. (See Chapter 16 for contributing causes of this war and its long-lasting impact on America.)

There is little or no detail on exactly which battles Anthony Hoskins was involved in during the war. Stiles also notes that no battles took place in the Windsor area, and yet the town lived "in a continual state of dread and alarm." Windsor cavalry "were constantly employed in rapid marches, bearing despatches and scouting parties."[21]

Connecticut troops did play a significant part in "The Great Swamp Fight" of December 19, 1675, near present-day South Kingstown, Rhode Island. They joined with the Plymouth militia to raid a Narragansett fort surrounded by a 12-foot palisade containing about 500 wigwams and several thousand people. The colonial troops set upon them, killing between 350 and 600 Native American men, women, and children. Connecticut's Major Treat reported that four of his five captains died in the fight, and 80 of his 300 soldiers were killed or wounded.[22] In fact, the Connecticut militia proportionally suffered the highest number of militia casualties in that raid.

Anthony Hoskins had no complaints or court cases against him at the time of this battle, possibly because he was away on military duty; however, there is no record of his involvement. I can only speculate that, given his character, he had strong survival skills and knew which fights to stay out of, if he could avoid them. His military superiors probably had grown tired of his argumentative nature. I wondered if his wives were worn down by him too.

Anthony's first wife, Isabel, died in 1698 and he took a second wife, Mary Griffin Wilson, sometime thereafter. Anthony died on January 4, 1707 at the age of about 75. He and his wives were probably buried in Palisado Cemetery at Windsor. Their burial sites are no longer visible, although many of their contemporaries were interned there.

In his will, Anthony Hoskins left considerable money and land to his children and second wife, Mary. His eldest son, John, received the lion's share of the property they lived on. My ancestor, Anthony II, received a comparatively smaller inheritance (Table 7). He remained a farmer in Windsor where he had a large family, including Anthony III, my 5th great-grandfather. Anthony III left Windsor, moving his family to nearby Harwinton, Litchfield County, Connecticut, including his son, my 4th great-grandfather, Micah Nathan (Chapter 12).

In retrospect, my visit to Windsor, and the professional research I commissioned, had been very fruitful. Even if John Hoskins is never proven to be a true ancestor of mine, I confirmed that Anthony Hoskins I, II, and III were progenitors of Micah Nathan, Nathaniel, David, and Lafayette Haskins, my great-grandfather who fought in the Civil War.

I wondered if I could discover any other New England pioneers to be true ancestors of mine. I decided to stay a little longer in Connecticut to investigate the history of the Robinson family, the ancestors of Abel Robinson, the Revolutionary War soldier whose life I explored in Chapter 10. Would I find more rowdy men among them?

# 14

## FINDING SOME "GODLY" ANCESTORS *in* MASSACHUSETTS

Old Scotland Cemetery (North), Windham County, Connecticut

LEAVING WINDSOR ON A SUNDAY AFTERNOON, I DROVE through southern Connecticut on country roads to the place where Abel Robinson was born on September 15, 1761, making him about the right age to join the Connecticut Army in the American Revolution (Chapter 10). The state of Connecticut is not large and I figured I could get there easily in an hour. My

GPS didn't work well in rural areas, so I ended up asking several people for directions. As luck would have it, the last man I asked lived near Old Scotland Cemetery, a place I had just whizzed by. Since he belonged to the local historical society, he gave me good directions and then went back to his football game on television.

By this time, wandering around ancient cemeteries had become second nature to me. I parked up the small lane, as directed by the helpful history buff, and reached the top of the hill, happy to find it full of Robinson tombstones. Because of waning light and a waxing full cloud cover, I took photographs of all the Robinson memorials I could see. I had studied Abel's genealogy and the pictures of the tombstones I could find online, but those were probably taken a decade or two before my visit. Now moss grows over many of the memorial inscriptions. I inspected the crowned circular faces used on the Robinson tombstones. To me, they looked more like Native American chiefs than depictions of God or Jesus. Finally, I found a tombstone I could read—that of Peter Robinson who died March 22, 1785. He was one of my 5th great-grandfathers.

I looked for his wife, Ruth Robinson née Fuller, but if her tombstone was still there, its inscription had been eroded by over 200 years of wind, sun, snow, sleet, rain, and moss. I did find two other Fuller tombstones, put in place in 1838 and 1860. I'd studied many Robinson family trees online which, along with a visit to the genealogical library in Hartford, confirmed my conclusions. Now I had my own visual confirmation that—like Allegany County in New York for the Haskins/Hoskins family—here was another crossroads for more of my New England ancestors: the Robinsons, the Fullers, and more.

My 2nd great-grandmother, Clarfira Robinson, who married my 2nd great-grandfather, David Haskins, connected me to her father, Abel Robinson, and to several other notable people

Inscription reads: "In Memory of, Mr Peter Robinson, who departed This Life, March 22$^d$, 1785 in the 89 Year of his Age"

in the founding of America. Abel Robinson's 3rd great-grandfather was none other than Reverend John Robinson, pastor to the *Mayflower* Pilgrims who landed at Plymouth in December 1620. He didn't join the voyage and never made it to New England, having died of the plague in Leiden, Holland in 1625. But before his death he had influence on the Pilgrims during their first years through his parting words and letters to the colonizers. His son, Isaac Robinson, came to New England in 1631, implanting his father's genes in North America. Even more interesting to me was the confirmation that Ruth Fuller's 2nd great-grandfather was Edward Fuller, a passenger on the *Mayflower*. He died in the early months of 1621, but his son, Dr. Matthew Fuller, a surgeon, came to New England in 1640.

Below is a brief outline of my *Mayflower* passenger connection, which I was able to confirm by hiring the professional researchers at NEHGS, in Boston. They found some missing documents on the connection between Abel Robinson and his daughter, Clarfira, as described at the end of Chapter 10. The additional proof confirmed the *Mayflower* links in my heritage and allowed me to join the General Society of Mayflower Descendants, as well as the Massachusetts and New Mexico chapters of the society. (See genealogical details in Table 8.)

### Neill McKee's *Mayflower* Ancestry

1.  **Edward Fuller** (b. ca. 1575, England - d. winter 1621, Plymouth, MA) He was a *Mayflower* passenger and he signed the *Mayflower* Compact, but he and his wife died in the first winter.

2.  **Dr. Matthew Fuller** (b. ca. 1603, England - d. 1678, Barnstable, MA) He came to Massachusetts in 1640, probably with his wife, Frances, and children.

3.  **Lt. Samuel Fuller** (b. ca. 1630, England - d. March 26, 1676, Central Falls, RI) He married Mary __?__, details unknown.

4.  **Samuel Fuller Jr.** (b. 1676, Barnstable, MA - d. 1716, Mansfield, CT) He married Elizabeth Thacher, b. March 1, 1672, d. by 1730.

5.  **Ruth (Fuller) Robinson** (b. 1706, Mansfield, CT - d. 1795, Windham, CT) She married Peter Robinson Jr. 1697-1785.

6.  **Samuel Robinson** (b. 1726, Windham, CT - d. 1792, Windham, CT) He married Mary (or Sarah) Kimball, 1720-91.

7.  **Abel Robinson** (b. 1761, Windham, CT - d. ca. 1835, Alfred, NY) Probably he married Rhoda Ormsby first,

ca. 1787, but then married Eunice Woodward (ca. 1772 -
1850) in 1795, in CT, after Rhoda's death.

8. **Clarfira (Robinson) Haskins** (b. ca. 1806, Pawlet, VT –
   d. 1867, Adams, WI) She married David Haskins, 1803-73.

9. **Lafayette Haskins** (b. 1844, Almond, NY - d. 1925,
   Waupaca, WI) He married Sarah Alma Catherine Thomas,
   1847-1931.

10. **Effie Jane (Haskins) Neill** (b. 1876, Cadott, Chippewa,
    WI - d. 1966, Kitchener, ON) She married John Addison
    Neill, 1870-1948.

11. **Alma Katherine (Neill) McKee** (b. 1920, Fenwick,
    ON - d. 2015, Elmira, ON) She married Russell Cadwell
    McKee, 1920-2007.

12. **Neill McKee, author** (b. 1945, Kitchener, ON) *General
    Society of Mayflower Descendants, Member no. 94515.*

My 9th great-grandfather, Edward Fuller, probably died of
scurvy and pneumonia after the long and arduous voyage on
the *Mayflower* over the North Atlantic. Records indicate that
Fuller's unnamed wife was on board and that she died during
the first winter as well. Also, on the ship were their youngest son,
Samuel Fuller Jr., and Edward's brother, Samuel Fuller Sr., who
cared for the younger Samuel after his parents passed away. The
*Mayflower* did not land at Plymouth until December 20, 1620,
in a season when the Pilgrims had inadequate clothing for cold
weather, insufficient food supplies, and no time and little energy
to build shelters. The ship served as a shelter for those most sick
or dying until it sailed in the spring.

At the time of discovering and verifying my *Mayflower*
connection, I reminded myself that every individual has four

grandparents, and if you multiply those by two, we each have eight great-grandparents, and if you keep on multiplying by two up to our 8th great-grandparents, we each have 1,024 of them, and 2,048 9th great-grandparents. Mathematically, I'm far from unique for finding an ancestor on the *Mayflower*. Recent estimates claim that there are approximately 35 million living people, worldwide, who had ancestors on the ship.[1]

The records of births, marriages, and deaths of those buried in Old Scotland Cemetery also revealed a connection to other notable people in the early history of New England. Ruth (Fuller) Robinson is an ancestor of particular importance for me. Besides being my connection to the *Mayflower*, she links me to other prominent New England families. Ruth's mother was Elizabeth Thacher (1672-ca. 1730),[2] whose mother was Ruth Partridge (1645-1717), daughter of George Partridge (ca.1617- ca.1695), an important pioneer of Druxbury, Massachusetts.[3] Elizabeth Thacher's father was Rudolphus/Ralph Thacher (ca.1647-1733), whose father was the Reverend Thomas Thacher (b. May 1, 1620 - d. Oct 15, 1678). He, another of my 8th great-grandfathers, became the first pastor of the Old South Boston Meeting House. (See Table 8.)

Until this point in my research, the only clergyman I had known about in my ancestry was my maternal grandfather John Addison Neill, the Methodist preacher who, through his wandering ways, connected me to the United States with his marriage to Effie Jane Haskins. Through all the generations after that, I had not discovered any other ancestor who had been a "man of the cloth" until I came to Rev. Thomas Thacher. Intrigued, I decided to investigate his life further.

From Connecticut, I traveled to the location of the Puritans' Old South Boston Meeting House at 310 Washington Street in downtown Boston, Massachusetts—the very place where Rev. Thomas Thacher once preached. The original cedar worship house, built in 1669, no longer stands. A newer church building replaced it in 1729. The Puritans called it the "Third Church" when its parishoners separated from the first and second congregations over theological differences, mainly concerning the separation of church and state and the qualifications for church membership. The older congregations had sided with a more authoritarian line on these issues, a philosophy that had driven away many families, such as John and Ann Hoskins, who settled in Windsor, Connecticut. This "Third Church" had a more favorable view of religious liberty.

The Old South Boston Church is now enveloped by modern downtown Boston. The advantage of physically exploring the ground on which your ancestors once stood, rather than only reading about them in books or online, is appreciable. I strolled around inside the church's great hall and read displays stating that Rev. Thacher had begun a more liberal tradition in the Puritan movement. His installation as minister took place on February 16, 1669, and he remained in that position for eight years, until his death.

Rev. Thacher's approach started this congregation on a path of involvement in social causes and progress, as well as rebellion against England. In 1773, the church's great hall held a gathering of thousands in a protest against Britain's unreasonable tax policies, most recently on the importation of tea. Men claiming to be "Sons of Liberty" took matters into their own hands, marching to the harbor to relieve three British ships of their tea by dumping 340 chests of this valuable commodity into the water—the famous Boston Tea Party.

Old South Boston Church erected in 1729

Old South Boston Church hall

American patriot leaders, including Samuel Adams and Benjamin Franklin, spoke at this church and partook in discussions on religious, civil, and political freedoms. As I moved through the hall, I read more displays that proclaimed how the place had served as a platform for the expression of ideas through the centuries, including those of the poet Phillis Wheatley, who published a book in 1773 while she was still enslaved. (Slavery was abolished in Massachusetts in 1781.) The display I saw, with its chronological list of people who had spoken here, read like a "who's who" in American revolutionary, intellectual, abolitionist, and social reformation history: John Adams, John Hancock, George Washington, Ralph Waldo Emerson, Henry Wadsworth Longfellow, Booker T. Washington, W.E.B. Du Bois, William Lloyd Garrison, Wendell Phillips, Mary Antin, Louisa May Alcott, Dorothy Day, Margaret Sanger, and more.

Digging deeper into the kind of person Rev. Thomas Thacher had been and what brought him to New England, I found some details in an old Thacher genealogy[4] and more in three sermons delivered by the pastor of the church, Benjamin B. Wisner, in 1830, on the 100th anniversary of the newer building.[5]

Thomas Thacher was born May 1, 1620 at Salisbury, England, where his father was a minister. After a good grammar school education, his father offered to send him to Oxford or Cambridge, but he refused due to his growing revulsion with the ecclesiastical tyranny to which he would have been subjected during that era. He opted instead to emigrate to America, arriving in Boston on June 4, 1635.

Thomas spent several years studying with the Reverend Charles Chauncey, then minister of Scituate, Massachusetts, and later president of Harvard College. By this association, Thomas studied Syrian, Arabic, and Hebrew, and he even wrote a lexicon of Hebrew language. In addition, he was a logician and well-versed in mechanics, both in theory and practice. He chose to concentrate his formal studies in theology and medicine, obtaining a high reputation in both.

After his studies, Rev. Thomas Thacher became the pastor at Weymouth, Massachusetts in 1644, where he served as a beloved minister to the people for 20 years. According to Wisner, he delivered elaborate and affectionate sermons. "His abundant labors in the ministry were crowned with signal success; as was evinced by 'the great growth of the church' in Weymouth while under his oversight."[6]

Rev. Thacher married Elizabeth Partidge, the youngest daughter of Reverend Ralph Partridge, the first pastor of Druxbury, Massachusetts, and they had five children. She died in 1664 and he remarried, but apparently had no children by his second wife. Rev. Thacher moved to Boston in 1664, possibly after his wife's death, where he practiced medicine full time until he was called to be pastor of the Third Church in 1669. But he apparently did not give up his medical career. He wrote the first medical treatise ever published in New England titled, *A Brief Rule To Guide the Common People of New England How to order themselves and theirs in the Small Pocks, or Measels* [sic]. This short broadside publication, with such a long title, was published on January 21, 1677 by John Foster of Boston.[7] Ironically, the old Thacher genealogy claims Rev. Thacher died of "a fever" on October 15, 1678, after being infected by a patient.[8]

I felt humbled by this man's accomplishments during his 58 years, and even more so when I read the following elegiac poem written by a Native American youth who was a student at Harvard College.[9]

### On the Death of that truly Reverend Man, Thomas Thacher, Who Departed this Life for His Heavenly Home, October 15, 1678.[10]

I sing of one, though tears bedew the page,
Mourned by the present, as the former age,
Mourned as was Memnon, by Achilles slain,
When o'er his corpse, his mother knelt in vain.
Mind, voice, and strength have lost their wonted fire,
As if the muse would weep, but not inspire.
Thacher, 'tis virtue that thy name endears,
Virtue, that climbs beyond the starry spheres.
To men of station, and of low degree,
Thy faith shines forth like beacons o'er the sea.
Though dead, thou livest! Victory crowns thy brow,
The grace that saved thee, glorifies thee now;
Thy cross of suffering thou shalt bear no more,
Temptations, perils, sorrows, all are o'er.
Death, the destroyer, dies—the last of foes—
And life renewed, to life immortal grows.
When the last trumpet, fearfully and loud,
Peals like thunder through the parted cloud,
And the great Judge of all shall spread his throne,
Thou shalt sit with him as a chosen son;
Then through the skies seek realms of endless day,
To which thy Savior hath prepared the way—
Then 'mid delights for human thought too sweet,
Thy rest is pure—thy pleasure infinite.

—Eleazer, an Indian Senior Sophister

In Rev. Thomas Thacher, I'd discovered a New England ancestor of whom I could be proud—a Renaissance man of sorts, knowledgeable in many fields.

I wondered if Rev. Thomas Thacher was one of a kind in my early American ancestry. An in-depth review of the people buried in Old Scotland Cemetery led me to another. Abel Robinson's mother was a woman by the name of Mary (or Sarah) Kimball, born ca. 1720, in Ipswich, Essex, Massachusetts. She died on December 15, 1791, in Scotland, Windham County, Connecticut. Mary's mother was Sarah (Burley) Kimball, whose mother was Mary (Conant) Burley, a granddaughter of another of my 8th great-grandfathers, Roger Conant, born in Devon, England in 1592. He was the founder of Salem, Massachusetts. (See Table 8.)

When I found this connection with Roger Conant and Salem, I wondered whether he had anything to do with putting those innocent people to death during the Witch Trials of 1692-93. I headed to Salem, an hour's drive from the center of Boston to investigate, and quickly found my ancestor's stately statue. The powers-that-be in Salem had parked him right in front of the Witch Museum—one of the main tourist attractions in town.

I discovered, however, that Roger Conant and his wife, Sarah, plus most of their children, passed away before the Witch Trials. This included my 7th great-grandfather, Lot Conant, who died before his father in 1674. One son, who had been given the interesting name "Exercise," was born in Salem in 1632 and died in Connecticut in 1722. With such a name, no wonder he succeeded in running away from Salem! Perhaps he had foreseen some kind of disaster coming, such as the Witch Trials, when 20 innocent people were put to death because of the delusions of hysterical adolescent girls and the ignorance and prejudice of the religiously-bigoted, male-dominated society in which they lived.[11]

I read the details of these unjust trials and the use of "specter

Statue of Roger Conant, Founder of Salem, in front of
Salem Witch Museum

evidence"—accusations that the witches sent out their "spec-
ters" or "shapes" with human powers of sight, hearing, speech,
and touch, as well as superhuman abilities of locomotion.[12] The
trial and death of Giles Cory brought the era alive in all its horror. He was the only man put to death and sole victim not to be
hung—a relatively quick ending. The magistrate ordered that
he should be slowly crushed to death with large stones, as the
popular ballad goes:

### The Ballad of Giles Cory[13]
—Anonymous

Giles Cory was a wizard strong,
A stubborn wretch was he;
And fit was he to hang on high
Upon the locust tree.

So when before the magistrates
For trial he did come,
He would no true confession make
But was completely dumb.

"Giles Cory," said the magistrate,
"What have thou here to plead
To these who now accuse thy soul
of crimes and horrid deed?"

Giles Cory—he said not a word,
No single word spoke he.
"Giles Cory," said the magistrate,
"We'll press it out of thee."
They got them then a heavy beam,
They laid it on his breast.
They loaded it with heavy stones,
And hard upon him pressed.

"More weight," now said this wretched man,
"More weight," again he cried,
And he did no confession make,
But wickedly he died.
Dame Cory lived but three days more,

But three days more lived she,
For she was hanged at Gallows Hill
Upon the locust tree.

This ballad—as a poem, song, and story—is familiar in American folklore. Giles Cory, 80 years old when he died, was known in the village as a cantankerous and obstinate character. Because of an on-going marital dispute, he testified against his wife in her witchcraft trial, but this backfired on him. He had relatively recently come from England to settle in Salem, and many in the village saw him as an eccentric outsider. Cory also had quickly amassed a significant amount of property. He calculated that if he testified and was found guilty, the sheriff could seize all his land and goods. On the other hand, if he remained silent, he could save his estate for his children. By piling more stones onto his chest, the sheriff hoped to get him to plead guilty. But Cory's only words were, "More weight!" in the hope of speeding up his death. Likely it took many hours to kill him, as his ribs slowly cracked. His tongue stuck out of his mouth as he gasped for air, and the sheriff used the end of his cane to push it back in.[14]

As I read more on Roger Conant in an old Conant genealogy[15] and other sources, it became evident to me that the act of placing his statue in front of the Salem Witch Museum might have caused him to roll over in his grave. He was a fair man and an excellent arbitrator, often settling arguments between warring groups of settlers. Besides being the first Governor of Salem, he was a leading church member and a representative to the First General Court of Massachusetts Colony in 1636. He also was appointed as a magistrate. Upon his death, he left a large estate to his family, including 200 acres (81 hectares) of land at Dunstable and another 77 acres (31 hectares) in the surrounding countryside. I found one passage which summed up his character:

Conant was moderate in his views, tolerant, mild and con-
ciliatory, quiet and unobtrusive, ingenious and unambi-
tious, preferring the public good to his private interests;
with the passive virtues he combined great moral courage
and indomitable will....Governor Conant's true courage
and simplicity of heart and strength of principle eminently
qualified him for the conflicts of those rude days of perils,
deprivation and trial.[16]

I wondered what had transpired in Salem only 13 years after
his death that led to the Witch Trials. Had Conant seen signs of
these developments during his life? I decided to find out more
about him. Conant had become a successful salter (expert at
preserving fish) in England, but in 1623, he and his family
immigrated to the Plymouth Colony. He was a nonconformist
who believed the Church of England should be reformed from
within, and these religious beliefs did not match those of the
strict Pilgrim Separatist society at Plymouth and their growing
mean-spirited fanaticism.

In 1624, Conant moved from Plymouth to Nantasket—present-day Hull, Massachusetts, on the southern peninsula of Boston
Harbor. By 1625, he had relocated once more to Cape Ann, a settlement created to service English fishermen by establishing provision stores and salt works to preserve fish. The place suffered
from a drunken leader and rowdy men, who had come only to
make quick fortunes. They fought with Plymouth over fishing
rights, a conflict which threatened to turn into all-out warfare.

Conant managed to negotiate a peace, but he didn't think
this setting was proper for his family. So, in 1626, he led an exo-
dus of about 30 settlers to the place called "Naumkeag," at the
base of the peninsula. (It was later renamed "Salem.") The Cape
Ann settlement fell apart and its investors in the Dorchester

Company, an English corporation of shareholders who were also looking for quick profits, refused to support those who moved to Naumkeag.[17]

I also found a passage on Roger Conant's life in Naumkeag at the Conant genealogy:

> Roger Conant, the first settler in Naumkeag, has built his dwelling, months ago, on the border of the forest-path; and at this moment he comes eastward, through the vista of woods, with his gun over his shoulder, bringing home the choice portions of a deer. His stalwart figure, clad in a leathern jerkin and breeches of the same, strides sturdily onward, with such an air of physical force and energy that he might expect the very trees to stand aside, and give him room to pass. And so, indeed, they must; for, humble as is his name in history, Roger Conant still is of a class of men who do not merely find, but make, their place in the system of human affairs; a man of thoughtful strength, he has planted the germ of a city. There stands his habitation, showing in its rough architecture some of the features of the Indian wigwam, and some of the log cabin, and somewhat too, of the straw-thatched cottage in Old England, where this good yeoman had his birth and breeding.[18]

In 1628, a new group of investors, less intent on quick profits, formed the New England Company which soon morphed into the Massachusetts Bay Company. New settlers, including families and skilled men, began to flood the settlement Conant had started. The company sent John Endicott to take over as governor. Conant had only been informally voted in by the community as the first governor of the colony, but Endicott's appointment was official. Although a capable and honest man, he had a very high opinion of himself and possessed a combative personality with very strong views on just about everything.[19] I found a passage in the Conant genealogy which is telling:

> Endicott was the opposite of Conant, arbitrary and sometimes violent, he ruled with a determined hand, and carried the sword unsheathed, quick to assert and ready to maintain his rights; firm and unyielding: a man of theological asperity and bigoted."[20]

Endicott fought with the original planters, led by Conant, who took their grievances back to England. Endicott had to modify his behavior, and eventually he and Conant came to an agreement. Together they renamed the place "Salem," meaning "peace" in Hebrew.[21]

In 1629, the Massachusetts Bay Company was granted a Royal Charter and John Winthrop was appointed as the new governor to oversee the process of organizing more ships with settlers and their belongings. Winthrop brought with him the original of the new charter for protection from the upheavals in England, due to the fight between King Charles I and Parliament. Winthrop had great authority and decided to move the colony's headquarters to Charlestown on the mouth of the Charles River, after which he shifted it to the opposite bank, where he founded the City of Boston.[22]

Roger Conant's early and moderate influence on Salem and New England dissipated. The town became a backwater. More people like Endicott took over. A later example is the Reverend Samuel Parris, who came to Salem to run the church only three years before the Witch Trails began. He brought along his wife, three children, and his 11-year-old niece, Abigail Williams. Parris' theology consisted of "terrifying absolutes of good and evil, sin and saintliness and heaven and hell," and he infected his nine-year-old daughter, Betty, and his niece with his beliefs.[23] They joined with other adolescent girls in conjuring up their hysterical accusations of witchcraft.

Compared to Parris and Endicott, I found that at least two of my ancestors had tried to counteract the negative trends in New England's Puritan society. I felt the need to explore the beginnings of these tendencies further at Plymouth Colony, Massachusetts, the settlement where my 9th great-grandfather, Edward Fuller, landed with the rest of the Pilgrims in 1620.

# 15

## HUMOROUS CONVERSATIONS *at* PLIMOTH PLANTATION

Red sky in the morning on Plymouth Bay, May 2017

I DROVE TO PLYMOUTH, MASSACHUSETTS AND CHECKED into the Pilgrims Sands Hotel overlooking Plymouth Bay. The next morning, I woke at five to look out upon a most glorious sunrise. I gazed at it for a while and imagined I could see in the distance the *Mayflower* sailing in to anchor, as it did nearly 400 years ago. I also thought of the old saying: "Red sky in the morning, sailors take warning." But I substituted the words in my head, "Pokanokets take warning."

The Pokanokets led a larger Algonquin tribe called the "Wampanoag," who had inhabited this area for hundreds of years. Their civilization, already tipping over, was about to be turned upside down by the arrival of this ship with its 130 English settlers and sailors. Up to 90 percent of the coastal Indigenous population had perished due to contact with European fishermen and explorers, especially during the years 1616 to 1619. Some accounts claim it was smallpox or the bubonic plague that struck them down,[1] while modern researchers have hypothesized it may have been Leptospirosis, a bacterial disease like the plague, carried by rats on European ships.[2]

I visited Plimoth "Plantation" (a word which meant "colony" in the 17th century). It is a built-to-scale re-creation of the village that the Pilgrims constructed. (The curators had respelled the place "Plimoth," in deference to historical accuracy, and I have used it here in historical references.) The site also included a replica of a Wampanoag village with realistic displays of the life of the Indigenous People in the 1600s. Educator-actors, some from the remaining Wampanoag community, added to the detail the curators put into the reconstruction.

The day I visited, I shared this interactive museum with only a few other tourists—great for photography. I talked to some of the educators playing various personalities who lived at Plimoth in 1623, two years after my 9th great-grandfather Edward Fuller had died.

My conversation with a woman playing Elizabeth Hopkins proved instructive. I said to her, "You're wearing such colorful clothes. How come you don't wear those black and white robes and shoes with buckles?" I had seen such clothing in story books as a kid and I knew it was a myth, but I wanted to see what she would say.

Re-creation of Plimoth Plantation, Plymouth, Massachusetts

A Living History Educator in the Wampanoag Homesite drying animal skins

Living History Educator playing the role of a Pilgrim woman

She looked at me as if I were a bit daft, and answered, "I haven't seen such clothes around here. Just what are you getting at?"

Feeling embarrassed, I changed the subject, "Did you know Edward Fuller and his wife?"

"Yea," she replied with a heavy 17th century English accent. "Poor souls died the first winter. Many passed then. Such a terrible time, it was. A bad time to come here, I should say."

"Edward Fuller was my 9th great-grandfather," I said. Elizabeth totally ignored my claim. She wouldn't engage in a conversation outside of the time frame she was playing.

I tried another line of enquiry, "Did many die that first winter?"

"Most certainly. Half of us. Bitter days they were, I can tell you. Young ones and older folks especially. We had no proper clothes and shelter. Little food—and so, so cold. Poor planning I would say."

"Why did you come in the winter?"

"Fanatics, half of them, these Separatists. Some of my neighbors are just that, fanatics. It is against my principles to speak ill of others, mind you, but they do not know how to think properly, that is for sure."

I knew Edward Fuller had been a Separatist. So, I dug a little deeper to understand what she was saying, "You mean you don't believe like they do—to separate from the Church of England."

She lowered her voice, "Not on your life, my dear man. King, God, church, and country is what I believe in. Keeps us on the straight and narrow. Makes us think properly, I would say."

I asked her, "Is your husband here?"

"He is off working our land—only six acres allotted to us. Misers they are. But we have to do our best to grow food for the winter. Such cold winters. If my husband had told me so, I might not have agreed to come."

I had read about her husband, Stephen Hopkins—quite a famous man.[3] In 1609, he left England to go to Jamestown Colony in Virginia as a minister's clerk, but their ship, the *Sea Venture*, encountered a powerful storm near the Bermuda Islands and nearly sank. At the last moment, the ocean calmed and they spotted land. Sailors had long called Bermuda the "Isle of Devils," thinking it to be inhabited by evil spirits and not fit for human habitation, but the castaways found it to be a tropical paradise—warm temperatures, palm trees, fruits, berries, fish, and birds of many varieties.

A group of men, including Hopkins, refused to continue on to Jamestown. The captain charged them with mutiny, and they narrowly escaped being put to death. (The tale of their battle to stay afloat in the storm and the story of their near shipwreck inspired William Shakespeare to write *"The Tempest,"* including a mutinous butler named "Stephano," fashioned after Stephen Hopkins.)

Hopkins carried on to Virginia with the party—a terrible

place, he found, with colonists starving to death, no trade with the native people, and no fish in the bay. He managed to stay for several years to help rebuild the colony until his first wife, Mary, died in England. He returned in 1614 to take charge of his three children. Then he married Elizabeth and they joined the Pilgrims—his second voyage to the New World.

I could find no such detail about my ancestor, Edward Fuller. I did find that he had been baptized on September 4, 1575 at Redenhall, Norfolk, England. Sometime after May 1614, he left England for Leiden, Holland, to join the congregation of Separatists led by Rev. John Robinson.[4] As first mentioned in Chapter 14, his son, Matthew, my 8th great-grandfather, remained in England to study medicine and came to New England in 1640. Even though he did not come on the *Mayflower* in 1620, he was my first genetic link to a passenger on that famous ship.

From the Hopkins' house, I walked down the hill to the Fuller cottage. No one was home. I asked a few of the educator-actors if they knew whether any member of the family would return to the cottage that day, but I only received vague answers. I guessed that Samuel Fuller Jr. and his uncle Samuel Fuller Sr. were also out working in their fields. The Pilgrims had begun by trying to work communally, with no individual land ownership, but this soon broke down due to quarrels. By 1623, they had divided up the land.

My conversation with Elizabeth Hopkins reminded me that she and her husband were two of the "Strangers" who had joined the *Mayflower* in England. Although the original intention of Rev. John Robinson, and the leading men in the Leiden congregation, was to only allow Puritan Separatists to join the voyage to North America, they had to compromise. They wanted to relocate all of the estimated 300 people in the congregation to North America, but only about 50 opted to depart in 1620. Robinson decided he had to stay with the majority of his flock, intending to follow later. Their investors in England allowed many non-Separatists to join the party in order to make up for those from Holland who decided not to join. Also, in their first attempt to leave, the *Speedwell,* a small ship the Separatists purchased in Holland for the journey, proved not to be seaworthy, forcing it and the *Mayflower* to turn back. At that point, some of the original group grew discouraged and opted out completely, leaving only 37 Leiden Separatists in the party of 102 passengers, including some servants. The others were so-called "Strangers."

The investors made a decision to pack everyone into the *Mayflower,* which did not finally leave Plymouth, England until September 6, 1620. Furthermore, on arrival, some of the 30 crew members of the *Mayflower* opted to stay in Plimoth Plantation—non-religious, uncultured, and lower-class people in the eyes of most Pilgrims.[5]

On my first visit to Plimoth Plantation, I had been disappointed not to meet any actor-educators playing Fuller family members. I decided I had to return. Meanwhile, I read much more about the history of the place and the immigrants my ancestors had joined. I learned that the settlement had endured for many years precisely because of its mixture of people. They were diverse compared to Jamestown, a settlement mainly composed of fortune-seeking men, two-thirds of whom died within a year of arrival, as noted earlier.

Before they landed, the leaders of the Plimoth Pilgrims had the foresight to ask all male passengers to sign the *Mayflower Compact,* which was aimed at regulating their behavior on land—a civil covenant rather than a religious one. Rev. Robinson, had "anticipated the need to create a government based on civil consent rather than divine decree."[6] Even marriages were to be civil agreements, not religious.

In June 2019, I returned to Plimoth Plantation to see if I could meet actor-educators playing the Fullers. This time I was in luck. I headed down the hill to the Fuller cottage where I met my ancestor's brother, Samuel Fuller Sr. and his nephew, Samuel Fuller Jr. They were now role-playing events in 1627, four years later than during my previous visit when they pretended it was 1623.

I had read that, although Samuel Fuller Sr. had little formal training in medicine, he had acted as a quack doctor for the Pilgrims, and had most likely witnessed the death of his brother, Edward. I engaged Samuel Sr. in a conversation, this time avoiding any mention of my relationship to his late brother. He had no problem in explaining how Edward had died, "It was lung fever that took him, and scorby too."

I knew he meant scurvy, a disease caused by a lack of Vitamin C in the diet. Normally people in 17th century England drank beer instead of contaminated drinking water, but the passengers had to ration it on the *Mayflower* because the journey took longer than anticipated.[7] At any rate, unless 17th century sailors followed the new practice of enhancing beer with pine or spruce needles, it would not have prevented scurvy. I pictured Edward Fuller and his wife shivering to death due to the damp cold winter, their gums bleeding, their teeth falling out, while they expelled foul breath.

Samuel Sr. went on, "Our beer supply was finished and we had no lemon beer or apple cider either—hard to fight the scorby."

"Where did you learn about all this?" I asked.

"Leiden. I spent some time at the university. You know, they actually send young men to study medicine at university in Holland. I am no physician, mind you, but I did attend lectures at

Living History Educator playing role of Samuel Fuller Sr.

their anatomy theater. I learned all about the body, including the brain. Did you know that snot is brain poop?"

"No," I replied with a smile. "Do tell me more."

"I saw it with my own eyes, I did. Brain poop coming out of my brother's skull. In Holland, those cadavers lay all around us on benches. Peculiar way to treat dead men, I should say. The Dutch are different—rather strange in their methods of education. To become a surgeon in England, a man only has to apprentice with a senior surgeon. My nephew Mathew is doing just that. He might come here someday."

I wanted to tell him that indeed, Mathew would come in 1640. But I knew from my previous visit not to go there, so I changed the subject, "Did you like it in Holland?"

"It was good to begin with, but then too many different kinds of dissenters came, including Scots, Presbyterians, Huguenots, Walloons, Lutherans, even Mennonites. I saw some Mennonites pumping water out of the ground with windmills. Can you believe it? Strange people. Pacifist, they are. Did you know, they will not even shoot Catholics?" (Catholicism had been outlawed in both England and Holland at the time.)

"You don't like Catholics?"

"Papists cannot be tolerated. We cannot trust them and their priests—devilish people. You will not find one here."

"So, you felt the need to leave Holland?"

"Most definitely. Too crowded, I would say. And we had to work in clothing factories to make a living. We did not like our young ones mixing with the Dutch. Too many strange ideas, those Dutch people have. Would you believe, the men get drunk and cavort with women on the streets?"

"How are you finding life here after almost seven years?"

"I must say, I cannot complain. We are far away from King Charles, as well. He can't tax us here, which makes it even better....By the way, do you have to pay heavy taxes? Why are you wearing such shoddy clothing?"

"What's wrong with my clothes?" I asked.

"Why even the cloth we spin right here is superior in grade to what you dress in," he answered. "I would not be caught in public dressed in such garments."

As I laughed at his comment, Samuel Jr. arrived at the Fuller abode. He was about 12 years old when he came in 1620. The educator-actor who now portrayed him in 1627 was a rather robust youth with a thick red beard. I greeted him and asked how he was doing.

"Not so well."

"Why is that?" I asked. "You don't look like you're starving."

"There is nothing much to do here."

Living History Educator playing role of Samuel Fuller Jr.

"Aren't you busy with farming and hunting?" I asked.

"Sure, there is definitely work to do. In fact, we work all the time. But there are few people my age, especially young women who are not already spoken for. I would like to have a family someday."

He seemed so depressed. I felt like cheering him up. I wanted to tell him that he would become a freeman in 1634, move away to Scituate in 1635, marry a lady by the name of Jane Lothrop, and that they would settle in Barnstable, Massachusetts and have nine children. Not only that, he would live to a good old age for that time, and die in 1683.[8] But I knew this kind of prophesizing would not be something these educator-actors could play to. Time travel wasn't in their briefs.

Just then, the educator-actor playing Myles Standish arrived to call the Fullers to militia training. Standish had been one of the most controversial of all the *Mayflower* passengers. By all accounts, he began his career as an English soldier, fighting against Catholic Spain's domination of Holland. In Leiden, he struck up a relationship with Rev. John Robinson, who recognized that his people would need a military man to accompany them on their adventures in the New World. All sorts of horrendous stories were circulating in England and Holland about the terrible reception the Virginia colonists had received from the Indians. The Pilgrims' original plan had been to land and settle in northern Virginia. (At the time, Virginia comprised a much larger territory and the Pilgrims aimed to start a colony near the mouth of the Hudson River, probably on Long Island.)

Living History Educator playing role of Myles Standish

They also calculated they would need protection from rival colonial powers—the Dutch, French, and maybe even the Spanish. So, the leaders put Myles Standish in charge of organizing a militia.[9] (Note: Myles was no blood relative of mine, but they lived in a small world, genetically speaking. One of his grandsons, who was also named Myles Standish, married my 6th great-grandmother, Elizabeth [Fuller] Thacher in 1724, after the death of Samuel Fuller Jr., my 6th great-grandfather in the Fuller line.)[10]

I followed Standish and the Fullers to watch the training exercise. Unlike my first visit to the plantation when I was practically alone, I happened to return on a "school day" with free admission to all. School children and tourists swarmed the place, so I found it hard to get photos of the educator-actors without the 21st century popping up in the background.

Standish put his militia men through their paces. He yelled at them to speed up their musket loading, as they stumbled through the steps. It was 1627, but they didn't appear to be very well trained after almost seven years of such drills. It took them five minutes to prepare and load their old matchlocks. Finally, he marched the small platoon off to a nearby field to have them practice firing and reloading. Standish had put Samuel Fuller Jr. in charge of the group, but that didn't give him any protection from Standish's tongue.

Standish yelled, "Fuller, form a proper line! Can you not remember what I said last time? No, not that way. Line them up pro-per-ly and fire!"

After the volley, Standish continued, "Now, you two should step back and reload while the others fire. How many times do we have to repeat this to get it into your small brains?"

Standish turned to the crowd, "You see, they are not real soldiers. Not military material, really. It is not in their nature. I have tried over and over and look at the results. These people are only

Living History Educators re-enacting militia training, loading muskets

good for manual labor. Such dull heads....Fuller! No Fuller, not that way!"

I turned to the crowd of tourists and said, "He's being very nasty with my ancestor's son." A few people laughed.

If this demonstration accurately reflected the Pilgrims' military abilities in 1627, I wondered how on earth they had survived. Indian arrows could surely have taken out many as they fumbled through the reloading process. On the one hand, this whole exercise ran counter to the pictures I originally had about the Pilgrims from childhood stories. Indeed, this dashing military man, Myles Standish, collided with those images. On the other hand, I had come more prepared on my return, having delved into the other myths besides their clothes and dispositions.

First of all, they never called themselves "Pilgrims" at all. For over a century they were called "Old Comers" or "Old Planters"

Living History Educators re-enacting militia training, firing muskets

until Plimoth Governor William Bradford's historical manuscript, *Of Plymouth Plantation,* was discovered and referred to in a 1793 sermon. Bradford had quoted the original version of the Geneva Bible, Hebrews 11:13: "but they knew they were pilgrims."

The myths continued to build through the centuries. According to the detailed book titled *The Times of Their Live: Life, Love, and Death in Plymouth Colony,* by James Deetz and Patricia Scott Deetz,[11] the Thanksgiving feast in the autumn of 1621, with Pilgrims seated at a table of plenty, surrounded by a few appreciative natives left standing, has to be turned on its head. About 90 Pokanokets, with whom they had signed a peace treaty, marched into their camp, bringing with them an abundant supply of fresh venison. They also roasted water fowl, fish, and cooked Indian corn. Perhaps they ate some tough wild turkeys. Cranberries and pumpkins are native to North America, but their use was not recorded. By that time, the settlers only had finished building a few cabins, so the celebration took place outdoors without the tables or tablecloths often depicted. Probably they did not all participate in a common prayer to thank God for their first harvest in New England. Contrary to the desires of the Pilgrim Separatists among them, the celebration took the form of a traditional three-day English harvest festival with beer drinking, singing, dancing, and contests—archery, shooting, leaping, vaulting, weight throwing, and ball games—the Pokanokets adding some new competitions to the revelry.

Most North Americans have not digested the truth about the beginnings of our now mainly commercial holiday of Thanksgiving, and if anyone tried to popularize the original scene today, it would probably be decried by some as "fake news."

Having witnessed the militia drill, I wanted to explore more about the militancy of the Pilgrims. Was this the intention of my ancestor, Rev. John Robinson? By all accounts, he had been a wise and effective leader who preached peace and tolerance. He had led his flock in their escape from the intolerant religious conditions of England under King James I, who, along with the Church of England authorities, had insisted that everyone follow the *Book of Common Prayer* and the King James version of the Bible, instead of the Geneva Bible with its Calvinistic commentary.[12]

The Puritans emphasized an individual's personal responsibility and relationship with God, not something to be defined by ecclesiastical authority or the King as head of the Church of England. Richard Bancroft, Archbishop of Canterbury, 1604 to 1610, the "chief overseer" of enforcing the use of the King James version of the Bible, "banished approximately 300 Puritan ministers from the Church, stripping them of their salaries and pulpits." Some were imprisoned, whipped, and made to perform hard labor.[13]

Rev. Robinson, with much of his congregation, escaped to Holland in 1608. They moved to Leiden in 1609, where he became very popular. In his farewell letter to the departing Pilgrims, read aloud to them at dockside in Holland, he "encouraged them to be tolerant of each other—not to 'give, no, nor easily take offense'— and to demonstrate 'wisdom and charity' to all. When the time came to establish a form of government—'a Body Politic,' he called it—he urged them to 'let your wisdom and godliness appear, not only in choosing persons as do entirely love, and will diligently promote the common good, but also in yielding to them all due honor and obedience....'"[14] Rev. Robinson further implored the Pilgrims to get along with the Strangers among them.[15] I wonder if that included the Native Americans they would meet.

Although the Pilgrims made a peace treaty with Massasoit, the leader of the Pokanokets, not all the Wampanoags recognized him as the legitimate *sachem* because of chronic divisions among Native American people. Massasoit saw the English settlers as excellent allies, given his politically weak position, largely due to his loss of many fighting men during the plague of 1616-19.

In addition, Plimoth Pilgrims did not have control over nearby English settlements and their inhabitants' attitudes and actions toward the natives. In 1623, skirmishes morphed into all-out war with the Massachusetts tribe to the north, and Myles Standish inserted himself into the thick of it when his militia fired muskets against oncoming arrows. Due to his aggressive commands, many natives died or were wounded. Some fled and hid in swamps.[16]

When Rev. John Robinson heard of this event some months later, he admonished Governor Bradford on his willingness to allow Standish to attack, writing that "the captain lacked that tenderness of the life of man (made after God's image)" and that "It is... a thing more glorious, in men's eyes, than pleasing in God's or convenient for Christians, to be a terror to poor barbarous people. And indeed, I am afraid lest, by these occasions, others should be drawn to affect a kind of ruffling course in the world."[17]

When I read these words, I had to cut through my ancestor's rather harsh phrase—"barbarous people"—to realize he had actually been advocating a relatively enlightened path for the era in which he lived. But how accurate he had been in his prediction about the "ruffling course in the world." Rev. Robinson's delayed letters from Holland had little force on the ground, as events unfolded in New England.

The natives soon acquired firearms. Thomas Morton, a man who couldn't abide the Puritan ethic, set up his own libertarian settlement of Merrymount, Massachusetts (present day Quincy), where he traded guns for furs with his native allies—especially beaver pelts, which were all the rage in English fashion in the early 1600s.[18]

The Plimoth Pilgrims also needed the fur trade to pay back their investors in England who had funded their voyage and settlement. As the trading of guns for furs became commonplace throughout New England during the 1600s, the English grew accustomed to seeing Indians armed with flintlocks, rather than the old matchlocks still held and used by many white settlers. Native Americans became more adept than the English at hunting with flintlocks,[19] and also repairing them.

When I read about this trading guns for furs, it sounded like a disaster in the making. I wanted to learn more about my ancestors' involvement in the early wars with Native Americans in New England.

# 16

# FINDING FOUR INDIAN
# FIGHTERS *in* MY GENES

Plymouth Rock at Plymouth Harbor

AFTER I LEFT PLIMOTH PLANTATION, I DROVE TO THE
waterfront of Plymouth town, a strip of restaurants and gift
shops serving the thousands of tourists who visit every year. The
*Mayflower II*, a replica of the original ship, was out for repairs until
the 400-year anniversary of its landing in 2020. But I knew that
the "Plymouth Rock" could be seen. When I arrived at the site,

I listened to a tourist guide briefing a crowd on the importance of this rock to America's history. He spoke with great authority:

> Here is a piece of the original Plymouth Rock where the Pilgrims landed almost 400 years ago. When you look at this rock, think of our veterans and all the wars we have won against our enemies through the centuries, starting here in this very town. It stands today as a symbol of our strength and to the glory of our great nation under God. Remember 9/11 and the enemies of our Republic. For almost 250 years since our nation's founding....

As he went on and on, I walked away shaking my head. I was dumbfounded to hear this stream of nonsense issuing from the guide's mouth and thought of its effects on the general public. The contents of his speech had nothing to do with Plymouth Rock. I wanted to cry out, "Stop!" The guide was in the process of adding new myths to old myths, which could have a further corrosive effect on the ability of many Americans to evaluate their history in a rational way.

The Plymouth Rock story is yet another myth about the origins of the US. There is no evidence the Pilgrims landed on any such thing. There may have been a large boulder near the place where a brook ran into the sea, but William Bradford's journal, *Of Plymouth Plantation*, the only eye-witness account we have of the time, makes no mention of such a rock or landing on it. Besides, the exhausted Pilgrims probably would not have ventured up a high piece of granite when they only had to wade in on the sandy shore.[1]

One story has it that the so-called Plymouth Rock of today is the remnant of an old boulder buried by sand under the town pier—a rock which the Sons of Liberty dug up and tried to move to the town square in 1774. As they attempted to raise it onto a wagon, it fell and split in half. They took the top part to display in various places over the years, and left the bottom for souvenir hunters to pick at for decades, until a barrier was raised to inhibit direct access.[2]

With such myths and distortions surrounding Plymouth's history, I wondered if I would ever find the truth about my Puritan ancestors' involvement in the early wars against the Indigenous People of New England. The short-lived Pequot War of 1637-38, briefly mentioned in Chapter 13, had been the first major conflict between the English settlers and Native Americans. The colonists won and claimed God was truly on their side:

> Let the whole Earth be filled with his Glory! Thus the Lord was pleased to smite our Enemies in the hinder Parts, and to give us their Land for an Inheritance: Who remembred [sic] us in our low Estate, and redeemed us out of our Enemies Hands: Let us therefore praise the Lord for his Goodness and his wonderful Works to the Children of Men![3]

After the Pequot War, relative peace returned to New England for 38 years, largely because the English put great effort into pacifying almost every *sachem* with treaties and rewards, and dividing the tribes against each other. But the poor treatment of Native Americans by Puritans, most of whom continued to consider Indians to be agents of Satan on Earth, provided the fuel for a fire that broke out in 1675.

At the time, there were an estimated 52,000 English and 20,000 Indians living in New England. This second major conflict, King Philip's War (1675-78), was the bloodiest in American history. An estimated 800 English and 3,000 Indians were killed. These numbers may seem small until they are measured as a percentage of the population: 1.54 percent of the English and 15 percent of the Indians died. Compare this to the American Civil War when only 0.856 percent of an estimated 35.6 million people perished.[4] Eleven colonial towns were reduced to ashes and abandoned for at least a decade, and many others experienced loss of life and property damage.[5]

One of the root causes of King Philip's War was the burgeoning English population's quest for new land. The conflict began when the relationship between the Plimoth Pilgrims and the Wampanoags began to break down. Massasoit, the *sachem* who had made a peace treaty with the Pilgrims, died in 1661. His oldest son, Wamsutta, then became *sachem*. Shortly afterwards, he requested that he be called "Alexander" and that his younger brother Metacom be known as "Philip" in order to gain more respect in English eyes. Much to the Plimoth colonists' dismay, these brothers flexed their muscles by selling some of their land to non-Puritan outcasts in Providence Plantations. This land sale led to the arrest and interrogation of Wamsutta (a.k.a., Alexander), during which time he died. Philip accused the colonists of poisoning his brother, but this was never proven. One report holds that Samuel Fuller Sr., my ancestor's brother and Plimoth's quack doctor, gave Alexander a purgative for a case of appendicitis.[6]

The truth of this accusation will never be known, but my humorous interaction with the educator-actor playing the part of this wordy and opinionated man, led me to believe that the real quack could easily have done such harm. I could easily imagine Samuel Fuller applying such theories as "snot is brain poop," which the educator-actor playing him related to me at Plimoth Plantation.

At the time, even educated doctors "believed that most medical problems were caused by an imbalance of the four 'humors,' namely blood, yellow bile, black bile, and phlegm. The way to cure disease was to determine which humor was out of balance, and then attempt to adjust it, either by laxative, inducing vomiting, or more commonly—draining off 'excess' blood."[7]

Tensions grew over the next decade until the powder keg exploded in June 1675, with the trial and execution of three Wampanoga men for the murder of John Sassamon, a Christian Indian who had fought alongside the English in the Pequot War.[8]

In my search through four centuries of North American history, I had found a few soldiers among my ancestors, but still had not discovered any fighting men who relished that occupation. I managed, however, to find four of them who were deeply involved in King Philip's War.

The first was Dr. Matthew Fuller, my 8th great-grandfather, who had stayed in England to complete his training as a surgeon and came to Plimoth Plantation in 1640. Being a real doctor, I expected the best from him—that he would do no harm. But as I read on, a different picture emerged. Fuller moved to Barnstable, Massachusetts, where he became a magistrate, a lieutenant in the militia, and later, Chairman of the Council of War. He was appointed Surgeon General of the colony's troops on December 17, 1673, and a captain in Plimoth's militia in 1675, at the outbreak of King Philip's War.[9]

Fuller claimed himself to be "too ancient and heavy to be chasing Indians," but in July 1675, he nevertheless joined Captain Benjamin Church in leading a troop of three dozen men to try to speak to a faction of the Wampanoga about maintaining peace—a fumbled move which resulted in one of the first scuffles of the war. Their miscalculation on the souring mood and mistrust of Native Americans led to the Battle of Almy's Pease Field on Sakonnet River near present-day Tiverton, Rhode Island. The Wampanoga launched a surprise attack on the militia from a hill, firing 50 or 60 muskets at them as they crossed an abandoned pea field. The militia had to take shelter behind a stone wall by the water's edge. Captain Roger Goulding, with his sloop, rescued them by using a canoe to bring them on board, two at a time. But when Church boarded the canoe, he remembered he had forgotten his hat and cutlass, so he rushed back to retrieve his gear. Somehow, he avoided being hit by a great volley of musket fire from the Wampanoag forces. Church attributed his survival to "the glory of God and His protecting providence." The troops also escaped harm, except for the wounding of two men under Fuller's command. Following this skirmish, the Puritan forces realized that the time for negotiation and diplomacy had passed. New England ignited into all-out war.[10, 11]

The second ancestor I found in the war was Captain John Gallop Jr. (sometimes spelled "Gallup"). His daughter, Elizabeth, married Henry Stevens, the first of my Stephens/Stevens ancestral line to settle in New England (Table 5). Elizabeth (Gallop) Stevens (ca. 1662-1726) was a great-grandmother of Joseph Stevens Sr., who fought in the American Revolution in the Hudson River-Lake Champlain Valley (Chapter 11). Therefore, Elizabeth's father, John Gallop Jr., was another of my 8th great-grandfathers. This finding confirmed, once more, that investigating female ancestral lines is a most fruitful genealogical endeavor, even if made more complicated by changes in surnames due to marriages.

John Gallop Jr. was born in 1620 at Bridport, Dorset, England, to John Gallop Sr. and his wife, Christobel. John Jr. came to Massachusetts Bay Colony in 1633 with his mother, brothers, and sisters, to join his father, whose name appears on the A-list of passengers (i.e., most certain) on the *Mary and John*, which arrived in 1630. John Sr. piloted ships and engaged in trading to make a living. In July 1636, he rammed his vessel into the light sailing ship owned by a fellow trader, John Oldham. Oldham had been overtaken by Pequot warriors off Block Island. They butchered Oldham, an incident that set off the Pequot War, as mentioned in Chapter 13. But Gallop, with a few native employees and two of his sons, one being John Jr., overpowered the Pequot pirates, shooting some, binding those who had not escaped, and throwing them into the sea to drown. Next, the colonial forces invaded the island and burned Pequot villages to the ground.[12]

John Gallop Jr. became known as a gallant Indian fighter during the Pequot War, and in recognition of his bravery, he was granted over 350 acres (142 hectares) of land in New London and Mystic River (now Stonington), Connecticut. He became a wealthy landowner and trader, like his father.[13] When King Philip's War broke out, John Gallop Jr. returned to fighting Native Americans, although about 55 years of age at the time. He had much experience and skill at warfare. But he may have underestimated the Narragansetts.

To explain the historical context of John Gallop Jr.'s involvement in the war, the Narragansetts remained the largest and most independent Native American tribe in New England. They lived at peace with Providence Plantations settlers, whose colony was founded by the Reverend Roger Williams, a clergyman who also believed in the complete separation of church and state. (He is known more for his political importance than his religious works and therefore is not addressed as "Reverend" in most historical accounts.) Arriving in 1631, he briefly tried to settle in Salem, then Plimoth, where he was an assistant minister until 1633, and then back to Salem, where he argued with the authorities over Indian rights and theology. He was prosecuted for his liberal beliefs and banished. Escaping the threat of being shipped back to England, he traveled south through the winter of 1635-36 with the help of Native Americans, who guided and sheltered him. He could not abide the Puritans' exclusionist theology. He argued in favor of religious liberty for all people, no matter how eccentric their beliefs. Even Quakers were allowed to settle in Providence Plantations, a sect which was despised by the Puritans. In Providence Plantations, Williams also wanted to practice more democratic government in which magistrates do not derive their power from God, but from the consent of citizens.[14]

As an aside, I was happy to find an account of how my 7th great-grandfather, Isaac Robinson, after arriving in 1631 and trying to settle in Plimoth Plantation, left the place in 1636 to settle in Barnstable and then Falmouth in 1669. There, he eventually grew sympathetic towards some of the beliefs of the Quakers and was disenfranchised for four years by the governor for his religious tolerance.[15] I like to think that Isaac heard the sermons of Roger Williams at Plimoth, for they overlapped there during 1631-33.

Williams learned Algonquin languages and wrote the first book on the subject, titled *A Key into the Language of America.*[16] He wanted others to better understand Native American culture and thought. He made land purchase agreements with the Narragansett based on their traditional customs, rather than the usual Puritan means of subterfuge or force. He returned to England in 1643 to lobby successfully for a separate Parliamentary Charter for the Colony of Rhode Island and Providence Plantations—the smallest US state today with the longest name. At the time, a Royal Charter could not be granted because the English Civil War had begun and King Charles had fled London for Oxford, which became his base for fighting parliamentary forces. (The so-called "Glorious Revolution" continued until 1649, when Charles was captured and beheaded by order of Parliament.)[17]

Williams' radical views, and the independent establishment of his colony, remained a thorn in the side of the Puritans' United Colonies of New England, which had been formed in May 1643 by Massachusetts Bay, Plimoth, Connecticut, and New Haven. Providence Plantations and their allies, the Narragansetts, posed a growing threat to the United Colonies' dominance in the region. The Puritans and their Indian allies made several attempts to take Narragansett lands during the tumultuous years of the Civil War in England, which lasted until the restoration of the monarchy with the coronation of Charles II in 1660. In 1663, on another voyage to England, Roger Williams managed to negotiate a Royal Charter for Providence Plantations to replace the Parliamentary Charter, which no longer had legal standing under the new king. In July 1664, a Royal Commission visited New England to put the Puritans in their place, declaring the United Colonies of New England illegal, and that Narragansett country would henceforth be under the jurisdiction of Charles II and administered by Providence Plantations magistrates.[18] But the Puritans continued to look for an opportunity to stop Roger Williams and the Narragansetts.

Returning to John Gallop Jr., he joined King Philip's War as Captain of the First Company of Connecticut forces from Stonington, under the command of Major Robert Treat. He fought in the "Great Swamp Fight" against the Narragansetts in

Rhode Island on December 19, 1675.[19] (This is the famous battle that my infamous 7th great-grandfather, Anthony Hoskins, probably managed to avoid, as I speculated in Chapter 13.) Despite the fact that the Narragansetts had not declared that they would side with King Philip, Connecticut and Plimoth troops entered a frozen swamp to attack a Narragansett fort populated by about 1,000 people. The colonial troops set upon them with hate in their hearts, killing between 350 and 600 native men, women, and children in fierce hand-to-hand combat using knives and swords, guns, and torches. They burned the village to the ground.[20]

Capt. John Gallop Jr. died in the battle during a charge by his Stonington militia. The soldiers carried his body, with about 40 others killed, back to their army's field headquarters at Smith's Castle. They were buried in a mass grave, which is marked by a rough granite column and the plaques pictured below.

John Gallop Jr. probably expected to survive the Great Swamp Fight, for he left no will. He had amassed considerable property and cash to pass on. By court order after his death, his money was divided as follows: "to his widow, £100; to his oldest son John,

Plaques marking the mass grave, including John Gallop—men who died in the Great Swamp Fight, Sources: Chapter 16 notes[21, 22]

£137; to Benadam, £90; to William and Samuel, each £89; to his five daughters, £70 each." In addition, the General Court, in recognition of his services to the colony of Connecticut, made further land grants to his widow.[23] Trading with and fighting wars against Native Americans had clearly become a means of wealth-building for this family.

The third ancestor I found in the war was Henry Stevens. As noted above, he married Elizabeth (Gallop) Stevens, daughter of John Gallop Jr.,[24] Although I didn't find details for his service, Henry Stevens received a land grant in Voluntown, Connecticut. Eventually, he became an extensive landowner, also acquiring lands in Stonington, North Stonington, and Plainfield, Connecticut.[25] Henry and Elizabeth both lived long lives and probably enjoyed their wealth—largely a bounty of war.

The fourth ancestor I found who fought in the war was Dr. Mathew Fuller's son, Lieutenant Samuel Fuller. He was born in England around 1630 and came with his father to New England in 1640. On March 26, 1676, he accompanied Captain Michael Pierce in a force of 63 Plimoth troops and 20 Wampanoag Christian Indians in pursuit of Narragansett warriors, who had attacked and burned several towns and attempted the same on Plimoth. Although Capt. Pierce's soldiers caught up with the Narragansetts, these clever warriors managed to ambush the militia near what is now Central Falls, Rhode Island. A battle raged for several hours before the outnumbered Plimoth troops were overpowered.

This encounter became known as, "Pierce's Fight"—one of the worst defeats for the colonial militia during the war. All but nine English soldiers were slain on the spot, including Capt. Pierce and about ten native allies. The Narragansetts lost only a handful of warriors. The nine surviving Puritan troops were taken prisoner, marched three miles north, scalped, and tortured to death. When the colonial militia found their remains several weeks later, they buried them on a rise of land in this swampy area. The site became known locally as the "Nine Men's Misery."[26] No record remains of the names of the nine men who were tortured to death, so it is not known whether Lt. Fuller died quickly in battle, or met the more gruesome end.

Fortunately for my family's history, Lt. Samuel Fuller's wife, Mary, had already given birth to another Samuel Fuller, born in Barnstable in August 1676. This Samuel Jr. was the father of Ruth (Fuller) Robinson, the key person who connected my genes to Edward Fuller of the *Mayflower* and also to Rev. Thomas Thacher (Table 8).

Unfortunately for Narragansett history, the tables had turned on them and most other Indian tribes of New England. King Philip's War resulted in the eradication of their political power

Plaque commemorating "Pierce's Fight," Rhode Island[27]

and cultural autonomy throughout the region. After King Philip was killed on August 12, 1676, the Pilgrims cut off his head and stuck it on a pike for display to all in Plimoth Colony.[28] There it remained for many years, a symbol of the disintegration of Native American civilization and the relationship between the colonists and the remaining Indigenous People.

Like the Gallop family and Henry Stevens, the father of Lt. Samuel Fuller, Dr. Matthew Fuller, survived the war, continuing to practice medicine in Barnstable. He acquired land and died a wealthy man in 1678. Among the items listed in his will were the following: "Pearls, precious stones and diamonds, at a guess, £200."[29]

The acquisition of wealth and Native American lands through war and shady deals became the major means for expansion of the New England colonies. The natives believed most land and water to be a gift to all, or at the very least to those in their tribe, and a blessing that should be used with reverence and protected. They had various customs of demarcating their land for different purposes, such as cultivation and hunting, but the English found it relatively easy to swindle them out of it, especially if they could not read. At first, many Native Americans couldn't understand the English concept of land ownership, and the colonists were sometimes surprised to find Native Americans returning to graze their animals, hunt, and fish on land that they had recently purchased from them.

To begin with, the Puritans justified their colonization of Indian lands through claims of their humanity and good treatment of Indigenous People, compared to the Spanish in Central America. Besides, by their perception, the Indians did not make proper use of the land, according to English standards, and therefore had no exclusive right to it. Roger Williams disagreed with this. He believed the colonists had no right to take Indian lands without their full understanding and agreement. He saw Native Americans as equal to the English in every way, as written in his book, mentioned above, *A Key Into the Language of America*, a blend of vocabulary, instruction, and untitled poems on native languages and cultures:

> Boast not proud English, of thy birth & blood,
> Thy brother Indian is by birth as Good.
> Of one blood God made Him, and Thee & All,
> As wise, as faire, as strong, as personall.
> By natures wrath's his portion, thine no more
> Till grace his soule and thine in Christ restore.
> Make sure thy second birth, else thou shalt see,
> Heaven ope to Indians wild, but shut to thee.[30]

While delving more deeply into this early period of our colonial history, I came across a passage that brought home to me, in a personal way, that it had been more than the colonists' hunger for land that drove them into these wars, and more than land that enriched them:

> In the autumn of 1675, Plimoth forces under Captains John Gorham and Matthew Fuller had moved into Narragansett Bay area in pursuit of Wampanoags and Pocassets who had fled to the Narragansetts. Both men would participate in the Swamp Battle in December. En route, however, they took captives for profit[31]....These men "kidnapped 'Jack an Indian & his Squa & papoose' from the estate of William Paine" and other natives working for settlers on agreements or bonds

that also gave them protection from enslavement or capture. After taking these people at gunpoint, Gorham and Fuller then put them on a ship bound for Fayal (Faial Island in the Azores, a Portuguese colony). The employers of these peaceful natives took court action against Gorham and Fuller for selling them into slavery, but their lawsuit was unsuccessful. "Gorham died of fever soon after the Swamp Battle, but Fuller continued to serve and win honors and position."[32]

Unless there were two Captain Mathew Fullers in the colonial militia at the time (an unlikelihood), my ancestor, Dr. Mathew Fuller, took part in the growing and lucrative Atlantic trade that involved shipping captured Indians, along with other commodities, to the Azores, Bermuda, Jamaica, and Providence Island, in exchange for African slaves, supplies of rum, and other cherished products. This is spelled out in succinct terms by Margaret Ellen Sewell in her book, *Brethren By Nature: New England Indians, Colonists, and Origins of Slavery in America.*

When I read her thorough work, cited above and below, I realized I could no longer take solace that my known American ancestors had not been involved in the slave trade. I had previously understood it to be only a feature of the history of America's southern colonies.

Even before the English settled in New England, sailors and adventurers had captured coastal Indians to sell in the growing international slave market.[33] After the Pequot War ended in 1638, Massachusetts Bay officials sent a shipload of Pequot captives to the Puritan settlement of Providence Island off the coast of Central America. Thus, began a slave trade that helped to pay for that war and created vacant lands for the English to claim.[34]

The English colonists sought more than land and monetary enrichment by selling people into slavery. They also had a growing labor shortage. Indentured household servants and laborers made up a good percentage of the immigrants who came to New England and, as their terms of service ran out, the colonist needed new indentured or slave labor to feed their expanding economy. Enslaving or indenturing captured Native Americans in wartime offered a major solution.[35]

Roger Williams claimed Native Americans were "our brethren by nature"—members of the same "miserable drove of Adam's degenerate seed" as the English, with the same potential to be subjects and citizens.[36] But such sentiments of equality did not take hold in most of New England. Rather, the Governor of Massachusetts Colony, John Winthrop, portrayed Indians as cultural inferiors with words such as "savage," "pagan," and "devil-worshipper."[37]

Such opinions later gave justification for the forced labor of male captives in ironworks, fisheries, animal husbandry, agriculture, and other enterprises.[38] Female native captives were sometimes placed in households to ease the burden of English housewives during pregnancies and child rearing, and their presence brought new foods, materials, methods, and technologies to them, resulting in the evolution of a hybrid English-Indian culture in foods and their preparation. But sometimes their presence resulted in sexual abuse by white men.[39] Living in English households also brought obvious benefits to Native Americans (language skills, literacy in some cases, knowledge of animal husbandry, and commercial trade), but it cut them off from their kin and changed traditional gender roles.[40] Unlike the English, in their own villages Native American women usually had the responsibility of growing food crops, harvesting, and managing the land.[41]

During King Philip's War and later conflicts, many English were also captured and held by Native Americans when they raided and burned towns and farms. Just as the Indigenous People had different concepts of land ownership from that of the English, they had quite different traditions concerning treatment of captured members of the enemy. In their own tribal wars, unless captives were seen as incorrigible (in which case they would usually be brutally tortured and executed), they were treated as valuable assets for the enrichment and replenishment of their own tribe. Young men could become fine warriors, hunters, and fishermen. Women were much sought after, not only for procreation, but for enriching tribal cultures—some of which were matrilineal.

As the orthodox Puritan religious tradition solidified in New England, Native Americans became more and more viewed with suspicion by opinion makers. To the Puritans, some Indians also appeared to have supernatural powers. Otherwise, how would they be able to influence some of the English captives to stay with them and adapt to Indian ways of living, rather than return home to their families, when given the choice?[42]

Probably some did not want to go home because, as it evolved, life under the Puritan regime in New England was almost devoid of joy, especially for women and children. An influential clergyman, author and scientist, Cotton Mather (1663-1728), practiced this rule: "rarely to let one of my children to come anear me . . . without some explicit contrivance and endeavor, to let fall some sentence or other, that shall carry a useful instruction with it."[43] The Puritans also believed in "original sin" at birth. As poet Anne Bradstreet (1612-72) wrote:

> Stained from birth with Adam's sinful fact,
> Thence I began to sin as soon as act:
> A perverse will, a love to what's forbid,
> A serpent's sting in pleasing face lay hid:
> A lying tongue as soon as it could speak,
> And fifth Commandment do daily break.[44]

The fifth commandment on obeying one's parents, no matter what they said or did, formed a solid cornerstone of Puritan culture. Likewise, obedience to a husband, regardless of how he mistreated his wife, was a set fixture. Some captive women and children who spent time with Native Americans experienced, for the first time, the real freedom and joy that life could hold. To illustrate this point, I have summarized below, *The Unredeemed Captive: A Family Story from Early America*, by John Demos.[45]

On February 29, 1704, Mohawk warriors, allied with the French in Canada, along with French-Canadians disguised as Mohawks, attacked, looted, and burned Deerfield, Massachusetts on the Connecticut River. They captured many people, including seven-year-old Eunice Williams, her siblings, as well as her Puritan preacher father, Reverend John Williams and his wife. The captors marched everyone north to Canada in the dead of winter. Mrs. Williams was killed by the Mohawks for falling behind and becoming a burden to the party. But Eunice and the other children were treated well, and even carried on the shoulders of strong Mohawk men.

After a long and cold trek through the wilderness, Eunice and the rest of the party reached Montreal, where they stayed for a year under the protection of French Catholic priests. Later, they were shifted to a place called "Kahnawake," a Mohawk longhouse settlement just across the St. Lawrence River from Montreal. The Puritans believed that Catholics were also agents of the devil on earth, so the surviving adult captives thought of this Mohawk papist village as a doubly satanic place.

Through negotiations, the Mohawks allowed many of the surviving adults, including Rev. Williams, to return to Massachusetts. But Eunice and many of her friends remained. They were adopted by Mohawk families, played with Mohawk children, and learned their language and customs, which included children taking part in conversations with adults. They were even given Mohawk children's names. Eventually, Eunice married a Mohawk diplomat, Arosen, and took on the new name "Kanenstenhawi," meaning "she brings in corn." Eunice also adopted a French first name, "Marguerite." She and Arosen had at least two known daughters. She lived a fulfilling life among the Mohawk, always pushing away pleas to return to Massachusetts in letters and personal representations from her family. The couple did pay a few awkward visits to see her family in Massachusetts during their later years, but she lived a long and happy life in New France, passing away at the age of 89.

After returning home to Albuquerque from my second journey to New England, I re-read *All the Wild and Holy: The Life of Eunice Williams, 1679-1785* by Gayle Lauradunn,[46] a New Mexico poet and author. Her evocative 83-page poem about Eunice's capture, march north, childhood, marriage, and adult life in New France, ends with these words:

> Father's voice comes back to me.
> His speech about subduing
> the wilderness. Did he not know
> he subdued the wilderness
> in me also?
> Ah, but I forget:
> that was the purpose.
>
> Among my people I breathe
> deep and spread my arms
> to embrace all the wild and holy.[47]

This poem feels historically authentic to me because of my connection to both the Puritans and to Canada. My American-born maternal grandmother Effie (Haskins) Neill, who lived with us after the death of my grandfather, Rev. John Addison Neill, was my most recent link to the Puritans. Thankfully, she, a Methodist, passed on no genetic Puritan propensity to "straight-jacket" children. She listened and respected everyone and seldom passed judgment. Likewise, my parents demonstrated similar child-rearing values.

I had comparable freedoms to those that Eunice Williams had in New France—to explore our rivers, forests, and hills, and to make friends with whomever I chose; although, like Eunice, I had been taught productive skills and given chores to perform, beginning at age four or five. Sure, I played the now frowned-upon game of cowboys and Indians with other boys, using cap-guns and homemade bows and arrows. In Western movies, I watched racist depictions of Indigenous People being subdued by armies of white men—a business which some of my Puritan ancestors began in New England. But I also understand now, that there was something "wild and holy" in my upbringing, which helped me escape any remaining social or genetic Puritan legacy, including the effects of their guns and their unforgiving and vengeful god I never knew.

# 17

# TO BE *or* NOT TO BE...
## *an* AMERICAN?

Cathedral at West Point United States Military Academy

DURING MY ROAD JOURNEYS FROM 2013 TO 2019, I clocked over 15,000 miles (about 24,000 km) searching for the guns and gods in my genes. I traveled to Ontario and 22 American states to find answers concerning what kind of people I came from. I took a much longer journey, time-wise, inspecting genealogical and other sources on the Internet and reading thousands of pages of reference books.

I believe that our parents' or caretakers' behavior and the social, economic, and physical environment in which we grow up, normally have a greater influence over who we become than the genes we inherit—although that may not hold for disadvantaged minorities in societies where inequalities are accentuated. At any rate, I didn't discover any "black sheep" in my ancestors, except perhaps, Anthony Hoskins, my rowdy 7th great-grandfather in Connecticut. All the others could be classified as "moderates" for the time and place they lived. I mean that in terms of both guns and warfare, as well as, gods—their religiosity.

I had discovered a huge gap in "men of the cloth"—217 years to be precise—between the death of my 8th great-grandfather, Rev. Thomas Thacher, in 1678, (Chapter 14) and the ordination of my maternal grandfather, Rev. John Addison Neill, in 1895 (Chapter 5). Throughout that long period, my other ancestors' records of religiosity are almost silent. The McKees did a little lay-preaching in the 1800s in Ontario, but I have not come across any evidence that they were radical, Bible-thumping fundamentalists. From what I have discovered, my early American ancestors were not attracted by the dictates of extreme orthodox religious leadership. The majority left the early Puritan Church that eventually became the Congregational Church, which, in turn, split and merged, creating various conservative to more liberal groupings. Many of my ancestors evolved into moderate Methodists in America, and remained Presbyterians and Methodists in Canada, where the Methodists, Congregationalists, and three-quarters of the Presbyterians formed the United Church of Canada in 1925, a very liberal institution today.

My own opinion is that, although my ancestors claimed faith in Jesus Christ, many attended church more for baptisms, weddings, funerals, social connections, and social work, rather than to listen to fiery sermons on damnation and salvation. But this conclusion is only speculation, based on the information I found.

Concerning guns, at least those used against other human beings, I discovered four ancestors who willingly fought the Indigenous People of North America, and two of those—Lt. Samuel Fuller and Capt. John Gallop—got their comeuppance. To put it simplistically, they met their deaths in battles against people whose land they were involved in stealing. Later ancestors fought in the French and Indian War, the American Revolution, and the Civil War. But even among these men, I discovered no professional soldiers regularly employed to raise arms against other human beings. Rather, they appeared to fulfill their duty, suffer wounds in some cases, and thank God when they returned home to their families. I'm sure that most of them owned guns for hunting—supplementing their diets with needed protein, there for the taking.

Having completed my search, I decided that I had inherited a lot of characteristics from my maternal grandfather, Rev. John Addison Neill. I believe my attitude towards firearms and blood sports to be about the same as his had been, and our life stories had many parallels, although I don't practice any particular faith. During my travels and sojourns around the world, I have seen the good and bad of many religions and found none that suited my personal universalist philosophy.

Like my grandfather, who left the family farm in Ontario to become a preacher in Wisconsin, I left my birthplace and my family's business. I first journeyed to a far more distant and alien land, Borneo, as a volunteer teacher, and then began a career as an international filmmaker and multimedia producer, always working for social and economic improvements and international understanding. Like my grandfather, I married an American woman, and Elizabeth and I have moved many times during my career—about half the number of moves my grandparents made, but our transfers were much more dramatic—to Malaysia, Bangladesh, Kenya, Uganda, and Russia, and then to the United States.

During my lifetime, there have been no great wars requiring or requesting my involvement—none like my Neill uncles experienced in the First and Second World Wars. As a Canadian, I never had to deal with the draft during the Vietnam War, for Canada stayed out of that mess, although 30,000 Canadians volunteered to join US forces, while 30,000 Americans headed to Canada to avoid the draft—an exchange that went in Canada's favor, I believe. I'm not a pacifist but have always wondered what I would have done if there had been an obligatory call to arms during my youth.

While in western Massachusetts, I visited the Springfield Armory National Historic Site. This museum contains a large part of the record of America's long love affair with guns. I walked through the comprehensive displays, making notes, taking photos, and listening to enthusiastic staff as they demonstrated the loading of old muskets.

Gunsmiths in New England began to make rudimentary firearms as early as the 1630s, and it remained a craft or cottage industry until the mid-1700s, when a plethora of new models began to flood the market, as thousands of Americans headed westward into the virgin frontier. The Springfield Armory, a Government-owned facility, was commissioned by George Washington in 1777 as an arsenal for army weapons, but it soon became a production factory. During the Civil War, my 3rd great-grandfather, Abel Robinson, and my 4th great-grandfather, Joseph Stevens, probably were issued rifles from this place for participation in the American Revolution. My great-grandfather, Lafayette Haskins, may have carried a powerful .58 caliber Springfield Model 1855 or 1861 rifle manufactured in the armory.

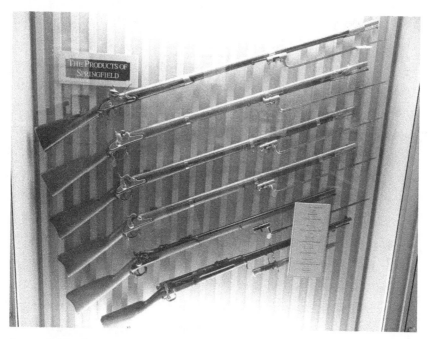

Springfield rifles on display at Springfield Armory

I knelt down to stare at these weapons through the glass, thinking of how their conical-shaped spinning bullets could easily decapitate a person if they directly hit the neck. I recalled the large holes I had put through the flesh of those two deer with my father's old Lee-Enfield .303 when I was a kid, as described in the opening pages of this book.

As I walked through the displays, I read how new machine manufacturing methods brought about a huge increase in output—from about 9,500 rifles in 1860 to 275,000 in 1864, largely due to demand during the Civil War. The Springfield Armory and private companies, like Colt Firearms of Connecticut, helped to spark the 20th century's assembly line production, with innovations such as interchangeable parts and hourly wages for workers. The armory designed new weapons throughout the late-1800s and the first half of the 1990s, the last one being the M-14, the precursor to the problematic M-16 used by American soldiers in the jungles of Vietnam.

The businessman, Robert McNamara, took over as Secretary of Defense and began ramping up the production of weapons for the Vietnam War. In 1968, he ordered the US Government to close Springfield Armory and turn over all military weapon manufacturing to the private sector, a trend that had started some years before. After all, wouldn't the private sector be a much more creative and cheaper option for the US Government's endless wars? Unit costs would surely go down, especially if new models of semi-automatic assault rifles, like the Colt AR-15, could be made widely available to just about anyone who wanted them—hunters, militia groups, target practice clubs, gun collectors, and misguided loners. And that brings us full circle to the ending of the first chapter of this book—Omar Mateen, who in June 2016 used his semi-automatic assault rifle and handgun to kill 49 people and injure 53 more at a gay nightclub in Orlando, Florida.

In the months and years since that attack, mass shootings, defined by the FBI as a single incident in which four or more people are killed and/or injured, have continued unabated in a plethora of American venues: on streets and highways, in train stations, car washes, restaurants and bars, hotels, cinemas, shopping centers, stores, pharmacies, gas stations, community festivals, municipal and other office buildings, schools and universities, parks, churches and synagogues, factories, homes, hospitals, nursing homes, veterans' homes, social clubs, nightclubs, strip clubs, libraries, sports events, airports, courthouses, and even on military bases. The number and variety of locations is mind-boggling. In 2019 alone, there were 435 incidents with a total of 517 killed and 1,748 injured.[1] In 2020, to date, the number of incidents has increased by 25 percent.

In recent years, mass shootings have been increasing in

Canada as well,[2] mainly perpetuated by lone wolf, misguided, and alienated men, as in the US, although the number of these incidents per year (only one in 2018, none in 2019, and one in 2020, to date) contrasts sharply with the number in the US. Furthermore, in America, the mass shooting statistics only account for a fraction of deaths due to gun violence each year—almost 40,000 in 2017—including criminal activity, police shootings, accidents, and suicides.[3] That's 12.21 deaths per 100,000 people each year in the US, as compared to 2.05 in Canada.[4] The number of guns per 100 people is estimated to be 120.5 in the US compared to 34.7 in Canada.[5] In the US, 30 percent of adults report that they personally own a gun, and an additional 11 percent say they live with someone who does.[6] In Canada, an estimated 26 percent of households have guns,[7] but Canada has strong gun control measures. The mass shooting of 22 people in Nova Scotia in April 2020, led to the banning of all assault-style firearms.[8]

The majority of Americans, including gun owners, support a variety of gun control laws, similar to many in Canada.[9] But at the time of writing, no great changes have been made to US national gun laws since "the individual's right to bear arms" side won the US Supreme Court case of 2008 on the Second Amendment to the US Constitution. Politics remains polarized and the carnage continues. In this regard, America, a relatively young country, is behaving like a grumpy old man, when it has so much more potential in the modern world.

Unlike my grandfather Neill, who took his American-born wife and children from the "gun-happy" American West, back to the relative safety of Canada in 1907, my wife Elizabeth, an American-Canadian dual citizen, and I had decided to finally settle in New Mexico in 2015. We now live only a short drive away from her brothers and family in Las Cruces, and an easy flight to see our daughter, living in Los Angeles with her American-born husband and children. (Unfortunately, we cannot be so near our son in Montreal, but remote connectivity is easy these days and we provide a sunnier climate and intriguing landscape for him on his visits, while he provides a stimulating urban setting for ours.)

Having traced and verified my American roots, I could certainly claim to be a true American. I joined the Mayflower Society to prove it, as well as to gain easier access to the information I sought. It worked on several occasions. But after returning to New Mexico from my last research trip, I began to consider, again, the decision on whether or not I should apply for US Citizenship and become a "dual citizen" instead of remaining only a US Green Card holder, a permanent resident. In addition to the right to vote, I thought that such a move might give me more of a voice in the fight for changes in gun laws and other anachronistic elements of the US Constitution. As I thought more about it, the whole issue on becoming a US citizen, or not, became a difficult internal pro-con debate for me.

The US Department of State's website declares that "Dual nationals owe allegiance to both the United States and the foreign country. They are required to obey the laws of both countries, and either country has the right to enforce its laws."[10] That sounds okay. So why so much angst over the decision? Well, on the con side, it's because I need to tell a lie to become an American citizen, if I wish to retain my Canadian citizenship as well. The oath of allegiance today is similar to that which Benedict Arnold had to swear during the American Revolution (Chapter 10). Below, I have underlined some of the troublesome wording for me:

"<u>I hereby declare, on oath, that I absolutely and entirely renounce and abjure all allegiance and fidelity to any foreign prince, potentate, state, or sovereignty, of whom or which I have heretofore been a subject or citizen</u>; that I will support and defend the Constitution and laws of the United States of America against all enemies, foreign and domestic; that I will bear true faith and allegiance to the same; that <u>I will bear arms on behalf of the United States</u> when required by the law; that I will <u>perform noncombatant service in the Armed Forces of the United States</u> when required by the law; that I will perform work of national importance under civilian direction when required by the law; and that I take this obligation freely, without any mental reservation or purpose of evasion; <u>so help me God</u>."[11]

American friends tell me that if I do decide to take the American oath and become a citizen, it will be in a crowd of people being sworn in, and I can avoid speaking the parts about no other allegiance, bearing arms, and God. "Just move your lips," they say. But I take oaths seriously. The greatest hero of all my reading and research for this book was Roger Williams, the clergyman who founded Rhode Island and Providence Plantations. He forbade civil oaths in his new colony, especially any involving mention of God.[12] In his relentless efforts to separate church and state, he once observed, "The truth is the great Gods of this world are God-belly, God-wealth, God-honour, God-pleasure, etc.[13]

With some difficulty, the US citizenship oath can be modified slightly, on formal religious grounds, to omit the words "so help me God" and "bear arms." Of course, I'm too old to be involved in carrying a rifle now. But even noncombatant service in the Armed Forces of the United States is not something I could do. As an internationally experienced person, I am well aware of America's long list of mistakes and meddling around the world during my lifetime—attempted coups, successful coups, and endless wars. As a former UNICEF (United Nations) employee, I am also fully aware that the US is the only country in the world that has not signed or ratified at least 46 international treaties concerning human rights, the environment, health, and how this world can be run more harmoniously.[14] For me, this kind of exceptionalism is a barrier to feelings of true allegiance. I believe all nations should work together for the health of our planet and its inhabitants. I am essentially an internationalist and have been so for most of my life.

Because of a reinstated Canadian law, I voted during October 2019 in the Canadian Federal Election for the first time since I gave up Canadian residency 30 years ago. In truth, I much prefer the parliamentary system of government where there is a ceremonial head of state (not necessarily a monarch) and a *de facto* head of government, a Prime Minister. The PM and cabinet must all be well-grounded in law, policy, and historical precedents, as well as in current events, in order to endure a daily barrage of questions from the opposition in the House of Commons, all of which is done in full view of the public in the galleries and on television. This process constitutes, in my opinion, the best possible insurance against ignorant and tyrannical leadership.

In the Canadian system, deputy ministers and senior staff in each department of government are permanent civil servants who normally remain in place with changes of government, even if it means a change of ruling party. They may be moved around to different portfolios but are rarely fired. The American system of "to the victor goes the spoils"—political appointments in the top ranks of all departments—has always seemed to be wasteful and inefficient to me.

Furthermore, in contrast to the American citizenship oath, when a person becomes a new citizen of Canada s/he only has to say these words:

> I swear (or affirm) that I will be faithful and bear true allegiance to Her Majesty Queen Elizabeth the Second, Queen of Canada, Her Heirs and Successors, and that I will faithfully observe the laws of Canada, and fulfil my duties as a Canadian citizen.[15]

Some of my American friends and acquaintances laugh when I tell them that Queen Elizabeth II is still the Queen of Canada—the head of state represented by a Canadian Governor General. She also remains head of state of the UK and 14 other former colonies: Antigua and Barbuda, Australia, the Bahamas, Barbados, Belize, Grenada, Jamaica, New Zealand, Papua New Guinea, St. Kitts and Nevis, St. Lucia, St. Vincent and the Grenadines, Solomon Islands and Tuvalu. Elizabeth II is also the Head of the Commonwealth of Nations, a free association of 54 sovereign nations, including those mentioned above. Many Americans find all this pomp antiquated, while others follow it with fascination. But most leaders of Commonwealth countries just go along with the old saying, "If it ain't broke don't fix it." Besides, they like the technical cooperation and close association with other English-speaking countries—a remnant of the British Empire which seems to do no harm today, and may do plenty of good in bringing nations together.

In truth, I find the American oath of citizenship more antiquated, when compared to the simple Canadian oath. Furthermore, dual citizenship is recognized as a right under Canadian law, whereas it is not recognized under American law. The US Government will only recognize you as a US citizen once you become one. There's no exact provision for dual nationality in the US Constitution, in spite of the fact that many Members of Congress are dual citizens of the US and other countries, including Israel. This fact, one of the many ironies of American political life, probably makes most Americans simply shrug and say, "So what?"

However, some conservative American opinion leaders agree with what John Fonte wrote in the *National Review* on August 23, 2013: "The concept of dual allegiance—the idea that some Americans…have political allegiance to a foreign state as well as to the United States—is inconsistent with the moral foundation of American democracy. Our form of government is based on equality of citizenship, and dual-allegiance citizens are by definition civic bigamists."[16] Some of these voices are now calling for any new US immigration bill to clear up such ambiguity.

Mulling it over still more, I wondered if I should throw caution to the wind and view the US Oath of Allegiance as an antiquated and quirky part of the American landscape that lives on in modern times, just like the Second Amendment on the right to bear arms. As a man in my mid-70s, this citizenship oath surely would never be my problem. Any change in the US Constitution will not happen in my lifetime. So why not become an American citizen so I can vote?

On the pro-side of the debate in my head, I have always loved a "can do" spirit, rather than more cautious approaches to life. During my first job after university, as a Canadian CUSO volunteer teacher in Borneo, it was my American Peace Corps buddy and housemate, who had lent me his 16mm movie camera and books on cinematography, saying, "Of course you can use it to make a film for CUSO. Why not?" This generosity got me started in my career.

Although I had little experience and no credentials, two "can do" British immigrants to Canada started me on my filmmaking career in CUSO and Canada's International Development Research Centre (IDRC) in the early 1970s. Their own early careers also benefitted by taking chances and venturing to far-flung corners of the world.

Next, two former American Peace Corps volunteers became my principal "can do" professors and mentors during my paid sabbatical from IDRC at Florida State University. They met me at the airport in Tallahassee at the end of a filming trip to Costa Rica, and persuaded me that I could complete a Master's in Communication in a year, if that's all the time I had and really applied myself. (The Canadian universities to which I had applied told me that my time frame was impossible. I would need two years, which I could not afford.)

As my career advanced to UNICEF Bangladesh, UNICEF in Eastern and Southern Africa, Johns Hopkins University in Baltimore and Moscow, Russia, and the Academy for Educational Development cum FHI360 in Washington, DC, it was mainly "can do" Americans who supported my multimedia innovations, and allowed me to take time to write work-related books and articles. But maybe I was just lucky in my career to have met so many facilitating Americans. I'm fully aware that common American culture is one of individualistic competition, which often detracts from collegial decision making—probably more a feature of Canada.

At any rate, by the end of 2012, I had worked for US organizations for 12 years, paid and continue to pay US taxes, and now benefit from US Social Security. As a permanent resident in the United States, I'm defined as a "US person," and can legally support candidates in US elections and whatever movements I want to be involved in for political and social change, including reasonable gun control, racial justice, equitable and affordable healthcare, as well as other social and economic rights for all, while reducing the crippling polarization in US society. I "can do" political and social good. I just can't vote.

Because of my strong and positive connection to many Americans, and my newly discovered, long-standing American heritage, the pro-con debate on becoming a dual citizen continues in my head for months. Then one morning in January 2020, while in the process of finishing this book, I wake up in Albuquerque thinking, *I really should make a decision on becoming an American citizen.* I go out for my usual walk up and down Nob Hill, on which our house is situated, exercising my legs, arms, and heart, while keeping an eye on the changing colors of the Sandia Mountains to the northeast, rising a mile above the Rio Grande Valley. In the morning, these mountains appear a hazy blue, and turn brown-green by midday. Then usually right before sunset, they transform to watermelon pink—the inspiration and meaning of their original Spanish name, *las montañas de la Sandía.*

As I trudge along, I think of the historic land I've moved to and long-ago conflicts among the original inhabitants: the many tribes and linguistic groups of the Pueblo, probably the oldest surviving human culture in North America; the Navajo and the Apache—Athabaskans who migrated from the north about 1,300 years ago. Then, in the mid-1500s, Spanish settlers arriving after the explorer, Francisco Vásquez de Coronado, with muskets, cannons, and Catholic priests; followed by Latinos, a few French-Canadians, English-speaking white Americans—so-called "Anglos"—some African-Americans, and more recently immigrants from just about everywhere.

Sandia Mountains a few minutes before sunset

I'm presently reading about all this: How the Anglos, who brought New Mexico a plethora of protestant churches, fought the Navajo and Apache in devasting wars. In the late 1800s, they also created or attracted many characters of America's gunslinging past—Billy the Kid, Pat Garret, Doc Holliday, Kit Carson, Jesse James, Bob Ford, Wyatt Earp, the Durango Kid, and Wild Bill Hickok—even Annie Oakley and Calamity Jane. These outlaws, killers, frontiersmen, freelance lawmen, sharp shooters, and bounty hunters, who sparked my childhood fascination with guns in the many movies and television shows I watched, had all been here. When I drive through the deserts, grasslands, and scrub forests of my new homeland, I can easily imagine them riding the range beside me.

As I head down the long hill toward our pueblo-style home with its stucco painted in an earthy-red color, the big blue open sky of New Mexico reminds me that there is much more to discover and write about in the final years of my life. While completing this second travel memoir, I reflect on how the stories of the lives and times of my American ancestors have taken up the majority of pages written, and on how my perspective on history and politics has broadened. My own life has become richer—but the process hasn't convinced me to become an American citizen.

Returning to my study, I see that an email has arrived, which propels me to a final decision. On my trip to Ontario last summer, I applied for a memorial plot in the Glen Allan Cemetery, described in the opening pages of this book. I read the email with great anticipation. The answer is positive. I sit back in my chair and think of all my travels with my ancestors through time and space. The writer in me approves of this ending. I like my new identity as the former globe-trotting Canadian man who has become a creative writer in the American Southwest—no need to be a US citizen. And when my life story ends, my ashes will rest with my Canadian ancestors, whose memory I have also helped to preserve, in the verdant Conestoga River Valley where I explored, hunted, fished, and swam as a child—another set of stories I must tell.

# TABLE 1
## McKee Family Tree in Canada
*Author's direct ancestors

**1st Generation: Thomas McKee\* b. ca. 1777-1867**
He came to Canada from Scotland ca. 1843; spouse: unknown

**2nd Generation: Children of Thomas McKee:**
1. **\*William McKee 1815-82** He came from Scotland in 1844; married ca. 1845 **\*Margaret Fleming 1829-1903**
2. Mary ca. 1821-88; sister Mary possibly came to Canada with William and husband, Thomas Wilson.

**3rd Generation: Children of William and Margaret McKee:**
1. Margaret (Mrs. R. King) 1846-97
2. **\*John** 1848-1929; married ca. 1874 **\*Mary Jane Doren** 1854-1932
3. Barbara (Mrs. T. Faulkner) 1849-1911
4. Thomas 1851-1926
5. Elizabeth 1853-70
6. James 1854-1918
7. Mary 1857-77
8. William 1859-76
9. Archibald 1860-1911
10. Alexander 1862-1915
11. David 1865-1938

**4th Generation—Children of John McKee and Mary Jane McKee:**
1. Harvey William 1878-1931
2. Frances May 1883-after 1949
3. Archibald James 1885-1951
4. **\*Alexander Ross** 1887-1933; married in 1913 **\*Mary Blanche Humphries** 1890-1979
5. Thomas John 1890-ca.1955
6. Margaret Amelia 1890-1968
7. Percy Austin 1893-1952
8. Jessie Mary 1895-1967

**5th Generation—Children of Alexander and Mary Blanche McKee:**
1. Doreen Margaret 1914-56
2. James Alexander 1916-95
3. **\*Russell Cadwell** 1920-2007; married in 1941 **\*Alma Katherine Neill** 1920-2015
4. Gerald Humphries 1920-2009
5. John Fleming 1921-2018
6. Lillian Blanche 1923-2017
7. Wellington Roy (Bud) 1925-2002
8. Archie Maxwell 1927-2009
9. David Adam 1929-2006

Sources: Family Records and Canadian Censuses, Birth, Marriage, and Death Records, 1841–2018

## TABLE 2

## Excerpt from the Final Will of William McKee

Executed on 16<sup>th</sup> of April 1883. *We the undersigned have this day made an inventory of Estate real and personal of the late William McKee Esq. of lot No. 14 west half in the third concession of the Township of Maryborough, March 14, 1883.* (Author's note: Original spelling retained.)

| Farm consisting of 100 acres | $5,000.00 | $5,000.00 |
|---|---|---|
| **Stock:** | | |
| 1 Pair of mares | 100.00 | |
| 7 Cows at $20.00 each | 140.00 | |
| 1 Bull | 10.00 | |
| 4 two year olds at $10.00 each | 40.00 | |
| 7 year olds at $8.00 each | 56.00 | |
| 16 Sheep at $4.00 each | 64.00 | |
| 7 Lambs at $3.00 each | 24.50 | |
| 1 Sow | 14.00 | |
| 1 Sow | 15.00 | |
| 1 Boar | 10.00 | $473.50 |
| **Implements:** | | |
| 1 Carriage | 70.00 | |
| 1 Reeper | 20.00 | |
| 1 Seed drill | 15.00 | |
| 1 Mower | 20.00 | |
| 1 Buggy | 5.00 | |
| 1 Turnip Scuffler | 5.00 | |
| 1 Waggon | 30.00 | |
| 1 Sleigh | 4.00 | |
| 2 Ploughs at $4.00 each | 8.00 | |
| 1 Gang plough | 4.00 | |
| 1 Pair iron harrows | 8.00 | |
| 1 Farming mill | 2.00 | |
| 1 Set double harness | 5.00 | |
| 1 Horse rake | 2.00 | |
| 1 Straw cutter | 2.00 | |
| 1 Horse porver | 5.00 | 205.00 |
| **Hay and grain** | | |
| 6 tons of hay at $7.00 per ton | 42.00 | |
| 30 bushels of peas at .70c per bush | 21.00 | |
| 20 bushels of wheat .90c per bush | 18.00 | |
| 200 bushels of oats at .30c per bush | 60.00 | |
| 10 bushels barley at .50c per bush | 5.00 | 146.00 |
| **Household furniture** | 20.00 | 20.00 |
| | **$5,844.50** | **$5,844.50** |

*Signed: Robert Hay & John Fleming, Maryborough, March 14<sup>th</sup>, 1883*

Source: Chapter 2 note 7

# TABLE 3
## John and Ellen Neill Family Tree in North America
*Author's direct ancestors

**1st Generation: *Ellen (Stott) Neill (1803-74), widow of *John Neill** (dates unknown) whom she married in Tandragee, County Armagh, Ulster ca. 1832. After John died, Ellen immigrated to Canada in 1860.

---

**2nd Generation: Children of John Neill and Ellen (Stott) Neill:**
1. Elizabeth 1836-1904
2. Jeremiah 1839-55, died in Ireland
3. James 1840-1908
4. ***William 1842-1909; married in 1869 *Eleanor Bruce** 1833-85
5. Jacob ca.1841-91
6. Joseph 1847-95

---

**3rd Generation: Children of William and Eleanor Neill:**
1. ***John Addison** 1870-1948; married in 1895
   ***Effie Jane Haskins** 1876-1966
2. Mary Eleanor 1874-after 1948

---

**4th Generation: Children of John Addison and Effie Jane Neill**
1. Millard Lincoln (1896-1994)
2. Leigh Vincent (1898-1963)
3. Eleanor (1902-18)
4. Ralph Leroy (1905-92)
5. Merrill Adrian (1906-67)
6. Addison Bruce (1908-49)
7. Mae Edythe (1907-94) adopted
8. Gerald William (1909-55)
9. Elsie Muriel (1914-2005)
10. John Wesley (1916-99)
11. ***Alma Katherine** 1920-2015, married
    ***Russell Cadwell McKee** 1920-2007

---

Sources: Family Records and Canadian Censuses, Birth, Marriage, and Death Records, 1841–2015

# TABLE 4
## Neill McKee's Haskins Ancestry, Part 1: 1735-1966
*Author's direct ancestors

**\*Micah Nathan Haskins Sr. (a.k.a., Hoskins)**
b. May 10, 1735, Harwinton, Litchfield, CT; d. before June 1820, Alfred, Allegany, NY
**\* Abigail Jewell**, married ca. 1760, CT
b. Mar 27, 1739, Plainfield, Windham, CT; d. before 1818, Almond/Alfred, Allegany, NY
Children: Dorcas, Roswell, **\*Nathaniel**, Micah Jr., Daniel, David, Eunice, Dorcas

---

**\*Nathaniel Haskins**
b. ca. 1768-1774, Salisbury, Litchfield, CT; d. May 15, 1805, Brookfield, Madison, NY
**\*Lydia Stevens**, married ca. 1800
b. Aug 27, 1778, Stillwater, Saratoga, NY; d. July 26, 1853, Almond, Allegany, NY
She married second, Enos Seward, and was buried with him in Merwin Cemetery, Almond, NY. *See Table 5.*
Children of Nathaniel and Lydia: Eri, **\*David**

---

**\*David Haskins**
b. ca. 1803, possibly Madison, NY; d. 1873, Jackson, Adams, WI
**\*Clarfira Robinson,** married ca. 1829, probably in Allegany, NY
b. ca. 1806, Pawlet, Rutland, VT; d. May 1867, Jackson, Adams, WI
Children: Rhoda, Bertha, Marcia, James, Nathaniel, Enos Seward, Martin Henry, Charles Wesley, **\*Lafayette**

---

**\*Lafayette Haskins**
b. Feb 10, 1844, Almond, Allegany, NY; d. May 19, 1925, King, Waupaca, WI
**\*Sarah Alma Catherine Thomas**, married July 26, 1868, Jackson, Adams, WI
b. March 29, 1847, Waterford, IN; d. Aug 21, 1931, Clintonville, Waupaca, WI
Children: Willis Adrian, Eli Thomas, Vernon Edward, **\*Effie (or Effa) Jane**, Harvey James, Ralph, Catherine Alma (a.k.a., Kittie)

---

**\*Effie (or Effa) Jane Haskins**
b. Feb 23, 1876, Cadott, Chippewa, WI; d. May 7, 1966, Kitchener, ON
**\*John Addison Neill**, married March 6, 1895, Cadott, WI
*See Table 3 for more details.*

---

Sources: Family Records and U.S. Censuses, Birth, Marriage, and Death Records, 1735–1966, relevant ones confirmed by New England Historic Genealogical Society researchers and the General Society of Mayflower Descendants, Neill McKee. Membership no. 94515.

# TABLE 5
## Neill McKee's Stevens Ancestors in North America
*Author's direct ancestors

**\*Nicholas Stephens/Stevens**
b. 1620, Gloustershire, England; d. Sept 27, 1670 unknown
**\*Elizabeth Starkey**, married in ca. 1641
b. ca. 1614, Gloustershire, England, d. unknown
Children: **\*Henry**, Nicholas Jr., possibly Thomas

---

**\*Henry Stephens/Stevens**
b. ca. 1644, Gloustershire, England; d. Aug 9, 1726, Stonington, CT
**\*Elizabeth Gallop** marriage date unknown (daughter of Capt. John Gallop Jr.)
b. March 8, 1662, Stonington, CT; d. ca. 1726, Washington Co., RI
Children: **\*Thomas**, Richard, Henry Jr., Elizabeth, Lucia/Lucy

---

**\*Thomas Stevens**
b. Dec. 14, 1678, Stonington, CT; d. Sept. 7, 1750, Canaan, CT
**\*Mary Hall**, married in 1702
b. June 1, 1677, Concord, Litchfield, CT; d. May 30, 1719, Plainfield, Windham, CT
Children: Thomas Jr., Phineas, Uriah, Andrew, Benjamin, **\*Samuel**, Zebulon

---

**\*Samuel Stevens**
b. March 6, 1714/15, Plainfield, CT; d. Sept 1754, possibly Stockbridge, MA
**\*Anna Segar**, married in 1740
b. 1718, Sheffield, Berkshire, MA; d. unknown
Children: Anna, Samuel Jr., Ruth, Silence, **\*Joseph**

---

**\*Joseph Stevens Sr.**
b. June 14, 1752, Sheffield, CT; d. 1830, Wheeler, Steuben, NY
**\*Naomi Mathews**, married ca. 1770
b. ca. 1754, Stillwater, Saratoga, NY; d. 1778, Stillwater, Saratoga, NY
Children: Joseph Jr., John, Rhoda, **\*Lydia**

Second spouse: Desire Waterhouse
b. 1757, Canaan, CT; d. 1804, Steuben, NY
Children: Noah, Elias, Naomi, Silence, Jesse, Isaac, Sarah, Ann, Chloe

---

**\*Lydia Stevens**
b. Aug 27, 1778, Stillwater, Saratoga, NY
d. July 26, 1853, Almond, Allegany, NY
**\*Nathaniel Haskins**, married ca. 1800
b. between 1768 and 1774, Salisbury, Litchfield, CT; d. May 15, 1805 Brookfield, Madison, NY
Children: Eri, **\*David** *See Table 4 for more details*

Second spouse: Enos Seward
b. Sept. 4, 1766, Hampden, MA; d. Aug 6, 1842, Almond, Allegany, NY
Children: Naomi, Amos, Enos, Joseph, Orin, Sarah

---

Sources: Chapter 11 notes 7, 8, 9.

# TABLE 6
## Neill McKee's Hoskins/Haskins Ancestry,
## Part 2, 1600-1760
*Author's direct ancestors

**John Hoskins (UNPROVEN ANCESTOR)**
b. About 1585, possibly Beaminster, Dorset, England; d. May 3-5, 1648, Windsor, Hartford, CT.
First spouse: unknown, died before 1630
Children: Thomas, John Jr. (possibly stayed in England)

Second spouse: **Ann Filer,** married May 6, 1630, Dorchester, MA
b. Between 1585 and 1610, Possibly in Cornwall, England
d. March 6, 1662, Windsor, Hartford, CT
Children: possibly ***Anthony**, Rebecca (Note: Ann may have had two daughters from her first marriage, but this is unresolved.)

---

***Anthony Hoskins I, (a.k.a., Anthony Sr.)**
b. About 1632, Dorchester, Suffolk, MA; d. January 4, 1707, Windsor, Hartford, CT
*** Isabel Browne**, married July 16, 1656, Windsor, Hartford, CT
b. June 9, 1636, Duxbury, Plymouth, MA; d. Oct 2, 1698, Windsor, Hartford, CT
Children: Isabel, John, Robert, *** Anthony II** [a.k.a, Anthony Jr.], Grace, Rebecca, Jane, Thomas, Joseph

Second spouse: Mary Griffin Wilson, Marriage: After 1698, d. January 1715, Windsor, CT
Children: Possibly one daughter, Mary

---

***Anthony Hoskins II (a.k.a., Anthony Jr.)**
b. March 19, 1664, Windsor, Hartford, CT; d. July 9, 1747, Windsor, Hartford, CT
*** Hannah Grimes (a.k.a., Hannah Graham)**; married ca. 1686 Windsor, Hartford, CT
b. Between 1664 and 1667, Wintonbury, CT; d. Dec 2, 1751, Windsor, Hartford, CT
Children: Anthony (died young), Noah (died young), Hannah, Mabel, *** Anthony III**, Zebulon, Amey, Dorcas, Alexander, Sarah, Jane, Joseph

---

***Anthony Hoskins III**
b. Jan 19, 1695, Windsor, Hartford, CT; d. ca. 1760, Harwinton, Litchfield, CT
**Mary Gillett**, married Dec 23, 1725, Windsor, Hartford, CT
b. July 9, 1705, Windsor, Hartford, CT; d. April 28, 1746, Harwinton, Litchfield, CT
Children: Noah, Asa, Anthony, *** Micah Nathan**, Daniel, Hannah, Benoni

Second spouse: Mary Burrell, Married Sept 29, 1748, Harwinton, CT, b. ca.1694; d. unknown

---

Source: Chapter 13 note 23.
Other sources: Family Records and U.S. Censuses, Birth, Marriage, and Death Records, 1632–1760. Confirmed by New England Historic Genealogical Society researchers and the General Society of Mayflower Descendants, Membership no. 94515.

# TABLE 7
## Summary of the Will of Anthony Hoskins I
*Author's direct ancestor

To his second wife Mary: £40** and "improvement of the north end of the house I purchased of Tahan Grant."

To his son John: £20**, "a double portion of his estate;" "my dwelling and barn and my homestead and orchard, about 10 acres;" "in the Meadow 5 acres;" "the rest of the sd. Parcel of land, being about 10 acres, which I purchased from Samuel Farnsworth;" and "17 acres of woodland on the north side of the riverlet at Rocky Hill, bought of Samuel Gardner of Salem."

To his son Robert: "All my land in Simsbury, the homelott, 4 acres, and 16 acres of meadow that I had of John Owen;" "10 acres of upland the Towne gave me;" and "My share of the commons."

To his son Thomas: "The homelott and orchard I bought of Simon Mills, about 7 acres, and 10 acres of upland in the woods;" and "in the Great Meadow 3 acres bought from Alexander Allyn, merchant, and all that he owes me."

**To his son \*Anthony: "All of the land I have at Greenfield, 10 acres of which I bought of Josiah Clarke and of Nathan Messenger I bought 10 acres more;" "The marsh at Wash Brooke which I purchased of Messenger;" and "the £12\*\* cash I paid for him to Stedman as attorney for Mrs. Wilson of Hartford."**

To his son Joseph: "The house and homestead I bought of Tahan Grant, excepting the north end of the house, which he is not to have during my wife's widow hood;" "My loft on the east side of the Great River, which I had of John Witchfield, being 30 rods in breadth and holding the same breadth for 3 miles."

To his daughter Grace Eglestone: £60** and "15 acres of land near Miles Hole."

To his daughter Jane Alford: £60** and "what I have already given her."

Source: Chapter 13 note 24
**English £1.00 in 1707 = US $2,209 in 2020, source: Chapter 13 note 25

## TABLE 8

### Robinson Family and related families in the author's New England Genealogy

| Robinson family | Fuller, Thacher, Partridge, and Conant families |
|---|---|
| **Rev. John Robinson** b. ca. 1576, England - d. March 1, 1625, Leiden, Holland. Pastor to the Plimoth Pilgrims who never came to America. **Bridget White**, spouse, b. ca. 1581, England; d. after Oct 28, 1643, probably Leiden, Holland | |
| **Isaac Robinson** b. Feb. 1610, Leiden, Holland; d. 1702-04, Barnstable, MA. Came to Plimoth Colony in 1631. **Margaret Hanford**, first spouse, b. 1619; d. 1649 **Mary** _____, second spouse, d. ca. 1664-69 | |
| **Lt. Peter Robinson Sr.** b. March 6, 1655-56, Barnstable or Falmouth, MA - d. between Feb 6 and April 15, 1740, Scotland, Windham, CT) Third child of Isaac and Mary **Mary Manter**, first spouse, b. 1665, Tisbury, Dukes, MA; d. before 1698, Palmerston, MA **Experience Manter**, second spouse, b. 1672, Tisbury, Dukes, MA; d. April 1727, Scotland, Windham, CT | |

*Table 8 continued*

| | |
|---|---|
| **Peter Robinson Jr.**<br>b. Dec 7, 1697, Tisbury, MA; d. March 22, 1785, Scotland, Windham, CT. Fourth child of Peter and Mary<br>**Spouse: Ruth Fuller**, married on June 30, 1725,<br>b. April 12, 1706, Mansfield, CT; d. Jan. 9, 1795, Scotland, Windham, CT | 1. Ascending through Ruth Fuller's father Samuel Fuller Jr., 1676-1716; to his father Lt. Samuel Fuller, ca. 1630-76; to his father Dr. Mathew Fuller ca.1603-78; to his father **Edward Fuller, ca. 1575-1621; passenger on the *Mayflower*** |
| | 2. Ascending through Ruth Fuller's mother Elizabeth Thacher, b. March 1, 1672, d. by 1730, Tolland, CT; to her father Rudolphus/Ralph Thacher, ca. 1647-1733; to his father **Rev. Thomas Thacher, b. May 1, 1620, England; d. Oct 15, 1678; First pastor of the Old South Boston Church** |
| | 3. Ascending through Ruth Fuller's mother Elizabeth Thacher, b. March 1, 1672, d. by 1730, to her mother, Ruth Partridge, 1645/47-1717; to her father, **George Partridge, ca. 1617-1695; Pioneer of Druxbury, MA** |
| | *Sources: See Chapter 14 notes 24, 25, 26, 27.* |
| **Samuel Robinson**<br>b. July 6, 1726, Scotland Windham, CT; d. June 11, 1792, Scotland, Windham, CT<br>**Spouse: Mary (or Sarah) Kimball**, married on Jan 2, 1748, b. ca. 1720, Ipswich, Essex, MA; d. Dec 15, 1791, Scotland, Windham, CT | Ascending through Mary Kimball's mother Sarah (Burley) Kimball, b. Oct 6, 1698, Ipswich, Essex, MA, d. July 30, 1788, Ipswich, Essex, MA; to her mother Mary (Conant) Burley, b. July 14, 1662, Beverly, Essex, MA, d. ca. 1743 probably Ipswich, Essex, MA; to her father Lot Conant, ca. b. 1624, Nantesket or Cape Ann, Norfolk, MA, d. Sept 29, 1674, Beverly, Essex, MA; to his father, **Roger Conant, baptized April 9, 1592, East Burleigh, Devon, England - d. Nov 19, 1679, Beverly, MA, Founder of Salem, MA** |
| | *Sources: See Chapter 14 notes 28, 29.* |

*Table 8 continued*

| | |
|---|---|
| **Abel Robinson**<br>b. Sept 15, 1761, Scotland, Windham, CT; d. ca. 1835, Alfred, Allegany, NY<br>*See Chapter 10*<br>**Rhoda (possibly Ormsby)**, first spouse, married possibly 1787. No confirmed dates available on birth or death.<br>**Eunice Woodward**, second spouse, married March 17, 1795, CT<br>b. ca. 1772; d. after 1850, WI | |
| **Clarfira Robinson**<br>b. ca. 1806, Pawlet, VT; d. 1867, Adams, WI<br>**David Haskins**, spouse<br>b. 1803; d. 1873, Adams, WI<br>*See Table 4*<br><br>*Robinson family sources: Chapter 14 notes 30, 31, 32, 33.* | |
| *All relevant records confirmed by New England Historic Genealogical Society researchers and the General Society of Mayflower Descendants; Neill McKee, Member no. 94515.* | |

# CHAPTER NOTES

## Chapter 1

1. "Glen Allan Union, Inventory CC#4355, Cemeteries of Wellington County, Township of Peel," (Wellington County Branch Ontario Genealogical Society, 1996), pp. 3, 8, 29.

2. Maryborough Township History Committee. *Through the Years: Maryborough Township, Vol. 2, 1851-1998,* (Hanover, ON: Skyway Printing, 2000), pp. 91-92.

3. "Barque Jane Duffus, from Glasgow, 2nd May to Quebec 16th June 1843." Montreal Gazette, June 19, 1843. Accessed October 20, 2013 at: http://www.theshipslist.com/ships/passengerlists/janeduffus1843.shtml

4. McKee, Raymond W. *The Book of McKee,* (Dublin, Ireland: Hodges Figgs & Co. Ltd., 1959), pp. 322-327.

5. Devine, T. M. *The Scottish Clearances: A History of the Dispossessed, 1600-1900,* (Penguin Books, UK, 2018), pp. 143-163.

6. Herman, Arthur. *How the Scots Invented the Modern World,* (New York, NY: MJF Books, 2001).

7. Maclean, Fitzroy. *A Concise History of Scotland,* (London, UK: Thames and Hudson, 1970), p. 15.

8. Herman, Arthur. *How the Scots Invented the Modern World,* pp. 337-339.

9. Moss, Michael. *The Glasgow Story: Industrial Revolution,* Accessed on September 20, 2017 at https://www.theglasgowstory.com/story/?id=TGSC0

10. Herman, Arthur. *How the Scots Invented the Modern World,* pp. 315-319.

11. Trevor-Roper, Hugh. *The Invention of Tradition: The Highland Tradition of Scotland,* Chapter 2 (pp. 15-41) of *The Invention of Tradition,* Eric Hobsbawm and Terence Ranger, eds. (Cambridge University Press,

1983). Accessed on October 21, 2013 at http://www.columbia.edu/itc/journalism/stille/Politics%20Fall%202007/readings%20weeks%206-7/Trevor-Roper,%20The%20Highland%20Tradition.pdf

12. Devine, T. M. *The Scottish Clearances: A History of the Dispossessed, 1600-1900*, p. 11.

13. Herman, Arthur. *How the Scots Invented the Modern World*, pp. 22-25.

14. "History of Firearms Control in Canada: Up to and Including the Firearms Act, November 9, 2004, Canadian Firearms Program, Government of Canada. Accessed on October 22, 2016 at https://web.archive.org/web/20110706182135/http://www.rcmp-grc.gc.ca/cfp-pcaf/pol-leg/pdf/histo_e.pdf

## Chapter 2

1.  Graham, Jean Lancaster. *Asphodel: A Tale of a Township*, (Peterborough, ON: RDS Maxwell Press for the Township of Asphodel, 1978), pp. 22-23.

2.  Ibid., p. 23.

3.  Rattenbury, Richard C. *A Legacy in Arms: American Firearm Manufacture, Design, and Artistry, 1800-1900*, (Norman, OK: University of Oklahoma Press, 2114), pp. 5-7.

4.  Warrick, Gary. "European infectious disease and depopulation of the Wendat-Tionontate (Huron-Petun)." *World Archaeology Vol. 35, No. 2, Archaeology of Epidemic and Infectious Disease*, Oct., 2003), pp. 258-275.

5.  Brown-Kubisch, Linda. *The Queen's Bush Settlement: Black Pioneers, 1839-1865*. (Toronto, ON: Natural Heritage Books, 2004).

6.  Prince, Bryan. *My Brother's Keeper: African Canadians and the American Civil War*, (Toronto, ON: Dundurn Press, 2015).

7.  William McKee, Deceased, Administration, Died September 8, 1882, Surrogate Court, County of Wellington, Ontario, 24th day of April, 1883. Accessed on microfiche at Wellington County Museum, ON.

## Chapter 3

1.  Cole, Jean Murray. *The Loon Calls: Rose Island* (Coe Hill, Hastings County, ON), p. 87.

2.  Ibid., p. 87.

3.  Ibid., pp. 87-88.

4.  Ibid., p. 87.

5.  Ibid., p. 87.


## Chapter 4

1.  Donoghue, Clayton N. *The Irish Empire: The Story of Niall of the Nine Hostages*, (Victoria, BC: Friesen Press, 2015).

2.  Hanks, Patrick; Hardcastle, Kate; Hodges, Flavia. *A Dictionary of First Names (2nd ed.)*, (Oxford, UK: Oxford University Press, 2006).

3.  Lingerfelt, Jim & Jenny Versteeg, eds. *The Lines of Howick: The History of Howick Township, 1856-1995, Vol. 1,* (Gorrie, ON: Howick Historical Society, 1996), p. 475.

4.  *Review of Textile Progress, Vol. 8.* (Manchester, UK: Textile Institute, 1956), p. 257.

5.  "History of Tandragee, Ballymore Parish, County Armagh, Ulster, Ireland." The Brown Family, Hamilton, ON. Accessed on October 25, 2013 at http://freepages.rootsweb.com/~rykbrown/genealogy/brown.htm#Tandragee,%20Ballymore%20Parish,%20County%20Armagh,%20Ulster,%20Ireland

6.  Moran, Heather. *The Canadian Army Medical Corps at Vimy Ridge,* in *Vimy Ridge: A Canadian Reassessment,* Hayes, Geoffrey; Iarocci, Andrew & Mike Bechthold, eds. (Waterloo, ON: Wilfrid Laurier University Press), p. 139.

7.  Christie, Norm. *For King & Empire: The Canadians at Amiens, August 1918.* (Ottawa, ON: CEF Books, 1999).

8.  "One Soldier's War: The War and Post War Memoirs of Major (Rtd.) by John W. Neill, PhD." Self-published with limited distribution in 1998.

9. Bothwell, Robert. *Your Country, My Country: A Unified History of the United States and Canada,* (New York: Oxford University Press, 2015), p. 121.

10. Donoghue, Clayton N. *The Irish Empire: The Story of Niall of the Nine Hostages.*


## Chapter 5

1. Timberlake Jr., Richard H. "Panic of 1893," in *Business Cycles and Depressions: An Encyclopedia,* Glasner, David & Thomas F. Cooley, eds. (New York: Garland Publishing), pp. 516–518.

2. Winkler, Adam. *Gun Fight: The Battle over the Right to Bear Arms in America,* (New York: W.W. Norton, 2013), p. 166.

3. Ibid., pp. 157-160.

4. Shillingberg, William B. *Dodge City: The Early Years, 1872-1886,* (Norman, OK: The Arthur H. Clark Company, an imprint of the University of Oklahoma Press, 2009).


## Chapter 6

1. Ubelaker, Douglas H. "Prehistoric New World population size: Historical review and current appraisal of North American estimates," *American Journal of Physical Anthropology, Vol. 45, No. 3,* Nov. 1976, pp. 661–65.

2. Dobyns, Henry. *Their Number Become Thinned: Native American Dynamics in Eastern North America,* (Knoxville, TN: University of Tennessee Press, 1983).

3. Toland, John. *Adolph Hitler: The Definitive Biography,* (New York: Anchor Books, A Division of Random House, 1992), p. 202.

4. Grant, Madison. *The Passing of the Great Race,* (New York: Charles Scribner's Sons, 1918).

5. Brown, Dee. *Bury My Heart at Wounded Knee: An Indian History of the American West,* (New York: Henry Holt and Company, Owl Book Edition, 1991), pp. 291-298.

6. Ibid., pp. 310-313.

7. Ibid.

8. "On the Nebraska Plains" by Viola Aday and Catherine Hicks, *The Village Missions Newsletter*, printed on the 50th Anniversary of the Extension Chapel, Whiteclay, NE, 1955.

9. "Dry for a year, Whiteclay has cleaned up. But some alcohol problems have moved elsewhere." by Paul Hammel, *Omaha World-Herald*, May 1, 2018. Accessed August 10, 2019 at https://www.omaha.com/news/nebraska/dry-for-a-year-whiteclay-has-cleaned-up-but-some/article_ccf057c7-d9f1-5661-aaad-23b8ccd15b74.html

## Chapter 7

1. "Black Hills & Badlands, South Dakota." Black Hills and Badlands Tourist Association, SD. Accessed on April 10, 2020 at https://www.blackhillsbadlands.com/lakota-sioux

2. Brown, Dee. *Bury My Heart at Wounded Knee: An Indian History of the American West,* pp. 38-65.

3. "Lakotas: Feared Fighters of the Plains," by Gregory Lalire, *Wild West* magazine, April 2001. Accessed on September 19, 2019 at https://www.historynet.com/lakotas-feared-fighters-of-the-plains.htm

4. Boyer, Lee R. *Conflict over Hunting Rights: Lightning Creek, 1903,* (South Dakota State Historical Society, 1993). Accessed on December 20, 2019 at https://www.sdhspress.com/journal/south-dakota-history-23-4/conflict-over-hunting-rights-lightning-creek-1903/vol-23-no-4-conflict-over-hunting-rights.pdf

5. "Just Another Country Doctor" by Nathan E. Wells, M.D. (unpublished, undated memoir), Courtesy of Anna Miller Museum, Newcastle, WY.

6. "Cambria, Wyoming," by Colleen Pollat, (self-published in 2011), Courtesy of Anna Miller Museum, Newcastle, WY.

7. River, Charles, ed. *Butch Cassidy & the Sundance Kid: The Lives and Legacies of the West's Famous Outlaw Duo,* (Charles River Editors, 2017).

8.  Griffith, Elizabeth T. *The House of Blazes: The Story of Johnny Owens,* (Newcastle, WY: News Letter Journal, 1990).

9.  Ibid., pp. 2-10.

10. Ibid., p. 22.

11. Ibid., p. 26.

12. Ibid., p. 39.

13. "Indian Act," by William B. Henderson, February 7, 2006, updated by Zach Parrott, *The Canadian Encyclopedia*, October 23, 2018. Paragraph 6. Accessed on December, 20, 2018 at http://www.thecanadianency-clopedia.ca/en/article/indian-act/

## Chapter 8

1.  Civil War Hardee Hat taken by Hal Jespersen at Gettysburg National Military Park Museum, June 19, 2005. Public Domain, Created: June 18, 2005. Accessed on December 20, 2019 at http://en.wikipedia.org/wiki/Iron_Brigade

2.  Herdegen, Lance J. *The Men Stood Like Iron: How the Iron Brigade Won Its Name,* (Bloomington, IN: Indiana University Press, 1997).

3.  Bilby, James G. *Civil War Firearms: Their historical background, tactical use and modern collection,* (Conshohocken, PA: Combined Publishing, 1996).

4.  Civil War Archive: Union Regimental Index, Wisconsin - 7th Wisconsin Volunteer Infantry Regiment. Accessed on December 1, 2017 at https://en.wikipedia.org/wiki/7th_Wisconsin_Volunteer_Infantry_Regiment#Colonels

5.  Langellier, John. *Second Manassas 1862: Robert E. Lee's Greatest Victory,* (Oxford, UK: Osprey Publishing, 2002), p. 50.

6.  "Casualties and Assessment: Second Battle of Bull Run, American Civil War," *Encyclopedia Britannica.* Accessed on April 27, 2020 at https://www.britannica.com/event/Second-Battle-of-Bull-Run-1862

7.  "Casualties and Assessment: First Battle of Bull Run, American Civil War," *Encyclopedia Britannica.* Accessed on April 27, 2020 at https://www.britannica.com/event/First-Battle-of-Bull-Run-1861

8. Dorwart, Bonnie Brice. *Death is in the Breeze: Disease During the American Civil War,* (Frederick, MD: National Museum of Civil War Medicine Press, 2009).

9. Rhea, Gordon C. *The Battles of the Wilderness & Spotsylvania,* (National Park Civil War Series, Eastern National, 2004), p. 11.

10. Rhea, Gordon C. *The Battle of the Wilderness, May 5-6, 1864,* (Baton Rouge, LA: Louisiana University State Press, 1994), p. 161.

11. Rhea, Gordon C. *The Battle of the Wilderness May 5–6, 1864,* pp. 400, 435-436.

12. Carmichael, Peter S. *The War of the Common Soldier: How Men Though, Fought, and Survived in Civil War Armies,* (Chapel Hill, NC: The University of North Carolina Press, 2018.)

13. Website of Department of Veterans Affairs, State of Wisconsin, Accessed on October 20, 2018 at: https://dva.wi.gov/Pages/veteransHomes/VeteransHomeKing.aspx

## Chapter 9

1. Minard, John S., County Historian. *Allegany County and its People: A Centennial Memorial History,* Georgia Drew Merrill, ed., (Alfred, NY: W.A. Fergusson & Co., 1896), p. 624. Accessed on October 20, 2018 at https://archive.org/details/alleganycountyit00mina/page/n7

2. Ibid., p. 16.

3. Howe, Daniel Walker. *What Hath God Wrought: The Transformation of America, 1815-1848,* (New York: Oxford University Press, 2007), pp. 285-327.

## Chapter 10

1. Record of service of Connecticut men in the I. War of the Revolution, II. War of 1812, III. Mexican War, (Hartford, CT: Authority of the General Assembly, 1889), p. 177. Accessed on March 16, 2018 at https://archive.org/details/waroftherevolution00recorich/page/n12

2. Ibid., p. 168.

3.  Lesser, Charles, ed. *The Sinews of Independence: Monthly Strength Reports of the Continental Army*, (Chicago: University of Chicago Press, 1976).

4.  Sheinkin, Steve. *The Notorious Benedict Arnold: A True Story of Adventure, Heroism & Treachery*, (New York: Roaring Book Press, 2010).

5.  André, John. *The Cow Chase*, Accessed on May 22, 2019 at https://en.wikisource.org/wiki/The_Cow_Chase

6.  Original Oath of Allegiance of the United States. Accessed on May 22, 2019 at https://en.wikipedia.org/wiki/Oath_of_Allegiance_(United_States)

7.  Abel Robinson, Revolutionary War Claim, Vermont, March 18, 1818. Accessed on March 25, 2019 on www.fold3.com/image/14005806 (record # 8444).

8.  Abel Robinson, Revolutionary War Pension Transfer from Vermont to Allegany, New York, March 24, 1830. Accessed on May 18, 2018 at www.fold3.com/image/14005853

## Chapter 11

1.  Wood, Gordon S. *Empire of Liberty: A History of the Early Republic, 1789-1815*, (New York: Oxford University Press, 2009), pp. 659-700.

2.  Bowman, Fred Q. "10,000 Vital Records of Western, New York, 1809-1850," Record no. 8560 p. 218. Accessed on September 20, 2019 at https://www.ancestry.com/interactive/61445/flhg_10000vrwestny-0001?backurl=&ssrc=&backlabel=Return#?imageId=flhg_10000vrwestny-0224

3.  "New York in the Revolution as Colony and State, Vol. 1: A Compilation of Documents and Records," (Albany, NY: J. B. Lyon Printers, 1904). Accessed on September 25, 2017 at http://dunhamwilcox.net/ny/ny_rev_levies_albany3.htm

4.  Corbett, Theodore, *No Turning Point: The Saratoga Campaign in Perspective*, (Norman, OK: The University of Oklahoma Press, 2012).

5.  "Fire at the New York State Library, 1911" New York Genealogical and Biographical Society, May 4, 2018. Accessed on April

27, 2020 at https://www.newyorkfamilyhistory.org/blog/
fire-new-york-state-library

6. Excerpt from song by Captain Smyth, Simcoe's Queen's Rangers, originally published in the Pennsylvania Ledger, 1778. Accessed on December 2, 2019 at http://www3.sympatico.ca/goweezer/theshack/songs.htm

7. Colonial Families of the USA, 1607-1775, Vol. 5 p. 468 accessed on Ancestry.com at https://www.ancestry.com/interactive/61175/colonialfamiliesv-003795_468/450067232?backurl=https://www.ancestry.com/family-tree/person/tree/78480922/person/242053253314/facts)

8. William-Lackey-Stephens genealogy website, Accessed on January 15, 2018 at https://www.genealogy.com/ftm/s/t/e/William-Lackey--Stephens/GENE20-0023.html

9. Nicholas Stephens family genealogy accessed on January 20, 2020 at Geni: https://www.geni.com/people/Nicholas-Stephens/6000000032483939617

## Chapter 12

1. Drew, Bernard A. *Henry Knox and the Revolutionary War Trail in Western Massachusetts, Chapter 8, The Seven Years War I: Fort Saint Frédéric (Crown Point) Campaign, 1755,* (Jefferson, Carolina and London: McFarland & Company, Ltd., 2012), p. 65.

2. Thomas Stevens gravesite, on Findagrave.com record. Accessed on January 21, 2020 at https://www.findagrave.com/memorial/34700275/thomas-stevens

3. Fischer, David H. *Champlain's Dream,* (New York: Simon & Schuster, 2008).

4. Ibid., p. 3.

5. Portrait of Samuel de Champlain accessed on December 15, 2019 at https://www.biography.com/explorer/samuel-de-champlain

6. Anderson, Fred. *The War that Made America: A Short History of the French and Indian War,* (New York: Penguin Books, 2005).

7.  Fischer, David H. *Champlain's Dream*, pp. 142-143.

8.  Colonial Soldiers and Officers in New England, 1620-1755, Massachusetts Soldiers and Sailors in the French and Indian Wars, 1755-1756. AmericanAncestors.org, New England Historic Genealogical Society, Micah Hoskins, 1985. Call number 199.M414 1985.

9.  Drew, Bernard A. *Henry Knox and the Revolutionary War Trail in Western Massachusetts, Chapter 8, The Seven Years War I: Fort Saint Frederic (Crown Point) Campaign, 1755*, p. 69.

10. Cooper, James Fenimore. *Last of the Mohicans: A Narrative of 1757*, (New York: Charles Scribner's Sons, 1937).

11. "The Maple Leaf Forever," accessed on September 16, 2019 at: http://www.ingeb.org/songs/indaysof.html

12. Middlekauff, Robert. *The Glorious Cause: The American Revolution, 1763-1789*, (New York: Oxford University Press, 2005), pp. 576-578.

13. Six Nations Lands & Resources Department, Land Rights, Ohsweken, Ontario, Canada: A Global Solution for the Six Nations of the Grand River. [Brochure n.d.]

## Chapter 13

1.  Stiles, Henry R. *The History and Genealogies of Ancient Windsor, Connecticut, 1635-1891*, (Hartford, CT: Press of the Case, Lockwood & Brainard Company), p. 405. Accessed on January 31, 2020 at https://archive.org/details/historygenealogi02stil/page/405/mode/2up

2.  John Hoskins (1701-1765) tombstone found on *Findagrave.com*, accessed on September 15, 2019 https://www.findagrave.com/cgi-bin/fg.cgi?page=gr&GSln=Hoskins&GSfn=John&GSiman=1&GS-cid=103567&GRid=52594922&

3.  Anthony Hoskins Project by Robert Haskins on Hoskins DNA accessed on January 20, 2018 at https://sites.google.com/site/anthonyhoskinsproject/Home/dna

4.  Kuhns, Maude Pinney, *The "Mary and John": A Story of the Founding of Dorchester, Massachusetts, 1630.* (Rutland, VT: Tuttle Publishing Co., 1943), p. 47.

5. Mary and John Passenger List. Accessed on May 15, 2017 at https://www.packrat-pro.com/ships/maryjohn1.htm

6. Barry, John M. *Roger Williams and the Creation of the American Soul: Church, State, and the Birth of Liberty,* (New York: Penguin Books, 2012), pp. 120-128.

7. *The New England Historical and Genealogical Register and Antiquarian Society Journal, Vol. III, No. 1,* January 1849, (Boston, MA: Samuel G. Drake, Publisher, 1849), p. 91.

8. Stiles, Henry R. *The History and Genealogies of Ancient Windsor, Connecticut, Vol. II, 1635-1891,* (Hartford, CT: Press of the Case, Lockwood and Bainard Company, 1892), p. 404. Accessed on January 31, 2020 at https://archive.org/details/historygenealogi02stil/page/404/mode/2up

9. The New England Historical and Genealogical Register, Society Windsor Connecticut Land Record 1:14. Accessed on May 15, 2017 at https://larkturnthehearts.blogspot.com/2011/01/john-hoskins-11th-and-11th-gr.html

10. Warren, James A. *God, War, and Providence: The Epic Struggle of Roger Williams and the Narragansett Indians against the Puritans of New England,* (New York: Scribner, 2018), pp. 77-93.

11. Ibid., 90-93.

12. Stiles, Henry R. *The History and Genealogies of Ancient Windsor, Connecticut, Vol. II, 1635-1891,* (Hartford, CT: Press of the Case, Lockwood and Bainard Company, 1892), p. 404. Accessed on January 31, 2020 at https://archive.org/details/historygenealogi02stil/page/404/mode/2up

13. A Digest of the Early Connecticut Probate Records, by Charles W. Manwaring, R. S., Ann Hoskins, 1663-1677. (Hartford, CT: Peck & Co. Printers, 1904, August 17, 1660), p. 207-208. Accessed on January 20, 2020 at https://archive.org/details/digestofearlycon00manw/page/206/mode/2up

14. "The Parentage of Anthony Hoskins, Windsor, Conn." by Genevieve Tylee Kiepura, *The American Genealogist,* No. 30 1954. American Ancestors by New England Historic Genealogical Society,

Boston, MA). Accessed on September 18, 2019 at https://www.americanancestors.org/databases/american-genealogist-the/image?pageName=191&volumeId=11829&rId=23573278)

15. "Anthony Hoskins DNA Signature," Anthony Hoskins Project by Robert Haskins accessed on May 7, 2020 at https://sites.google.com/site/anthonyhoskinsproject/Home/dna#TOC-Anthony-Hoskins-DNA-Signature-

16. Stiles, Henry R. *The History and Genealogies of Ancient Windsor, Connecticut, Vol. II, 1635-1891*, (Hartford, CT: Press of the Case, Lockwood and Bainard Company, 1892), p. 404-406. Accessed on January 31, 2020 at https://archive.org/details/historygenealogi02stil/page/404/mode/2up

17. Anthony Hoskins Sr.'s Timeline by Robert Haskins. From *History of Ancient Windsor, Hartford County Connecticut Court Minutes, Volumes 3 & 4*, accessed at https://sites.google.com/site/anthonyhoskinsproject/Home/timeline

18. Barry, John M. *Roger Williams and the Creation of the American Soul: Church, State, and the Birth of Liberty*, p. 244.

19. Stiles, Henry R. *The History of Ancient Windsor, Connecticut: Chapter X. King Philip's War, 1675-6*, p. 196. Accessed on February 10, 2018 at: https://www.google.com/books/edition/_/Qg0WAAAAYAAJ?hl=en&gbpv=1

20. Philbrick, Nathaniel. *Mayflower: A Story of Courage, Community, and War*, (New York: Penguin Books, 2006), p. 205.

21. Stiles, Henry R. *The History of Ancient Windsor, Connecticut: Chapter X. King Philip's War, 1675-6*, p. 195. Accessed on February 10, 2018 at: https://www.google.com/books/edition/_/Qg0WAAAAYAAJ?hl=en&gbpv=1

22. Philbrick, Nathaniel. *Mayflower: A Story of Courage, Community, and War*, pp. 278-279.

23. Hoskins Family Tree with original sources found on Ancestry.com. Accessed on September 15, 2019 at https://www.ancestry.com/family-tree/person/tree/101911747/person/210012859380/facts

24. A Digest of the Early Connecticut Probate Records, 1700-1710, Anthony Hoskins Sr.'s Will. Accessed on Ancestry.com at https://www.ancestry.com/mediaui-viewer/tree/44514995/person/6879089761/media/ad81f70b-4d06-4dce-a776-7ccf749fe6a3

25. Conversion rate English pounds of 1707 to 2020 US dollars. Accessed on internet September 17, 2020 at https://gbp.currencyrate.today/usd/1707

## Chapter 14

1. "Was one of your ancestors on the *Mayflower*? You can find out now." By Doyle Rice, *USA Today*, June 13, 2018. Accessed on January 10, 2020 at https://apnews.com/6d093e5a5beb416dbd30922a68a903bf

2. Elizabeth (Thacher) Fuller on Findagrave.com. Accessed on May 12, 2018 at https://www.findagrave.com/memorial/44258989

3. *Partridge Genealogy: Descendants of George Partridge of Druxbury Massachusetts*, by George Henry Partridge. Privately printed, 1915. pp. 1-5. Accessed on September 12, 2019 at https://babel.hathitrust.org/cgi/pt?id=wu.89092814789&view=1up&seq=21

4. *Genealogy, and Biographical Sketches, of the Descendants of Thomas and Anthony Thacher, From their Settlement in New England, June 4th, 1635*, (Vineland, NJ: Independent Printing House, 1872). Accessed on September 15, 2019 at https://archive.org/details/genealogybiograp00inalle/page/n4/mode/2up

5. Wisner, Benjamin B. *The History of the Old South Church in Boston: In four sermons, delivered May 9, & 16, 1830*, (London: Forgotten Books, 2015).

6. Ibid., pp. 11-12.

7. Thacher, Thomas. *A Brief Rule To Guide the Common People of New England How to order themselves and theirs in the Small Pocks, or Measels*, on Library of Congress website. Accessed on January 20, 2020 at https://www.loc.gov/resource/rbpe.03300900/?sp=1

8. *Genealogy, and Biographical Sketches, of the Descendants of Thomas and Anthony Thacher, From their Settlement in New England, June 4th, 1635*, p. 8.

9.  "Ceremony Honors Early Indian Students," Boston Globe, May 18, 1997. Accessed on January 10, 2929 at https://www.massmoments. org/moment-details/ceremony-honors-early-indian-students.html

10. *Genealogy, and Biographical Sketches, of the Descendants of Thomas and Anthony Thacher, From their Settlement in New England, June 4th, 1635,* p. 9.

11. Hill, Frances. *A Delusion of Satan: The Full Story of the Salem Witch Trials,* (Cambridge, MA: Da Capo Press, 1997).

12. Ibid., pp. 66-73

13. Ibid., pp. 185-186.

14. Ibid., pp. 184-186.

15. Conant, Frederick Odell. *A History and Genealogy of the Conant Family in England and America, Thirteen Generations 1520-1887,* (Portland, ME: Privately printed, 1887.

16. Ibid., p. 110.

17. Barry, John M. *Roger Williams and the Creation of the American Soul: Church, State, and the Birth of Liberty,* pp. 97-99.

18. Conant, Frederick Odell. *A History and Genealogy of the Conant Family in England and America, Thirteen Generations 1520-1887,* p. 124. Accessed on August 31, 2019 at https://archive.org/details/ historygenealogy00cona/page/126/mode/2up

19. Barry, John M. *Roger Williams and the Creation of the American Soul: Church, State, and the Birth of Liberty,* p. 100.

20. Conant, Frederick Odell. *A History and Genealogy of the Conant Family in England and America, Thirteen Generations 1520-1887,* p. 110. Accessed on August 31, 2019 at https://archive.org/details/ historygenealogy00cona/page/110/mode/2up

21. Barry, John M. *Roger Williams and the Creation of the American Soul: Church, State, and the Birth of Liberty,* pp. 100-101.

22. Ibid., pp. 115-130.

23. Hill, Frances. *A Delusion of Satan: The Full Story of the Salem Witch Trials,* p. 2.

24. MacGunnigle, Bruce Campbell, ed. *Mayflower Families Through Five Generations, Descendants of the Pilgrims who landed at Plymouth, Mass., December 1620, Vol. 4, Third Edition, Family of Edward Fuller,* (Plymouth, MA: General Society of Mayflower Descendants, 2006), pp. 3, 5-6, 9-10, 26-27, and 86-87.

25. *Vital Records of Duxbury, Massachusetts to the Year 1850,* New England Historic Genealogical Society, Boston, MA, 1911; Elizabeth Thacher, p. 173

26. *Genealogy, and Biographical Sketches, of the Descendants of Thomas and Anthony Thacher, From their Settlement in New England, June 4th, 1635,* pp. 3-10. Accessed on January 20, 2020 at https://archive.org/details/genealogybiograp00inalle/page/n9/mode/2up

27. Partridge, George Henry. *Partridge Genealogy: Descendants of George Partidge of Druxbury Massachusetts,* privately printed, 1915. pp. 1-5. Accessed on Sept. 1, 2019 at https://babel.hathitrust.org/cgi/pt?id=wu.89092814789&view=1up&seq=18

28. Morrison, Leonard Allison, and Stephen Paschall Sharples, *History of the Kimball Family in America, From 1634 to 1897, and its ancestors, The Kemballs or Kemboldes of England, with an account of the Kembles of Boston, Massachusetts,* (Boston: Damrell & Upham, Old Corner Bookstore, 1897), pp. 75-76. Accessed on August 20, 2019 at https://archive.org/details/historyofkimball00morr/page/n5

29. Conant, Frederick Odell. *A History and Genealogy of the Conant Family in England and America, Thirteen Generations 1520-1887,* pp. 101-131, 155-156. Accessed on Aug. 20, 2019 at https://archive.org/details/historygenealogy00cona/page/n3

30. "Robinson Genealogy, Descendants of the Rev. John Robinson, Pastor of the Pilgrims, Vol. 1." (Robinson Genealogy Society, Newcomb & Gauss, Salem, MA, 1926).

31. "Robinson Genealogy, Descendants of Rev. John Robinson, Pastor to the Pilgrims" *The American Genealogist,* Vol 17, 1940, pp. 207- 215. Accessed on August 20, 2019 at https://www.americanancestors.org/databases/american-genealogist-the/image?pageName=207&volumeId=11861

32. "Robinson Genealogy, Descendants of Rev. John Robinson,

Pastor to the Pilgrims" *The American Genealogist, Vol. 18, 1941*), pp. 45-55. Accessed on August 20, 2019 at https://www. americanancestors.org/databases/american-genealogist-the/ image?pageName=45&volumeId=11852

33. *The Great Migration Begins: Immigrants to New England 1620- 1633, Volumes I-III.* (Online database: *AmericanAncestors.org,* New England Historic Genealogical Society, 2010), (Originally Published as: New England Historic Genealogical Society. Robert Charles Anderson, *The Great Migration Begins: Immigrants to New England 1620-1633, Volumes I-III,* 3 vols., 1995). Accessed on June 14, 2020 at https://www.americanancestors.org/databases/ great-migration-begins-immigrants-to-ne-1620-1633-vols-i-iii/ image/?volumeId=12107&pageName=1

## Chapter 15

1.  Philbrick, Nathaniel. *Mayflower: A Story of Courage, Community, and War,* p. 48.

2.  "New Hypothesis for Cause of Epidemic among Native Americans, New England, 1616–1619," by John S. Marr and John T. Cathey, US National Library of Medicine, National Institutes of Health, Emerging Infectious Diseases. Feb., 2010, 16 (2): pp. 281–286 accessed on Sept, 17, 2020 at https://www.ncbi.nlm.nih.gov/pmc/articles/ PMC2957993/

3.  Johnson, Caleb H. *The Mayflower and Her Passengers,* (Xlibris Corporation, 2006), pp. 160-168.

4.  Ibid., pp. 144-146.

5.  Philbrick, Nathaniel. *Mayflower: A Story of Courage, Community, and War,* pp. 3-30.

6.  Ibid., pp. 40-42.

7.  Ibid., pp. 3-4.

8.  Johnson, Caleb H. *The Mayflower and Her Passengers,* p. 145.

9.  Ibid., pp. 210-212.

10. MacGunnigle, Bruce Campbell, ed. *Mayflower Families Through Five Generations, Descendants of the Pilgrims who landed at Plymouth, Mass., December 1620, Vol. 4, Third Edition*, p. 26.

11. Deetz, James and Patricia Scott Deetz. *The Times of their Lives: Life, Love, and Death in Plymouth Colony*, (New York: Anchor Books, A division of Random House, Inc., 2000), pp. 1-29.

12. Gragg, Rod. *The Pilgrim Chronicles: An Eyewitness History of the Pilgrims and the Founding of Plymouth Colony*, (Washington, DC: Regnery History, Regnery Publishing, 2014), p. 43.

13. Ibid., p. 44.

14. Ibid., pp. 118-119.

15. Ibid., p. 114.

16. Philbrick, Nathaniel. *Mayflower: A Story of Courage, Community, and War*, pp. 148-153.

17. Ibid., p. 156.

18. Ibid., pp. 187-188

19. Ibid., p. 242.

## Chapter 16

1. Philbrick, Nathaniel. *Mayflower: A Story of Courage, Community, and War*, p. 75.

2. Ibid., pp. 350-351.

3. Mason, John with Paul Royster, eds. *A Brief History of the Pequot War*, (Lincoln, NE: University of Nebraska, 2009), p. 21. Accessed on December 15, 2019 at https://digitalcommons.unl.edu/cgi/viewcontent.cgi?article=1042&context=etas

4. Schultz, Eric B. and Tougias, Michael J. *King Philip's War: The History and Legacy of America's Forgotten Conflict*, (New York: The Countryman Press, 1999), p. 5.

5. Ibid., p. 2-3.

6. Ibid., pp. 22-24.

7.  Johnson, Caleb H. *The Mayflower and Her Passengers*, p. 148.

8.  Schultz, Eric B. and Tougias, Michael J. *King Philip's War: The History and Legacy of America's Forgotten Conflict*, pp. 25-29

9.  MacGunnigle, Bruce Campbell, ed. *Mayflower Families Through Five Generations, Descendants of the Pilgrims who landed at Plymouth, Mass., December 1620, Vol. 4, Third Edition*, p. 5.

10. Schultz, Eric B. and Tougias, Michael J. *King Philip's War: The History and Legacy of America's Forgotten Conflict*, pp. 238-241.

11. Philbrick, Nathaniel. *Mayflower: A Story of Courage, Community, and War*, pp. 246-251.

12. Oakes, Rensselaer Allston. *Genealogical and Family History of the County of Jefferson, New York, Volume 2* (New York: Higginson Book Company, 1905), pp. 1243-1248. Accessed on Sept. 25, 2019 at https://archive.org/details/genealogicalfami02oake/page/1243

13. Hayes, William. *Captain John Gallop: Master Mariner and Indian Trader,* (Stonington, CT: The Pequot Press with The Gallup Family Association and the Cocumscussoc Association, 1964), pp. 3 and 27. Accessed on Sept. 25, 2019 at: https://www.tomgallup.com/john-gallup-jr--hannah-lake.html

14. Warren, James A. *God, War, and Providence: The Epic Struggle of Roger Williams and the Narragansett Indians against the Puritans of New England.*

15. "Robinson Genealogy, Descendants of Rev. John Robinson, Pastor to the Pilgrims" *The American Genealogist, Vol. 18, 1941*), pp. 45-46.

16. Williams, Roger. *A Key into the Language of America,* (New York: Cosmo Classics, 2009).

17. Warren, James A. *God, War, and Providence: The Epic Struggle of Roger Williams and the Narragansett Indians against the Puritans of New England*, pp. 143-152.

18. Ibid., pp. 153-204.

19. Haynes, William. *Captain John Gallop: Master Mariner and Indian Trader,* (Stonington, CT: The Pequot Press, Inc., with Gallup Family Association. Stonington), p. 30.

20. Philbrick, Nathaniel. *Mayflower: A Story of Courage, Community, and War*, pp. 278-279.

21. "The View From Swamptown: Remembering the Great Swamp Fight," by G.T. Cranston Special to *The Independent*, Rhode Island, December 9, 2018.

22. Tom Gallop's memorial by Midge Frazel, Professional Genealogist. Accessed Sept. 8, 2020 at https://www.flickr.com/photos/midgefrazel/6062762787/in/photostream/

23. Genealogy of the Gallop Family, North America, Family Histories, 1500-2000, pp. 21- 25. Accessed on Ancestry.com on Sept. 5, 2019 at https://www.ancestry.com/interactive/61157/46155_b289923-00022/1361617?backurl=https://www.ancestry.com/family-tree/person/tree/78480922/person/242053253314/facts

24. Henry Stephens and Elizabeth Gallop, Geni a MyHeritage Company, accessed June 21, 2020, https://www.geni.com/people/Henry-Stephens/6000000010916775474

25. Colonial Families of the USA, 1607-1775, Vol. 5 p. 468. Accessed on Ancestry.com at https://www.ancestry.com/interactive/61175/colonialfamiliesv-003795_468/450067232?backurl=https://www.ancestry.com/family-tree/person/tree/78480922/person/242053253314/facts)

26. Schultz, Eric B. and Tougias, Michael J. *King Philip's War: The History and Legacy of America's Forgotten Conflict*, pp. 276-282.

27. Historic Marker Database website, Pierce's Fight plaque, accessed on Sept. 25, 2019 at https://www.hmdb.org/marker.asp?marker=45093

28. Schultz, Eric B. and Tougias, Michael J. *King Philip's War: The History and Legacy of America's Forgotten Conflict*, p. 69.

29. Plymouth Colony Wills and Inventories, Volume lll, Part ll, pp. 127-129.

30. Williams, Roger. *A Key into the Language of America*, p. 53.

31. Newell, Margaret Ellen. *Brethren by Nature: New England Indians, Colonists, and the Origins of American Slavery*, (Ithaca, NY: Cornell University Press, 2015), pp. 183.

32. Ibid., pp. 184-185.

33. Ibid., pp. 18-20.

34. Philbrick, Nathaniel. *Mayflower: A Story of Courage, Community, and War*, p. 253.

35. Newell, Margaret Ellen. *Brethren by Nature: New England Indians, Colonists, and the Origins of American Slavery*, pp. 43-45.

36. Ibid., p. 8.

37. Ibid., p. 9.

38. Ibid., p.5.

39. Ibid., pp. 5-7, 82-83, 230.

40. Ibid., p. 14.

41. Deloria, Philip J. & Neal Salisbury, eds. A Companion to American Indian History, (Blackwell Publishers Ltd, 2002), p. 157.

42. Hill, Frances. *A Delusion of Satan: The Full Story of the Salem Witch Trials*, p. 40.

43. Mather, Cotton. Broadstreet, "Diary" II' quoted in Edmund S. Morgan, *The Puritan Family*, (New York: Harper & Row, 1966), p. 98.

44. Bradstreet, Anne, "Childhood," from Works; quoted in Edmund S. Morgan, *The Puritan Family* (New York: Harper & Row, 1966), p. 93.

45. Demos, John. *The Unredeemed Captive: A Family Story from Early America*, (First Vintage Books, 1994).

46. Lauradunn, Gayle. *All the Wild and Holy: The Life of Eunice Williams, 1679-1785*, (Kanona, NY: Foothills Publishing, 2017).

47. Ibid., p. 94.

## Chapter 17

1. List of mass shootings in the United States in 2019, available on Wikipedia.com. Accessed on February 25, 2020 at https://en.wikipedia.org/wiki/List_of_mass_shootings_in_the_United_States_in_2019

2. List of Mass Shootings in Canada, available on Wikipedia.com. Accessed on April 15, 2020 at https://en.wikipedia.org/wiki/ List_of_massacres_in_Canada

3. "Nearly 40,000 People Died from Guns in U.S. Last Year, Highest in 50 Years," The *New York Times,* by Sarah Mervosh, Dec. 18, 2018. Accessed on October 19, 2019 at https://www.nytimes. com/2018/12/18/us/gun-deaths.html

4. United Nations, *World Population Review, 2020.* Accessed on April 15, 2020 at https://worldpopulationreview.com/countries/ gun-deaths-by-country/

5. United Nations, *World Population Review, 2020.* Accessed on April 15, 2020 at https://worldpopulationreview.com/countries/ gun-ownership-by-country/

6. Pew Research Report, 2017. Accessed on March 11, 2020 at https://www.pewsocialtrends.org/2017/06/22/ americas-complex-relationship-with-guns/

7. "Firearm Ownership in Canada." Department of Justice, Government of Canada. Accessed on April 15, 2020 at https://www.justice.gc.ca/ eng/rp-pr/csj-sjc/jsp-sjp/wd98_4-dt98_4/p2.html

8. "Canadian PM Trudeau Bans All Assault-Style Firearms," National Public Radio, by Austin Horn, May 1, 2020. Accessed May 2, 2020 at https://www.npr.org/2020/05/01/849236738/ canadian-pm-trudeau-bans-all-assault-style-firearms

9. "Majority of Americans, Including Gun Owners, Support a Variety of Gun Policies," Johns Hopkins University, Bloomberg School of Public Health, Hopkins Bloomberg Magazine, September 9, 2019. Accessed on April 15, 2020 at https://www.jhsph.edu/news/news-re- leases/2019/majority-of-americans-including-gun-owners-sup- port-a-variety-of-gun-policies

10. U.S. Department of State, Bureau of Consular Affairs' website. Accessed on Oct. 21 at https://travel.state.gov/content/travel/en/ legal/travel-legal-considerations/Advice-about-Possible-Loss-of-US- Nationality-Dual-Nationality/Dual-Nationality.html

11. U.S. Citizenship and Immigration Services, Today's Oath of Allegiance. Accessed on May 22, 2019 at https://www.uscis.gov/us-citizenship/naturalization-test/naturalization-oath-allegiance-united-states-america

12. Barry, John M. *Roger Williams and the Creation of the American Soul: Church, State, and the Birth of Liberty*, p. 310, 365.

13. Williams, Roger. *The Complete Writings of Roger Williams*, Chapter 4, (New York: Norton, 1967), p. 206.

14. List of international treaties unsigned or unratified by the United States. Accessed on Wikipedia on April 19, 2020 at https://en.wikipedia.org/wiki/List_of_treaties_unsigned_or_unratified_by_the_United_States

15. Public Works and Government Services Canada (2006), Citizenship Rights and Responsibilities, (Ottawa: Queen's Printer for Canada), p. 40. Accessed on February 27, 2020 at https://www.canada.ca/en/immigration-refugees-citizenship/news/2019/05/the-oath-of-citizenship.html

16. "Let's Talk about Dual Allegiance," *National Review*, by John Fonte, Aug. 23, 2013. Accessed on May 22, 2019 at https://www.nationalreview.com/2013/08/lets-talk-about-dual-allegiance-john-fonte/

# SELECTED READINGS

Anderson, Fred. *The War that Made America: A Short History of the French and Indian War,* (New York: Penguin Books, 2005).

Barry, John M. *Roger Williams and the Creation of the American Soul: Church, State, and the Birth of Liberty,* (New York: Penguin Books, 2012).

Bilby, James G. *Civil War Firearms: Their historical background, tactical use and modern collection,* (Conshohocken, PA: Combined Publishing, 1996).

Bothwell, Robert. *Your Country, My Country: A Unified History of the United States and Canada,* (New York: Oxford University Press, 2015).

Brown, Dee. *Bury My Heart at Wounded Knee: An Indian History of the American West,* (New York: Henry Holt and Company, Owl Book Edition 1991).

Brown-Kubisch, Linda. *The Queen's Bush Settlement: Black Pioneers, 1839-1865,* (Toronto, ON: Natural Heritage Books, 2004).

Carmichael, Peter S. *The War of the Common Soldier: How Men Though, Fought, and Survived in Civil War Armies,* (Chapel Hill, NC: The University of North Carolina Press, 2018.)

Christie, Norm. *For King & Empire: The Canadians at Amiens, August 1918,* (Ottawa: CEF Books, 1999.)

Cooper, James Fenimore. *Last of the Mohicans: A Narrative of 1757,* (New York: Charles Scribner's Sons, 1937).

Corbett, Theodore, *No Turning Point: The Saratoga Campaign in Perspective,* (Norman, OK: The University of Oklahoma Press, 2012).

Deetz, James and Patricia Scott Deetz. *The Times of Their Lives: Life, Love, and Death in  Plymouth Colony,* (New York: Anchor Books, A Division of Random House, Inc., 2000).

Devine, T. M. *The Scottish Clearances: A History of the Dispossessed, 1600-1900,* (Penguin Books, UK, 2018).

Donoghue, Clayton N. *The Irish Empire: The Story of Niall of the Nine Hostages,* (Victoria, Canada: Friesen Press, 2015.)

Fischer, David H. *Champlain's Dream,* (New York: Simon & Schuster, 2008).

Gragg, Rod. *The Pilgrim Chronicles: An Eyewitness History of the Pilgrims and the Founding of Plymouth Colony,* (Washington, DC: Regnery History, Regnery Publishing, 2014).

Herdegen, Lance J. *The Men Stood Like Iron: How the Iron Brigade Won Its Name,* (Bloomington, IN: Indiana University Press, 1997).

Herman, Arthur. *How the Scots Invented the Modern World,* (New York, NY: MJF Books, 2001).

Hill, Frances. *A Delusion of Satan: The Full Story of the Salem Witch Trials,* (Cambridge, MA: Da Capo Press, 1997).

Howe, Daniel Walker. *What Hath God Wrought: The Transformation of America, 1815-1848,* New York: Oxford University Press, 2007).

Johnson, Caleb H. *The Mayflower and Her Passengers,* (Xlibris Corporation, 2006).

Langellier, John. *Second Manassas 1862: Robert E Lee's Greatest Victory,* (Oxford, UK: Osprey Publishing, 2002).

Lauradunn, Gayle. *All the Wild and Holy: The Life of Eunice Williams, 1679-1785,* (Kanona, NY: Foothills Publishing, 2017).

Maclean, Fitzroy. *A Concise History of Scotland,* (London, UK: Thames and Hudson, 1970).

Mason, John & Paul Royster, eds. *A Brief History of the Pequot War,* (Lincoln, NE: University of Nebraska, 2009).

Middlekauff, Robert. *The Glorious Cause: The American Revolution, 1763-1789,* (New York: Oxford University Press, 2005).

Newell, Margaret Ellen. *Brethren by Nature: New England Indians, Colonists, and the Origins of American Slavery,* (Ithaca, NY: Cornell University Press, 2015).

Philbrick, Nathaniel. *Mayflower: A Story of Courage, Community, and War,* (New York: Penguin Books, 2006).

Prince, Bryan. *My Brother's Keeper: African Canadians and the American Civil War,* (Toronto, ON: Dundurn, 2015).

Rattenbury, Richard C. *A Legacy in Arms: American Firearm Manufacture, Design, and Artistry, 1800-1900,* (Norman: University of Oklahoma Press, 2114).

Rhea, Gordon C. *The Battle of the Wilderness, May 5-6, 1864,* (Baton Rouge: Louisiana University State Press, 1994).

River, Charles, ed. *Butch Cassidy & the Sundance Kid: The Lives and Legacies of the West's Famous Outlaw Duo,* (Charles River Editors, 2017).

Schultz, Eric B. and Tougias, Michael J. *King Philip's War: The History and Legacy of America's Forgotten Conflict,* (New York: The Countryman Press, 1999).

Sheinkin, Steve. *The Notorious Benedict Arnold: A True Story of Adventure, Heroism & Treachery,* (New York: Roaring Book Press, 2010).

Shillingberg, William B. *Dodge City: The Early Years, 1872-1886,* (Norman, OK: The Arthur H. Clark Company, An Imprint of the University of Oklahoma Press, 2009).

Trevor-Roper, Hugh. "The Invention of Tradition: The Highland Tradition of Scotland," Chapter 2, pp.15-41 of *The Invention of Tradition,* Eric Hobsbawm and Terence Ranger, eds., (Cambridge University Press, 1983). Accessed on October 21, 2013 at http://www.columbia.edu/itc/journalism/stille/Politics%20Fall%202007/readings%20weeks%206-7/Trevor-Roper,%20The%20Highland%20Tradition.pdf

Waldman, Michael, *The Second Amendment: A Biography,* (New York: Simon & Schuster Paperbacks, 2004).

Warren, James A. *God, War, and Providence: The Epic Struggle of Roger Williams and the Narragansett Indians Against the Puritans of New England*, (New York: Scribner, 2018).

Williams, Roger. *A Key into the Language of America*, (New York: Cosmo Classics, 2009).

Winkler, Adam. *Gun Fight: The Battle over the Right to Bear Arms in America*, (New York: W.W. Norton, 2013).

Wood, Gordon S. *Empire of Liberty: A History of the Early Republic, 1789-1815*, (New York: Oxford University Press, 2009).

# ABOUT THE AUTHOR

Neill McKee is a creative nonfiction writer based in Albuquerque, New Mexico. His first travel memoir, *Finding Myself in Borneo*, won a bronze medal in the Independent Publishers Book Awards, 2020, as well as other awards. McKee holds a Bachelor's Degree, from the University of Calgary and a Master's Degree in Communication from Florida State University. He worked internationally for 45 years, becoming an expert in the field of communication for social change. He directed and produced a number of award-winning documentary films/videos and multimedia initiatives, and has written numerous articles and books in the field of development communication. During his international career, McKee worked for Canadian University Service Overseas (CUSO); Canada's International Development Research Centre (IDRC); UNICEF; Johns Hopkins University, Baltimore, Maryland; Academy for Educational Development and FHI 360, Washington, DC. He worked and lived in Malaysia, Bangladesh, Kenya, Uganda, and Russia for a total of 18 years and traveled to over 80 countries on short-term assignments. In 2015, he settled in New Mexico, using his varied experiences, memories, and imagination in creative writing.

CPSIA information can be obtained
at www.ICGtesting.com
Printed in the USA
FSHW010224161220
76760FS

9 781732 945739